HALINA

To Sister Immaculata
with love
Halina

HALINA BRATKOWNA JOHNSON

HALINA

GROWING UP IN OCCUPIED POLAND DURING
WORLD WAR II

TATE PUBLISHING
AND ENTERPRISES, LLC

Published by Tate Publishing & Enterprises, LLC
127 E. Trade Center Terrace | Mustang, Oklahoma 73064 USA
1.888.361.9473 | www.tatepublishing.com

Tate Publishing is committed to excellence in the publishing industry. The company reflects the philosophy established by the founders, based on Psalm 68:11,
"The Lord gave the word and great was the company of those who published it."

Book design copyright © 2014 by Tate Publishing, LLC. All rights reserved.
Cover design by Rtor Maghuyop
Interior design by Mary Jean Archival

Published in the United States of America
ISBN: 978-1-63306-891-9
Biography & Autobiography / Personal Memoirs
14.08.21

To the memory of
the two million Polish children and teenagers
who died as a result of Nazi occupation

I am here in the hope that it is possible to start anew and heal your own life by thinking very strongly about the things you used to know, so strongly that the places and people time cannot takeaway, will last even more real than they were.

—Czesław Miłosz

CONTENTS

Part III
We Have Something to Fight and Die For

ACKNOWLEDGMENTS

I would like to express my gratitude to Gene Allen, who inspired and encouraged me to write this book about my experiences while growing up under the Nazi occupation of Poland during World War II. I realized that bringing up the memories that had been suppressed for years would be emotionally stressful and to recall the dramatic historical events I had been closely observing would demand a detailed study of historic development taking place during that time. Yet I was eventually convinced to share my story with people who know little about the Poles' stubborn perseverance in selfless struggle for their homeland's freedom and sovereignty as well as justice and personal dignity.

After I was diagnosed with macular degeneration, I had made the mistake of giving up my computer. Gene graciously offered to type my writing on his computer. During the first phase of my writing, he made helpful suggestions for some phrases and colloquial expressions in English. It had been a long and emotional journey.

I also acknowledge my debt to Ryszard Jacek Dumalo, my colleague from the underground gymnasium. His book, *War, Occupation, Liberation—Lubartow 1939–1949*, published in Polish in 2003 shortly before his death, had been sent to me by his wife, Danuta. It provided me with the records of events going on in Lubartov during five and one-half years of the German occupation followed by the no-less oppressive dictatorship of the Polish Committee of National Liberation, which was organized in Moscow and arrived on the heels of the Soviet army.

Finally, I am grateful to the staff of the Museum of Warsaw Uprising in Warsaw for sending me the original photos from The Uprising, 1944.

—Halina Bratkowna Johnson

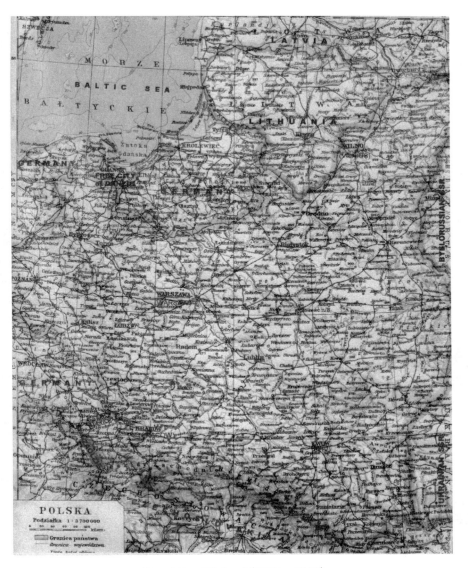

Republic of Poland (1921 - 1939)

As far as I remember, our mom always had time for us. She was a spring of energy, the heart, the cement, and the Band-Aid of our family.

When I was in first grade, some charitable organization in town was staging a Christmas play for the children of disadvantaged families. My part, actually not related to the Christmas story, was added a day before the performance. That winter, there had been a lot of talk about vitamins and their role in nutrition. I was to be an orange since oranges are a good source of vitamin C and bioflavonoids. I had just a few hours to memorize my lines, but it was St. Nicholas' Day, December 6, and my mind was on the stocking I had found that morning at the foot of my bed, so I did not apply myself properly to the task before me.

My costume was a short puffy skirt, velvety top with a green ruffle around the neck, a cute pointed hat with a green leaf, all in matching shades of orange. Little imitation oranges dangled around the cuffs of my sleeves. I was to arrive on stage riding my little tricycle to indicate that I had come from far away. I rode in, got off my tricycle, and approached the front of the stage. It was then that I saw the hall was filled to capacity. I had never performed before such a crowd, but there was no going back. I started my lines—something like:

I am a little orange
From a sunny country
Bringing you good tidings...

I stopped. No more words were coming. My mind was a complete blank. I was waving my hands to the audience, not knowing what else to do, when I heard Mom's voice from the prompter's box, whispering the words of the next line. But my brain was hopelessly frozen. What embarrassment!

But Mom didn't give up. "Get back on your tricycle, ride three times around, and start to dispense the oranges," she whispered again.

That was easy to do. I was saved! Three large baskets of oranges were placed on the stage. I rode up to the baskets and started to throw the oranges, one by one. The audience became ecstatic, everyone trying to catch an orange. Those children knew oranges only from the display windows of the stores lavishly decorated for Christmas. The more they cheered, the harder and faster I threw. I had no idea how many were caught or how many landed on heads instead of in hands. When I ran out of oranges, I started pulling the little decorative oranges off my cuffs and throwing them. The audience cheered all the more.

When the play was over, the actors came out for their bows, first Mary and Joseph followed by the three kings. I was next. When the children caught sight of me in my orange splendor, they started to stomp their feet and shout, "Po-ma-rancz-ka! Po-ma-rancz-ka!" which means "Little Orange! Little Orange!"

Nobody paid any attention to the angels or the shepherds or the donkey or the ox. Mommy's secret help turned my would-be defeat into success.

"Vox populi," she said as we were leaving. "That was the voice of the people."

I knew, even as a child, the face of poverty in our seemingly prosperous town. From time to time, Yanush and I saw a group or two of disheveled men, usually in the same place—idle, talking, and arguing for hours. They were our jobless people: frustrated, desperate, and sometimes angry and tipsy. One day, we confided to Mom what we had painfully observed.

"As you know, our country only recently regained independence," she said, "after more than a hundred years of being partitioned." She went on to explain that Poland was surrounded by powerful countries such as Russia, Austria, and Prussia. Their despotic monarchs resisted the political and social reforms proclaimed by Polish Sejm (elected Assembly) and, in a despicable act of treachery, simultaneously invaded our country and divided it among themselves.

"More recently, our country was devastated during the World War," she said. "Now we are going through a worldwide depression. No wonder we have many problems to face, among them high unemployment and poverty. You see, the task of helping poor people lies exclusively on the shoulders of churches, charitable organizations, and individuals willing to help. This is what I am doing. But how lucky you are, my children, to be growing up in a free Fatherland!"

She turned suddenly to Yanush. "Who are you?" she asked him.

"A little Pole," came the prompt reply. This question and answer was from a patriotic rhyme we both knew by heart.

Mom obviously had something on her mind as she continued questioning Yanush. The last question was whether he loved his country.

"I love it with all my heart," Yanush's voice was ringing with fortitude and elation.

"Then don't ever forget that," Mommy concluded pointedly, giving her young son a warm embrace.

Our mom didn't take her charitable work lightly. Known as the gracious lady, she lived her heart's call to help those less fortunate. My mother's warmth and dedication attracted some influential ladies to the local chapter of St. Vincent de Paul. Funds were urgently needed for the charitable projects; therefore, shows, lotteries, and plays were being organized.

One of the most successful events was the "Doll's Open House" staged at the Under Golden Lion Hotel on Krolovka Street. For weeks, the volunteer sponsors were busy sewing gorgeous outfits for the dolls, which were then sold to raise money for the poor. The beautifully arranged exhibit attracted so many people that it was a sold-out event.

Mom included Yanush and me in her ongoing charitable activities. We danced a graceful *polonaise* and folk dances, recited patriotic poems, and found that our efforts to help a good cause turned out to be fun.

My parents entertained often, but the biggest feast was the celebration of New Year's Eve. The whole house was made sparkling for the arrival of the guests, some of them from the nearby cities of Bydgosh and Torun. Polish hospitality is proverbial: "Guest home, God home." The tables were exquisitely laid with white damask linen and silver tableware. The golden chrysanthemums, beautifully arranged in a carved crystal bowl, added a touch of freshness. The genuinely Polish dishes for this occasion were served: borsch (beet soup) and bigos, which was made of sauerkraut cooked in dry wine or Madeira, with assorted meats and a variety of other ingredients. The recipes for these were well-guarded secrets of each household.

Course followed course, accompanied by wines suited to the character of each. The dinner was crowned by the roasted suckling piglet brought in on a large tray to the acclaim of the revelers. The sweets and coffee and liqueurs followed. The feast took hours.

Through all of the merriment, the great old grandfather clock, standing between two large windows in the dining room, ticked away the final minutes of the old year. Just as it was about to strike midnight, there came the popping of champagne corks, the outbursts of laughter, and the exchange of greetings. And slowly, solemnly, the clock struck twelve. As if on cue, the party grew quiet.

Tucked in bed in my room, I had been waiting for that moment. I listened intently for the haunting strains of the nostalgic song I knew they would sing:

> *How fast life is passing*
> *As torrent time flows by*
> *In a year, a day, a moment*
> *In vain to look for us.*

Graphic sign of celebration of 800 years of Inowroclaw

Our family, late summer of 1938

2

The last day of school came, as usual, in late June, shortly after my twelfth birthday. To celebrate the occasion, my Uncle Stefan invited me for a special ice cream treat at a popular in-town coffee house, A Sweet Little Hole.

Uncle Stefan, Mom's younger brother, held a position of bookkeeper in my parents' store. Since he was still a bachelor, he often dined with us. Taller than all the salesclerks, he wore glasses that only enhanced the aura of authority and reserve so specific to him. Few people knew of his love of poetry.

There was a special bond between Uncle Stefan and me. When I was in the first grade, I came down with scarlet fever, a dreadful childhood disease in those days. There were no antibiotics then, so I was very ill for a long time, and my recovery was slow. When my parents were thanking Dr. Mieroslawski for saving my life, he said, "It's not me, but Providence."

It was Uncle Stefan who helped me step by step to catch up with the weeks of schoolwork I missed. He was such a good tutor that by the end of the second grade, I received the school award as the best student in my class.

As soon as we were seated in the coffee house, I said, "Uncle, we had an assignment at school to write a letter to a soldier of the border guard. They selected mine to be sent."

"That's wonderful!"

"There are rumors that war is hanging by a hair, but I don't want to believe that. I don't understand why the grown-ups don't learn to live in peace." He nodded in agreement, but said nothing.

"Oh, I almost forget to tell you that we are going to vacation at the sea after all. We'll be going back, as usual, to Hel, but this year, Dad had to get a special permit from the Municipal Office. Something about Hel being strategically located. What does 'strategically located' mean?"

Uncle Stefan reflected for a moment and then went on to explain in his usual deliberate voice. "Your quaint fishing village occupies the tip of the Hel peninsula, which commands the entrance to Gdansk harbor. Gdansk is known in German as Danzig. Hitler has recently demanded that it be turned over to Germany."

"But I've been there! Gdansk has the status of Free City."

Uncle nodded in agreement. "As a matter of fact, Poland is in charge of its foreign policy." He took a sip of coffee and calmly resumed. "We will never surrender Gdansk to Germany. But if there is going to be a war, the Germans will surely attack the Hel peninsula. Naturally, the Polish government doesn't want any German to spy on the defenses. That is why your father had to get permission to go on vacation there."

He paused, then gazed at me with a smile, and said reassuringly, "I believe you will have a wonderful vacation on Hel as usual."

"I hope so, Uncle," I said. But I was not so sure.

✂◦✂

Our summer vacation began with the arrival of my brother, Emil, or Milek, as we usually called him. Milek was five years my senior. From childhood, he had been doggedly determined to be a missionary.

"What does it mean to be a missionary?" Yanush once asked. We looked it up in the dictionary and found that it meant to be sent out, to perform a special duty.

Milek prevailed, and at twelve years of age, he was taken to Cracow, where for three years, he studied at the missionary school. He came home for summer vacations, Christmas and Easter holidays. One December, he arrived a little earlier than planned, in cold weather, and wearing an old, outgrown coat.

"My son," I heard Mom saying, "why are you in this old coat? Didn't we send you a beautiful new coat? People seeing you like this will think I am not taking good care of you. What has happened?"

Milek tried to wriggle out of the question for some time, but the truth came out when his classmate, Wojciechowski, arrived home in Milek's new coat. His mother, greatly embarrassed, told our mom. She was a poor widow with a prematurely wrinkled face, who sometimes did alterations for our household.

"Why didn't you tell me this?" Mom asked Milek. "Why didn't you give him your old coat if he was so cold in his light jacket?"

Milek hesitated for a while. "How could I give him the worst one?" I still recall his protest. "Don't you see, Mommy, this would mean that I have no respect for him?"

I loved my mother with all my heart and admired her generosity, but I had been reading a book on St. Francis of Assisi and was overwhelmed by his compassion. So I was rather surprised that Mom didn't sense that Milek could be on his way to sainthood. On second thought, however, I had to admit that not all I knew about Milek indicated saintliness, so I was not sure. How could one ever be sure of things like that? At least both St. Francis and Milek were sons of merchants and textile merchants at that!

Milek continued his studies in Cracow, and then one day, he came home and announced that he had decided to be a sailor. We never knew why he changed his mind. Trying to grasp the reason for this inconsistency, we concluded that, after all, he had remained faithful to his call—to the spell of the unknown.

In Ino, as our city of Inovrotslav was called for short, Milek attended Jan Kasprowicz Gymnasium, which means six years of high school. Soon after his return from Cracow, it became evident that he was totally immersed in his own world, interested in anything related to the sea. Yanush, Georgy (our cousin), and I caught this romance of the sea. Milek taught us to recognize the flags of many countries, to tie different marine knots, and to tap out short messages in Morse code. From Milek, I heard for the first time the name of a famous Pole, sailor, merchant marine officer, and writer, known to the world as Joseph Conrad. We were told that his full name was actually Jozef Teodor Konrad Korzeniowski.

"Remember!" on some occasion Milek exclaimed. "He wrote the most adventurous and thrilling sea tales ever written!"

In our family album was a photo of a little girl with curly blond hair sitting in the shallow water on the Baltic shore playing with wet clumps of sand. The sun was dancing on the drops of sea water on her wet face and on the glowing orange balls of the amber earrings dangling from her little ear lobes. "Gdynia, July 1929," Mom recorded under it. I was then two years old! Those earrings belonged to Mommy. As far as I remember, amber jewelry was always her favorite.

Oh! Amber! From our earliest age, all three of us were bewitched by this precious mineral washed up from the depths of the sea on the southern shore of the Baltic.

"Amber is magical!" we kids used to claim.

If you hold a piece of amber in your hand for some time, it warms up. When we rubbed it against our woolen sweaters, it released a pleasant scent and acquired a magnetic power. A small scrap of newspaper was lifted from the table before our eyes and stuck to it. Proof of amber's authenticity! We had heard that some Baltic folks still believe that amber protects against evil and relieves pain and suffering. Others laughed at that, but our dad said that in old folk stories, there is always a grain of truth.

During one of our summer vacations at Hel on the Baltic, we watched a craftsman working a raw lump of amber. "It is during the polishing process," he told us, "that sometimes a surprised craftsman finds a mosquito, ant, or other insect, or a scrap of plant trapped in it. This was possible because amber is the fossilized sticky resin of pine trees. They grew here some forty or fifty million years ago, long before humans walked the earth."

I was enchanted. With my eyes fixed on the now polished piece, golden like the sun, I tried to imagine a world so distant, with no man in sight.

When Milek was due home from Gdynia, the newly built Polish port on the Baltic coast, Dad, Yanush, and I went to pick him up at the station. We took a droshky, a horse-drawn four-wheeled coach. The coachman, Mr. Lewandowski, was our favorite. When Milek got off the train, he presented a dashing figure in his brand-new white marine uniform, the little sheathed dagger dangling by his side. I was very proud to have him as my brother.

Back home, we gathered in Dad's study. I still vividly remember that beautiful summer evening. Rozalia, our housekeeper, was serving us tea as we settled in the comfortable leather armchairs. Milek's face was beaming. He was telling Daddy that passing the exam didn't guarantee acceptance to the Naval Academy since there were only a limited number of spaces.

"I will soon be off on the training vessel, *Gift of Pomerania*. This is one of the most beautiful three-masted frigates the world has ever seen!"

"I'm proud of you, my son."

"I only hope my dreams come true." Milek's tone suddenly changed. "All the people's attention is presently centered on Gdansk. You cannot imagine, Daddy, how Gdansk has changed!"

He told us that the atmosphere of the city was charged with emotion. "The Nazis are provoking constant skirmishes and confrontations, setting the German inhabitants against the Polish. In the meantime, the German newspaper headlines are screaming about a growing mortal danger to Danzig's ethnic German population." He paused for a long while and then added reflectively, "It looks to me that all those incidents are to arouse sympathy for the German Danzigers."

Dad nodded in agreement. "What I believe," he said, "is that Hitler's recent demand for Gdansk and a wide zone across our Pomerania to East Prussia is only an excuse for his far more ambitious territorial aims. He has already occupied the Rhineland, Austria, and Czechoslovakia without resistance. He will not stop now. The British tell us, 'Don't be obstinate. You don't want to give him an excuse for starting a war.'"

Milek moved impatiently in his chair. "Haven't we learned anything in a thousand years? Doesn't their *Drang Nach Osten!* (Push to the East) call ring in our ears?"

Listening attentively to Daddy and Milek's conversation, I suddenly became aware that there were terribly difficult things going on that could not be prevented from happening. I turned to Daddy, eager to hear what he was going to say. Dad took a final puff on his cigarette and, extinguishing it in the ash tray, concluded thoughtfully.

"We cannot yield to Hitler's demands. We know from the experience of Czechoslovakia that any concession to him will be followed by further demands."

The next day was Sunday, and around one o'clock, we assembled for dinner at the table covered by a white linen tablecloth. One seat, occupied for years by Mom, was vacant, but we children pretended not to notice it, knowing how much Dad struggled being left alone. Because of Milek's arrival, Rozalia served a delicious dinner. The mood was soothing and joyful.

Since it was St. Peter and Paul's feast, traditionally the day of Dad's rifle fraternity festival, we all went to the Rifle Range Park. Dad looked splendid in his green uniform, white shirt with a stiff high collar, white gloves, and a dazzling hat adorned with a white plume. The Poles are known as sharpshooters, I had been told, and my dad was one of the best! However, I had to admit that I was glad that his targets were only cardboard.

3

In July, we were on the train starting our vacation, just the three of us. Milek was at his scout camp in the High Tatra Mountains. For the first time, Mom was not with us. It was a very new experience for us kids as well as for Dad.

"One can get to Hel by going on the train to Gdynia and then taking a boat to our village on the tip of the peninsula," Dad said. "This time, we will stay on the train all the way." We loved the boat ride and knew that the train passage along the peninsula would be tedious, but we did not complain.

"You may want to know, Halinka," Dad noticed our sagging spirits, "that Gdynia seaport was opened the very year you were born. For centuries, Gdansk was our country's only natural seaport and its window on the world."

"Gdansk? Mom took us there last year during our vacation on Hel," I said cheerfully, animated by the happy memories. "It's a beautiful city, but what I remember best is the medieval crane with its majestic silhouette mirrored in the Motlava River."

"For centuries, it was lifting heavy cargo, loading and unloading barges and ships," Dad said with his eyes on my glowing cheeks. He reached into his pocket and brought out a silver cigarette box. He took one out, lighted it, and continued. "Poland was traditionally an agricultural country. It has been the granary of Europe since the Middle Ages. The grain was loaded on flat-bottomed barges and floated through tributaries to our mighty Vistula River, which empties into the Baltic at Gdansk."

"Daddy, do you remember our nanny, Irene?" Yanush got interested. She had grown up in a rafter's family. Her tales about their adventurous vagabond life were so exciting. She taught us a song I still remember:

> *Hey, you rafter folk*
> *Hey, further and further go on*
> *With beech, pine, and oak*
> *To Gdansk on rustling wave float...*

The train had just stopped at Tchev, the last major station on a new railway connecting Silesia and Gdansk. Yanush rolled down the window, and we both looked for a familiar little mobile restaurant on the departure platform. It was there! We ordered delicious veal hot dogs served with crisp rolls on disposable plates. It seemed that nothing had changed, that life was going on as usual. It was a comfortable feeling.

To catch a glimpse of Gdansk, we both moved to the corridor and squeezed our noses against the large window. In the distance, spread out on a vast green field, a large group of young men were training. We managed to open the heavy window and were about to wave to them. Then we realized they were Nazis. When they saw the Polish train, they started to shake their fists at us. They shouted something we couldn't hear, but their venomous hostility was evident.

I felt the blood pounding in my temples as I looked into the face of hatred for the first time in my life.

We were staying in a little boarding hotel called Villa Mimosa, a fancy formal place. Yanush and I were longing for the white family house, set in a lovely garden, where we had stayed in past years with Mom. The sweetest memories of those vacations would be always linked to that place.

"Let's go see it!" Yanush always liked action.

We walked the main thoroughfare of Hel, the Village Street, and just before the post office building, we turned into a small lane that was overgrown on both sides by weeds. A short walk, and there it was, just as we remembered it! I pushed the gate to find that it was locked. Without thinking twice, we climbed over the fence, rushed to the familiar door, and knocked. But we knocked in vain. No one seemed to be home.

"Where are they?" Yanush asked, not expecting an answer. And at that moment, we realized: They were Germans! What happened to them? Where did they go? Now we noticed that the flowerbeds were neglected, although it looked as if someone was watering them occasionally.

The charming gazebo where we had taken our breakfast and our evening meal was deserted, and a layer of dust covered the table and benches. Undaunted, we passed the vegetable garden and entered the wide green meadow. How often we played ball here with children of Mom's friends who came on vacation to Hel at the same time.

On the opposite side, the meadow ended abruptly against a thick green wall of majestic pines. A light breeze brought their familiar scent. In the shade of this pine grove, we often took our afternoon tea, enjoying pastries we had bought in a little bakery on our way back from the beach. A winding path meandered through the forest, and we knew it well. It led to the lighthouse and, further away, to the wild beaches of the open sea.

This lighthouse had always held a special attraction for us. Each night, it sent, like clockwork, dazzling rays of light shooting across the dark mysterious sea. However, now a large sign warned us:

No Passage
Restricted Military Area

We had seen similar signs the previous day. This morning, we noticed, with dismay, that the thick pine groves on both sides of the catwalks leading over the sand dunes to the open beach were bordered by a mesh fence topped with barbed wire. To our surprise, the vast gorgeous beach of finest sand was practically deserted.

Now we stood here, in front of the unfriendly sign, wondering who was trying to spoil our vacation. My eyes found the house and focused on the faraway front door. Maybe Mom would open it and call, "Halinka! Bobus!" The door remained closed. I knew then that we came here not only wanting to visit the place we liked, but also hoping to see once more the lovely, warm, encouraging smile on our mom's face. I turned to Yanush and gently took his hand in mine.

"Come, Bobus," I said as she would have said. "Dad must be looking all over for us."

"Daddy, Daddy, guess who is here on Hel! Mrs. Pilsudska[1]! We saw her passing in a carriage on the Village Street," Yanush announced, entering the room.

"Look who is here," Dad reciprocated.

It was Mr. Skrzypinski, our next-door neighbor, who only recently moved out from Ino. We were so glad to see his friendly face.

"Did you come with Mrs. Pilsudska?" Yanush asked him.

"Not at all. I am here because my doctor wants me to stop smoking, relax, walk a lot, and inhale pristine sea air, rich in iodine."

Mr. Skrzypinski was a broad-shouldered handsome man. He used to run a jewelry store in Ino, but his military bearing revealed the years he spent in Pilsudski's Legion. He had always been proud of his long service to the Fatherland. As usual those days, the talk turned to the clouds on the political horizon.

"Did you see today's newspaper?" Mr. Skrzypinski asked Dad. "Since Stalin replaced Litwinow with Molotov, there are disturbing signs of a clear rapprochement between the Soviet Union and Germany." Dad stared at him, obviously concerned.

"This rapprochement doesn't indicate anything good for our country." Dad wrinkled his brows. "Both Stalin and Hitler are unscrupulous men lusting for power. They are dangerous."

"What is even more alarming," Mr. Skrzynski was deeply troubled, "is that Hitler has stopped talking about the menace of world Bolshevism, and there are negotiations going on to improve Soviet-German trade relations. What are Hitler and Stalin plotting? Hitler is a villain, but Stalin… those rumors about new purges in Russia…"

Dad looked at me and Yanush and changed the subject. "What a beautiful evening! Let's go for a walk on the pier!"

On the way, we found a little bench and stayed on the beach to watch the sunset. The air was pleasant, with a refreshing breeze. The waves were rippling, gently spreading over the fine sand. A few seagulls held their last debate before nightfall.

∽o∾

"You were with Pilsudski's Legion, Mr. Skrzypinski, during the famous Battle of Warsaw. I've always wondered why it's called the Miracle on the Vistula. Oh, tell us, tell us what it was like." I couldn't have pleased him more.

"Let's then go back to 1920," he began. "After taking power in Russia, the Bolsheviks decided to spread the flames of revolution to the capitalist countries of Western Europe. Poland stood in their way. How vividly I remember that spring!" Mr. Skrzypinski continued. "The Red Army, some one million strong, crushed over the eastern frontier of our just recreated republic. Their battle cry, 'We will drown the Polish army in its own blood!' sometimes still arouses me from sleep."

Mr. Skrzypinski told us about the battles that had been fought with distinction to repulse the swarming Bolshevik invaders. Nonetheless, by August, the Red Army under General Tukhachevsky was within shelling distance of Warsaw.

"Our commander-in-chief, Marshal Pilsudski, knew how outnumbered and exhausted our soldiers were. A miracle was needed to save the capital from being engulfed by the Bolsheviks."

Yanush listened breathlessly, his face tight with emotion. "And what...what did he do?"

"He devised a brilliant and daring maneuver. He quickly moved his assault force units to the rear of the front...over a hundred miles southeast of Warsaw. My First Infantry Regiment of the Third Army under Major Kozicki, was put on alert in Lubartov on the River Wieprz, which was the headquarters of the chief of staff of the Middle Front."

"Lubartov?" I repeated. "I've never heard of it."

"A backwater town just north of Lublin. Let's see now, when General Tukhachevsky's army began its offensive on Warsaw on August 13, Marshal Pilsudski was inspecting his units in the rear. Although he found the morale of his soldiers was better than expected, he was deeply concerned about serious deficiencies in armament and equipment. During the parade of the unit stationed at Firley, near Lubartov, he observed with dismay that almost half of the proudly marching soldiers were barefoot!"

"That only proved," Dad remarked, "how eager and dedicated the volunteers were."

"In the meantime, the fate of Poland and of Europe had been hanging in the balance," Mr. Skrzypinski said. "It was on August 16, 1920, that Pilsudski's offensive was launched. Our assault forces unexpectedly sliced through Tukhachevsky's rear, severing his army's communication lines."[2]

"And was that what won the battle?" Yanush was on fire.

"Yes!" Mr. Skrzypinski exclaimed.

Encircled, the Russians panicked, and the Poles rode on their necks. Tens of thousands were taken prisoner, tens of thousands annihilated, and the rest were retreating in total disarray. General Budenny's Cossack cavalry defeat at Zamost concluded the war.

"The Polish victory was stunning. Lenin begged for peace. Not only Poland, but all of Western Europe was saved from the Bolshevik terror," Mr. Skrzypinski said proudly. "That is why," he turned to me, all smiles, "this battle is called the Miracle on the Vistula."

"Our nation learned over the centuries how to persevere in the most threatening invasions," Dad remarked. "Surely we don't want the Russians on our soil now any more than we did in 1920. At least then, the defeated Germany was no threat to Poland."

Our mood became much brighter as we kids sang along with Mr. Skrzypinski's legionary songs. For him, they brought back memories of the World War.

Here the white roses
Are in full bloom
Return, my Yasio
Return from war soon…

He was so pleased that he offered to take all three of us on a trip to Gdynia. The next morning, we boarded a steamboat ferrying between Gdynia and Hel. Yanush and I were standing in the bow, watching with delight the dance of wavelets formed by the passage of the boat and laughing at the playful swirls of white foam. The Polish flag was proudly fluttering in the light breeze. The blue summer sky overhead and the immense vastness of the open sea combined to create a feeling of serenity. Yet deep down, I realized how deceptive this sense of peace really was. Our frequent referrals to the threat of war, the foreboding signals of what might come, overshadowed the wonderful experience of being back on our beloved sea. How different this vacation was from all those happily spent on Hel in years gone by!

4

I was deeply asleep, carried into a realm of rest and dreams. I wanted to stay there a little longer, but something was pulling me away. I recognized my dad's voice. He said softly, "Wake up, Halinka!" I opened my eyes, and in the dim light coming from the slightly ajar door, I saw his silhouette as he bent over me.

"Get up, my child, and get ready! We'll be leaving soon," he said and was swiftly gone. Not once in my entire life had my dad ever come into my room to wake me up. This must be something very important. In a flash, the word from the newspaper headline, printed in gigantic black letters, leapt to my mind:

WAR!

Momentarily, I recalled yesterday's bombing of the town, the blackout, the disconnected electricity and gas. It was on September 1 that the foreboding news of Germany's attack on Poland came over the radio. I jumped from my bed and saw Milek and Yanush pass by my door carrying some luggage. Our housekeeper Rozalia came in. "Do you need any help? We must hurry! Here's a bag with some things you'll need."

I was obviously the last one Dad had awakened. With my bag slung over my shoulder, I ran down the stairs and out into the street that was enveloped in a cool, pre-dawn darkness. To my surprise, at the curb just in front of our house, stood a large sturdy wagon. Hitched to it was a pair of husky Percheron horses, stomping their feet and snorting impatiently. We had never owned even a single horse, so I was puzzled.

I turned to Yanush. "Where did these come from?"

"Don't you recognize them? Only recently they were hauling barrels of beer all over town. Daddy bought them from Mr. Truszkowski."

"Yes, of course," I mumbled. There was still a lot I didn't understand, but obviously, Dad had been planning all this ahead. Milek was coming out of the house carrying his bicycle. I knew he had been keeping up with the latest news.

"Milek, why are we leaving in such a hurry?"

"The Germans are already in Bydgosh. The frightened, often wounded escapees are arriving here in waves, telling bloodcurdling stories about the murder of the civilian population there."

"Why would the Germans shoot our people?" I was horrified.

"There's a rumor that it is a reprisal for the killing of some local Germans who were firing on the Polish soldiers."

Just then, Dad came down, followed by the Pankowski family with their older daughter, Lena, and son, Yulek.[3]

They were our new neighbors, who had recently moved into a large apartment across the hall from us. Yulek is going with us! I confess that despite the grave situation, this was a welcome surprise. I knew Yulek only from our occasional encounters on the staircase, but there was no doubt that he, in his smart gymnasium uniform, had been the center of my attention for the last few weeks.

"Time to go," Dad announced. "Milek will ride his bicycle. The rest of us, for the time being, will ride in the wagon."

"Dad," I pleaded, "can't I also take my bicycle? It would be easier on the horses."

"All right, but hurry!"

I dashed back into the house and grabbed the bicycle that had been a recent birthday present. By the time I reached the street, the wagon was already pulling away from the curb with the big beautiful horses straining at their harness.

I pedaled up beside Milek, and we were on our way. I could not help feeling that we were off on some exciting outing to the countryside. After only a few blocks, I found that riding my bicycle on our cobblestone street was too hard. I decided to put it on top of the wagon and climbed on myself.

We were passing the outskirts of town when it became evident that we were not the only ones who had heard of the bloody terror in Bydgosh. From side streets, other escapees were joining the procession, and soon, the road was overflowing with all manner of vehicles laden with children and hectically packed belongings. Whole families were on the move, trying to keep track of each other in the confusion.

By daylight, we were well out into the countryside, and looking ahead, I could see a long stream of human misery moving along the road. The pace was very slow, so the grown-ups walked now behind the wagon. At times, the column stopped for no apparent reason. Then somewhere up ahead, the people would begin to move, and we would follow until it would come to a halt again.

Fortunately, the weather was splendid. The sky was a brilliant, almost cloudless blue, and the temperature was unusually warm for September. We stopped for lunch in the cool shade of a grove of trees. Everybody was hungry since we had all missed breakfast.

"The weather is a blessing," Mrs. Pankowska said. But her husband and Dad, who had military experience, held that this perfect weather only facilitated Hitler's onslaught on Poland.

The mention of Hitler's name caused a cold shiver to run through my spine. In recent months, I had been collecting and pasting in my scrapbook clippings from the illustrated weekly magazine, *Swiatowid* (World View). I recalled the Führer's tense face, fiery eyes, and wild gestures at a mass rally when he addressed a rapt German crowd. They were assembled under a sea of red banners marked with huge black swastikas. Snatches of his hateful, threatening speeches came back. Now the threat was real.

Dad soon had us back on the road. The news was depressing. German armies were advancing, with thunderous speed.

"If they catch up with us, their tanks will sweep us from the road," Mrs. Pankowska said, fear in her voice.

However, Milek was hopeful. "I heard that Britain is honoring its guarantees to Poland and has declared war on Germany. France followed only hours later, however reluctantly. As our Allies, they will certainly launch an offensive from the west, and the Germans will be caught fighting on two fronts."

Milek had taken the Allies at their word, but I was aware that Dad remained strangely silent, evidently concealing his opinion.

The afternoon was exhausting as we walked mile after mile. This was not going to be the adventure I had naively imagined at the start. We stopped for the night at a farmhouse just off the road. The farmer and his family shared our feelings and worries about the Germans. They rented us one room and offered their kitchen so that Mrs. Pankowska and Rozalia could prepare supper for us. They graciously accepted payment for their hospitality. Milek and Yulek were in charge of caring for the horses, getting them unhitched from the wagon, and feeding and watering them.

When we retired to our room, Mr. and Mrs. Pankowski were offered a bed, Dad was given a cot, and the rest of us were going to sleep on the floor, on hastily arranged straw pallets.

I was too exhausted to eat very much. It was a long emotional day. I wished, oh how I wished, for a bath and my soft comfortable bed. I fell into a fitful sleep. I must have been uncomfortable because I woke up a couple of times, but eventually, I dropped off into deep slumber.

The next morning, after an early breakfast, we were well on our way. To my surprise, I felt rested, my confidence restored. For the first time since the beginning of our trip, Yulek walked close to me. For some time, neither of us said a word. But when he glanced at me with his sincere hazel eyes, my heart fluttered a bit. Yulek was three years my senior, and at the age of twelve, I was flattered by his attention. It was a ray of sunshine in our tiresome pursuit of a safer place in the path of a quickly approaching storm.

One late afternoon, we stopped to rest on the side of the road under the shade of nearby trees. Next to us, a unit of Polish soldiers were bivouacked on the grass. In their uniforms, they seemed to be as tired, dusty, and hot as we were, yet they smoked their cigarettes and chatted with good humor. I was too shy to talk to them, but Yanush started a conversation right away. One of them took a fancy to him and stroked his wavy blond hair.

"Have you kids had anything to eat today?"

"Not much," Yanush replied. "Some potatoes and cabbage." It turned out the man was a cook.

"Well," he said, "go get me a couple of bowls."

We dashed to our wagon and retrieved the bowls. The cook filled them with hot pea soup with generous pieces of bacon in it. We agreed we'd never tasted any better soup in our lives!

The previous day, an encounter with our army had been less fortunate. We were stopped, and one of the soldiers approached Dad.

"Sir, I'm very sorry," he said, "but we are going to have to requisition your horses. We will give you two of our horses. As you can see, they are too worn out to do military duty. I hope you understand."

What could Dad say? He understood and knew that the horses we got in exchange would barely be able to pull the wagon with our luggage, but not with people on it. Now everyone would have to walk. Yet they still were better than no horses at all. Yanush and I adopted them and petted them often. We fed them apples and even sacrificed little cubes of sugar from our daily allotment.

At the beginning of our journey, Dad and Mr. Pankowski decided to avoid the cities and towns that from the first day of the war had been bombed by the German planes. Passing a fair distance from Kutno, we heard the far-off roaring of artillery. We didn't know then that they were the sounds of battle.

It was impossible to distinguish between solid news and rumors. But they were all grievous. Even Milek admitted that not only were the Polish soldiers outnumbered, but also the Germans had impressive technical superiority.

"Now more than ever," Mr. Pankowski said, "it won't be the dedication or bravery of soldiers or even the military genius of a commander that will decide the outcome of war. It will be technical superiority. The high speed and flexibility of the German tank formations, supported by the air force, is unprecedented."

It was another of those beautiful September days. I remember most clearly our column of people moving in the general direction of Warsaw. We were passing through flat cropland. There were no trees in sight, not even bushes. The crops had been cut, leaving just a yellow stubble on the fields. The road was straight and flat. Somewhere ahead of us was a family with two small children. Their horse pulled a small cart and a cow followed, presumably to provide milk for the children. Suddenly, the column stopped. I noticed that people walking ahead of us were looking at the sky before we heard the faint sound of engines. It grew louder and then we saw planes, flying toward us. My father was one of the first to see the black crosses on the wings.

"They're German planes," he shouted. "Run to the ditches!"

We tumbled into the drainage ditch on our side of the road. Yanush and I were clinging to each other, covering our heads with our hands as though that would provide protection from danger. The weeds blanketing the ditch were moist and cool. The roar increased. The planes circled our road, dipping lower, and now there was the unmistakable sound of machine gun fire and the thudding impact of bullets hitting the ground all around us. I could hear men calling, women screaming, children crying, and horses neighing. Suddenly, it was over. By the time the sound of the engines faded away, the people were on their feet, and I heard shouts of frustration.

"Barbarians! They shoot at civilians!"

Yanush and I jumped out of the ditch to find that, thank God, Dad, Milek, Rozalia, and Pankowski's family were unharmed. A man was lying on the road just ahead of us, his wife bent over him, sobbing. A cow stood patiently dying, with its head down, its blood slowly running out onto the ground.

People were helping each other, and somehow, in a surprisingly short time, the lengthy column of refugees was again moving ahead. After the plane's attack, uncertainty besieged our minds. What should we do? Continue to travel and be an easy target for the German shooting? Our food supplies continued to dwindle. We needed some reliable information about the current political situation. After serious deliberations, Dad decided that he and Milek would ride on bicycles to a town visible in the distance. The rest of us, with Mr. Pankowski, would forge ahead. We were to meet that evening at a designated location a few miles away.

It was early evening when we reached our destination and settled down in a farmer's house close to a crossroads. We expected Daddy and Milek to show up shortly. We hoped they would bring some food. But they did not come. This was my longest, most anxious night. We waited all of the following day in vain, worrying about what had happened to them. The farmer was obviously eager to have us go on our way. He was even willing to provide some food for our journey.

It was in the third week of the war that we heard the heartbreaking news. Warsaw, our capital, encircled by the German armies, was in flames, burning under incessant bombardment from the air and by artillery, but still heroically fighting on against the odds. Soon, more heart-crushing news reached us. On September 17, the Soviet army, unannounced, crossed the Polish frontier and was occupying our eastern provinces. I instantly recalled Daddy's fear of Soviet invasion when he talked with Mr. Skrzypinski in Hel.

"Our forces are now caught in two claws of a pincer," Mr. Pankowski said in a deep voice. "There is no reason for us to continue our journey. Who knows what may happen next? We have to seriously consider going back home."

The next morning, I was watching Yulek hitching the horses to the wagon, when I noticed a quickly approaching cloud of dust on the country road. I alerted Yulek. We stood there petrified as a column of three motorcycles emerged from the dust, each with a sidecar bearing a soldier armed with a machine gun and belts of ammunition.

Will they shoot? We quickly got inside the farmhouse, and they followed us. I could roughly understand that they were asking about Polish soldiers. Rozalia, who had learned German in the Prussian school, told them that we hadn't seen any soldiers in days. "Where are you going?" one of the Germans inquired.

She explained that we didn't know what to do but that we were considering just going back home.

"Yes, by all means," he advised. "You should go home. It's too dangerous to be on the road. Go home."

We were all surprised at the gentle tone of his voice and the obvious concern for our safety. At least some of the Germans were decent people. We were soon going to find out that he was an exception.

Once we headed home, the roads were much less crowded. It was as though the refugee throngs had just dissipated, leaving no trace of their passing. I never knew how it happened. The journey was easier now, but evidently, we were more exhausted. Maybe it was because of a total lack of hopeful news. Yanush and I were craving normal meals, and we talked often about food.

All this time, the unbearable anxiety about what had happened to Dad and Milek weighed heavily on our minds. Yulek must have seen how difficult all this was on me because he began to spend more time talking with me. The long eventful journey had drawn us closer together.

One day, I could hardly put one foot in front of the other. Evening was approaching, and we could not find a place to spend the night. There were no farm buildings anywhere in sight. Finally, we simply pulled off the road just as darkness fell and, for the first time in our entire journey, decided to spend the night in the open. I was sitting down, leaning up against a fence with my eyes on the glow of houses burning in the distance, obviously hit in an air raid. I had been feeling unwell all day. Something was wrong with me! If only Mom were here she surely would help me, I thought. Finally I went to Rozalia, although very reluctantly.

"Oh, Halinka dear," she said tenderly. "You have just become a woman. Come with me, and we will take care of this."

After returning to my place by the fence, I felt very exhausted. Surely, things couldn't get any worse. We were caught in the vortex of uncertainty in the midst of a raging war, not knowing what had happened to Dad and Milek. How different was our world only a year ago. Then suddenly, I recalled a game I had played with Yanush on some occasion: What tree would we like to be, given a chance? Yanush wanted to be a sturdy oak. I wanted to be a weeping willow. I knew better now. I was none of those beautiful trees. I was only a fallen leaf, tossed by the winds of war. With my back up against the fence, I fell asleep.

One evening, we stopped at a large farm where the family took us in. The farmer turned to Yulek and me. "Why don't you kids walk down to the orchard and pick some fruit for tonight?"

Once in the orchard, we started to gather the sun-blushed apples and the purple perfectly ripe plums, laughing playfully until our baskets were full. Yulek slid down from a tree and landed right in front of me. We found ourselves standing face-to-face.

"The sun is playing on your hair," he said and, at the same moment, extended his hands to snatch mine. We were walking back to the house, hand in hand. It was very comforting. When we got close, we walked slightly apart. I am sure I was still smiling.

5

We were approaching Inovrotslav, dragging our sore feet behind the wagon pulled now by two horses that were skin and bones, partly blinded, and pushed to their limits. The Germans had taken our horses at the first roadblock and given us these miserable creatures instead. We picked up our pace when, over the flat Kuyavian plain, we saw the outlines of the city's buildings. The autumn air seemed sweet-scented now. We were almost home!

Once we reached our Holy Ghost Street, Yanush and I decided to run ahead. It was a long street, and we had to stop sometimes to catch our breath, but then we pushed ahead again. Reaching the Town Square, we found that Dad's store was closed. In no time, we were climbing the stairs of our house, taking two steps at a time. We rang the bell, again and again, but in vain. This was a very frustrating development. We still didn't give up. Aunt Marysia, our mom's sister, lived on the second floor of our large apartment building. More stairs up, and we were knocking on her door. This time, a door opened, and we were face-to-face with her.

"Am I ever glad to see you both back!" she exclaimed, her arms around us. "Georgy!" she called our cousin, "come and see who is here!"

"Auntie, where is Daddy?" I asked impatiently.

Her face suddenly saddened. She murmured, "He is in prison. The Germans seized several men in town as hostages. I am so sorry to tell you that upsetting news, but we are hoping they will be released soon."

This couldn't be true! I was shocked to the core after all we had been through.

"And Milek?" I still managed to ask.

"Milek is working in the bakery. He will be back soon."

She went downstairs with us to open the door to our apartment. "Welcome home," she said, and her voice was warm and encouraging. "Let me know if you need anything."

I entered my room. Everything was there as I had left it. I approached the case that held my books, slid open its glass door, and ran my fingers over the backs of volumes neatly stacked on the shelves. Yes, I was home among all the familiar things. Suddenly, a thought pierced my mind. Without Daddy, this home is like a roofless house. Passing by the mirror, I noticed my tumbled hair and realized how dirty and tired I was. More than anything, I needed a bath!

Rozalia busied herself about the kitchen preparing to serve a quick meal, and when it was nearly ready, Milek came in. Both Yanush and I were overwhelmed with joy to see him. He took us both in his outstretched arms, and his embrace was more affectionate than usual. After we finished our dinner, he said, "We will talk some more tomorrow.

Now, to bed! You must be terribly tired. But how glad I am that you are safely back!"

We slept like logs until noon the next day.

After exhausting days of wandering and uncertainty, we appreciated being back home. It was so good to be able to sleep in one's own bed and to be served normal meals. Rozalia had been very resourceful. It was also helpful that she spoke fluent German.

Yet in no time, a grim reality showed its ugly face, and we realized that the world to which we had returned was hostile. The Germans renamed Inovrotslav, Hohensaltza, and the Poles were supposed to survive on much-reduced food rations than those allowed to the Germans. Luckily, our cupboards were full to capacity because on the first day of the war, Dad bought a large supply of provisions from his friend, Mr. Bukowski, who had a "colonial" store at the Town Square. The cellar was well stocked for winter with coal and wood, a barrel of sauerkraut, and apples lined up on the shelves. For the time being, we were safe and well supplied.

After a long vacation, Yanush and I were eager to get back to our normal routine. It was the end of September, yet the only schools open in town were for the German children and youth. What about us? One by one, very quickly, we had to absorb scores of new rules and regulations imposed by the German occupiers on the Poles. We were ordered to stick to our areas, not to congregate in groups larger than three persons, except in church, to strictly observe the nightly curfew…and that was only the beginning of the litany of the rules.

It was late afternoon when the three of us gathered in Milek's room. The last twilight shafts of daylight were flickering on the map spread out on his desk.

"The situation is grave," Milek said. I had never seen him as serious as he was at that moment. It didn't escape me that my brother, who was only seventeen and not so long ago had played tricks with us, now spoke as a grown-up. With his head bent over the map, he continued. "Look here! By now, one-half of our country is occupied by Nazi Germany and the other is in the iron grip of Soviet Russia."

It took me a moment to collect my thoughts. I recalled that Mr. Pankowski decided we should return home to Ino after we had heard the shocking news that on September 17, the Russian army had invaded Poland from the east.

"I am still a kid," I said shyly, "but this is nothing less than a new partition of Poland."

"You are right, Halinka," Milek agreed, "Hitler prepared for this war ever since he came to power. The Polish soldiers fought valiantly[1], but they fought alone. England and France did not keep their promise to stand by their Ally. The Soviet invasion was the final blow. We are facing a hard time."

For a while, we all sat very quietly. It was Yanush who broke the silence.

"In times like these, we need Daddy to be with us. We came here hoping to find out what you know about him."

"You already know that he is in prison," Milek spoke calmly. "He is held there with some other well-known citizens to deter the Poles from carrying out any resistance or sabotage against the occupying forces." As he looked at each of us reassuringly, he said, "At least their detention is publicly known. We have to hope that he will be released soon."

❦

We were home at last, but our home turned out to be a bird cage because of the many things we couldn't do. When Rozalia went out next day on some errands, Yanush got an idea.

"Why don't we go see a bit of the town?"

We couldn't go to Solanky Park, our favorite place, because it was *Nur fur Deutsche* (Germans only). To ride a bicycle was out of the question. A Pole could not even own a bicycle unless it was used to ride to work. Could we take the tram? The first wagon was now only for the Germans, and the second one for the Poles with work passes. We had been warned that a Pole could be shot if he was wandering around the train station or caught on a train without a work pass!

"Let's just go for a walk downtown," I decided.

The house at the corner of Market Place and Queen Yadviga Street was a heap of rubble. We had known that lovely building well since it used to house the Under the Eagle pharmacy, the oldest in Ino. Georgy had already told us that the Germans had set it on fire only a day after the town was occupied. Workmen were busy clearing off what was left of the building. A couple of them were trying to bring down a white eagle carved in stone, Poland's national emblem, which was still perched over the ruins where the entrance to the pharmacy had been. The scene was heartbreaking.

Walking down Queen Yadviga Street, we heard only German. Its harsh sound hurt my ears. All shop signs were in German. From some store display windows, the mustached face of Adolf Hitler scowled at us.

"Let's go home," I said, seeing that Yanush was as bewildered by the new face of our Inovrotslav as I was.

Momentarily, I recalled that speaking Polish in public places was strictly forbidden.

On entering our area, we noticed that the plate bearing the name of our street had been replaced. I read it in disbelief: Horst Wessel Strasse. When had this happened? We decided to go straight to Aunt Marysia to seek an explanation.

"Aunty, who is this Horst Wessel after whom our Holy Ghost Street was renamed?" I was trying to speak calmly.

"I wanted to know that myself," she said. "It wasn't difficult to find out because Horst Wessel was Hitler's darling. You see, he composed the most popular Nazi song sung right after the German National Anthem at the National Socialist Party's meetings."

She reflected for a moment or two. "He was a member of the SD—as I now recall—so no wonder he had some enemies. When he was killed by an enemy bullet, Hitler declared him a national hero."[2]

"And what is this SD?" Yanush asked.

"It is The Nazi Internal Security. Plainly speaking, it is a bunch of informers and scums. They are called brown shirts, distinct from the black shirts, which are worn by the SS (*Schutzstaffel*)."

But I was still not satisfied. "Please, Aunty, I have one more question. Is it true that when the *Wehrmacht* (German army) was entering the town on September 8, shots were fired at the soldiers from the house where the Under the Eagle pharmacy had been?"

She turned to me. "We neighbors don't believe a word of it. It is pure Nazi propaganda, blown up in the German paper *Veolkischer Beobachter*, claiming that it was a pocket of resistance supposedly nestled there. The only shooting we heard of in Ino that day was from the Trade School at Sienkiewicz Square."

"The shots were from the school?" Yanush was choked with emotion.

"We actually know very little of what exactly happened there," Aunt Marysia hesitated to share the heartbreaking story with us, but seeing our persistence, she relented.

Muted by the passage of time, her voice still brings back a memory of Ino's youthful scouts' desperate act of defiance against the overwhelming Nazi deluge.

6

The Nazis held our town in an iron grip.

It was my outing day. Rozalia collected a small loaf of bread, some sausage links, homemade cookies, and a pack of cigarettes and put them into a little linen sack with Dad's name, Jan Bratek, printed on it in thick black letters. In the autumn chill, I stood in line by the high prison wall with other women. Their weary faces marked by anxiety, they were besieged by the same thought: Will the guard take the parcel? Will he deliver it to my dear one?

How I longed to have our daddy back with us. How I hoped that he was still alive in one of the murky cells, in the belly of this detested monster, the Nazi prison.

∽o∽

Marylka and Leshek, our cousins, surprised us by coming to say good-bye. If I remember correctly, Marylka was four years my senior and Leshek two years older than me. Since early childhood, they had been our play leaders. Marylka was very creative with her hands; Leshek had a boundless imagination and a knack for drawing. He was fun to be around because of his pleasant personality.

They taught Yanush, Georgy, and me how to make and fly kites, create gorgeous Christmas tree ornaments, and later how to manage a kayak on the River Notec. When we played Indians and our team of Mohawk braves was being attacked by those hateful Hurons waving their tomahawks, Leshek would come to my rescue, even if I were held captive on top of our highest wardrobe standing in the hall.

"Where are you going?" I asked Marylka, hugging her warmly. I had not seen her for weeks. "And how did you manage to get permission from the Germans to travel?"

"Where have you been?" she laughed at my naïve question. "My transport is leaving next week. My best friend will be going along. Haven't you heard about the mandatory conscription of Polish youth for work in the Reich?"

"No. What are you supposed to do there?"

"We are going to work on their farms. Hitler is a megalomaniac, obsessed with power and warfare. Many thousands of German *bauers,* that means farmers, were drafted to the army or assigned to armament factories. The Third Reich desperately needs rural laborers, and the authorities decreed that we Poles from the occupied territories would provide slave labor."

I looked at Marylka in disbelief. "This is highly unethical."

"They've been away," Leshek came to my aid, "and may not know what is going on here."

He turned and said to me, "Did you hear, Halinka, that all of Poland's western provinces, including Pomerania, Great Poland, and Silesia were incorporated this month into the Deutsche Reich? As Poles, we now have no rights whatsoever and are obliged to work for our German masters."

"But you passed with distinction your entrance exams to gymnasium in June."

"There will be no more Polish schools. Polish children will not be encouraged to read."

Marylka, an avid reader, had been listening, her chin propped up on her hand. "All Polish public libraries in town are closed," she said. "The books are being loaded on trucks and hauled away to be burned."

"How can Poles be expected to work if they aren't able to read?" Yanush was anxious to know.

"All they are supposed to do," Leshek clarified German intentions, "is to follow their masters' orders."

Rozalia entered the room with a tray. "Hot chocolate and some home-baked cookies," she announced. "Enjoy them while they last. Who knows what tomorrow will bring?"

"How pleasant our life seemed to be only a couple of months ago," Marylka tried to change the subject, but in vain. We had to be able to understand the meaning of this new reality, no matter how gloomy it was.

"You're a scout, Leshek. Did you hear what happened here on September 8 in the Trade School?" Yanush restarted the painful topic.

"Those boys are in the hearts and prayers of all Poles in Ino. What is even more outrageous and painful is that their ordeal was not isolated."

He told us that in Bydgosh, the Boy Scouts were the first victims of the Nazi occupiers. They were herded to the marketplace, put against the wall by an SS firing squad, and shot—the whole group of them! And this was only the beginning of gruesome mass arrests and murder.

"How do you know what happened in Bydgosh so well?" Yanush was puzzled. "Not from the radio, because a Pole caught listening to a radio would surely be killed on the spot."

"You don't ask questions like that these days, Yanush. The point is, you have to pretend to know nothing about anything. This is our new rule." Marylka was very serious.

"What the Germans are doing to us," I sighed, "is an evil thing."

"I have been thinking a lot recently about war, any war," Leshek spoke with a voice charged with emotion. "War breeds hatred and brings destruction and death where once people lived in peace."

"It takes only one megalomaniac," Marylka concluded, getting hastily to her feet. It was time to part.

"Farewell!" I had been fighting back tears.

"Are we going to see each other again?" she asked as we reached the door. It was a question not one of us could answer. After Marylka and Leshek left, I stood restlessly for a while, and then, with uneasy steps, I approached the sliding glass door leading to the balcony and looked out. It was getting dark, and I could see the dried-out stalks of the petunias bending in the cold autumn wind. No one had thought to remove the flowers from the boxes, and now they were brownish skeletons with no trace of their summer beauty. Something began to stir within me. I wouldn't open the door because outside was a hostile world. The world I used to know was crumbling under my feet.

That night, my pillow was wet with tears. The cruel occupation, Daddy in prison. Would he come out of it alive? What will happen to all of us?

I fell on my knees and prayed with all my heart for deliverance.

﹏∽o∽﹏

One evening, just before All Saints' Day, I heard a gentle knocking on our front door. Because of the mandatory curfew, this was unusual and disquieting. It was Mr. Pankowski, our next-door neighbor.

"Is Milek around?" he asked in a hushed voice. Only when he entered the room did I notice his furrowed brow.

Milek came in, and after a brief exchange of greetings, they were seated together, heads close, engrossed in whispered conversation. I pretended to be totally immersed in my reading, but out of the corner of my eye, I saw Milek's face soon turn somber. This was enough to give me the jitters. What was bothering them? Some time passed before Mr. Pankowski, aware of my presence, apologized.

"It was just a brief compatriot's talk."

Mr. Pankowski had hardly left when I turned anxiously to Milek. "What has happened? What news did Mr. Pankowski share with you, coming so late at night?"

He looked straight into my eyes; I noticed that his cheek muscles twitched. "Promise me not to share with Yanush or Rozalia what I will tell you."

"I promise," I said.

"Something most gruesome happened in the prison. It's impossible for the Germans to hide it all from the Poles."

"Oh my god!" I gasped.

"Sunday night, two well-known Germans in town returned to Ino after a hunting party and, heavily drunk, forced their way into the prison. The prisoners, the town's elite, were brutally dragged from their cells, mauled, and chased through the corridor with intoxicated German madmen shooting indiscriminately at them."[1] Milek had anguish written all over his face. I stared desperately at him, asking no further questions. He couldn't know the names of the prisoners who were killed. Like me, he must be worried about Dad, I thought, prayerfully hoping that our father was not among the victims. With his jaws tightened, he put his hand on my shoulder.

"Let's pray," he said.

7

Our Parish Church of St. Nicholas, rebuilt in a Gothic style in the late Middle Ages, had been a beacon of the town's spiritual life for 700 years. I was baptized there. I had been one of the flower girls in the traditional feast processions. Wearing our white dresses, white stockings, and white shoes, and with our heads crowned with wreaths of green, we sprinkled handfuls of fresh flower petals on the road. We were followed by our parish pastor, who held in his hands the golden monstrance with the Blessed Sacrament. It all seemed eons ago.

Now on a cloudy Sunday morning, I was kneeling before the large crucifix set above the side altar. This crucifix dated from the fourteenth century, and generations of people before me had sought help here. I folded my hands and prayed ardently with the total confidence of a child, "O, Lord, Daddy was snatched from us during this terrible time when we need him most. Deliver him from the hell of prison. He must be worrying himself sick about us. O Lord, I implore you to hear my prayer and bring him back home."

I stayed to hear the Mass. The Church of St. Nicholas was the only Catholic church in our town still open for the Poles. In the first months of the brutal Nazi occupation, Poles had come here seeking spiritual encouragement and reassurance in being together, united by community bonds. Leaving the church, I saw people who, only months ago, were confident and cheerful. Now, their faces were ravaged by anguish and fear, eyes blurred by grief. Some women were discretely wiping away their tears. I heard the familiar voice of Ms. Lewandowska, my godmother. "How are you coping, Halinka?"

"I have been praying for Dad's deliverance from the prison," I whispered back. "Do you know the Father who celebrated the Mass? And what has happened to our pastor Father Jaskowski?"

Ms. Lewandowska lived at the marketplace not far from us so we were walking home together. "Don't you know?" she said in a hushed voice, checking cautiously around to make sure there was no one near. "Soon after the *Wehrmacht* occupied the town, he was arrested, and no one has heard from him since."

I lapsed into a worried silence as she kept talking about the hundreds of Ino's Polish citizens who were seized and herded to the vacant army barracks at Railway Street, where some were executed by SS firing squads and many others loaded into trucks and taken to Gnievkovo forest and summarily shot.

I could barely continue walking, my limbs suddenly strangely heavy, but Ms. Lewandowska continued on, apparently eager to share the overheard news with someone she could trust.

"To tell the truth, I've been afraid even to come to church today after what I heard happened in Bydgosh. The Nazi terror surpasses anything we have ever known," my godmother concluded, her voice charged with emotion.

Noticing my pale face, she apologized. "I'm so sorry, my child," she said. "I've upset you by sharing these horrible stories. Forgive me, please. You are young. You will survive. Somebody has to survive to bear witness to what we went through. Give my love to Milek and Yanush, will you?"

I returned home terribly shaken by the news of raging Nazi terror, hurt to the very depths of my being. In my room, I broke down and wept. I refused to eat, which made Rozalia unhappy. I declined to play Chinese checkers with Yanush. I didn't touch my books.

"You have been crying. What happened?" Milek noticed my distress.

Reluctantly, I told him what I had heard from Ms. Lewandowska, and then with eyes flashing, asked the burning question, "Why did you not tell me about those gruesome murders? Why should I learn this from other people? Do you believe that your little sister should be spared upsetting news?"

"This must have been a nasty shock for you," he said calmly. "What good does it serve to dwell on the bestial slaughter of our intellectual leadership, the best among us?"

He told me that he had just heard that his favorite professor, Father Demski,[1] had been arrested and sent to the concentration camp. "He is a man of exceptional erudition and culture," he said. "It hurts. It was he who, not so long ago, told me that an idea that is imposed by violence collapses under it."

Milek believed that so many German people were misled by Hitler's thundering orations, full of lies. Someday, the Nazi's totalitarian regime would collapse. In the meantime, we had to keep our sanity intact. That night, I couldn't go to sleep. I was tossing and turning in my bed, frightening reflections spinning in my head. In the pitch black of the night, I was looking into a glaring, demoniac face, viciously laughing. Scared to death, I crossed myself, saying aloud: "In the name of the Father and the Son and the Holy Ghost…" The apparition disappeared! Morning came, and I was not yet over my solitary struggle. Yet I did not share the night's experience with anyone. In a painful way, I have tried, oh, I have tried to endure.

Not long after that, Daddy showed up, almost as if by magic. In the first moment, I couldn't believe my eyes, it seemed so unreal; the last time I had seen him, it was as in another life. I raced up to him with my heart bursting with joy and threw myself into his open arms. Wiping my tears with the palm of his hand and being deeply moved, he kissed me on the forehead, murmuring, "My little girl…my little daughter."

Yanush, who was obviously alerted by Rozalia, burst into the room. He was very excited and enthusiastic as he greeted his long-missed Daddy.

My eyes fixed on him, I noticed his emaciated figure and his pale face, although it was lit at the moment with gladness. The prison had undoubtedly wearied him. That night, after Milek returned from work, we were all four together for the first time after a long painful separation. Even though we talked and talked, Dad was quiet about his experience in the prison. I realized that he had put up with a lot while there.

Let him bask in cheer and the consolation of being together, I thought. Let him put away whatever he endured there, if only for a while.

It was a memorable night of thankful prayers followed by the first blissful sleep for many weeks. I learned quickly that we should never be caught up in total despair.

The unrelenting persecution and massive extermination of the Poles was considered far too savage even for some of the Germans. Their disgust was so profound and convincing that it deserved to be presented, even though at that time, we Poles were not aware of it. Lily Jungblut, the wife of a German landowner in Hohensalza (Inovrotslav) district, was a Party member. Nonetheless, she became profoundly outraged by the massacre of her innocent Polish neighbors. Mrs. Jungblut wrote a sharp letter directly to Goering, one of Hitler's key henchmen and the Third Reich's Minister of Aviation. In this letter, she complained that "thousands and thousands of innocent men are being shot."

She knew that many of those murders, prompted by hatred, greed, and revenge, had been committed by members of a paramilitary organization known as *Selbstschutz* (Self-Defense), drawn by the hundreds from the fanatical local German Minority[2] and led by SS-men trained in the *Deutsche Reich*.

Still, the pitiless liquidation of Jews, Polish intelligentsia, gentry, priests, and "troublemakers" suspected of any sign of resistance or opposition, was assigned by Heinrich Himmler, the Grand Master of the SS Order, directly to the dreaded

Einsatzgruppen. They were the mobile killing units of the *Sicherheits Polizei* (SIPO).[3] During the invasion of Poland, they followed the *Wehrmacht* advances and were feared for their ruthless mass executions.

The boldest critic of these "SS" units was the *Wehrmacht* General Johannes Blaskowitz[4], the same Blaskowitz who imposed the act of capitulation on mutilated Warsaw on September 27, 1939. Blaskowitz systematically collected the *Wehrmacht's* reports on the crimes committed in Poland on the civilian population and, with his memorandum, sent them to the army headquarters in mid-November 1939: "Great concern over illegal shooting, arrests and confiscations; risk to the discipline of the troops who see the thing happening...request for re-establishment of the rule of law...executions only to be carried out on sentence by a court."

Blaskowits, undeterred by Hitler's furious reaction to his memorandum over such "childish ideas" on the part of the army, continued to collect further evidence against the SS. Soon, the reports were pouring in from different units.

Following are quotes from two reports Blackowitz found on his desk:

In his report, General Petzel Wehrkreis, Commander of *Warthegau,* November 23, 1939, said, "In almost all major localities, the organizations (SS and Police) referred to carrying out public shootings. Selection is entirely arbitrary, and the conduct of the executions in many cases disgusting. Arrests are almost invariably accompanied by looting." In a letter dated February 2, 1940, General Ulex wrote: "The recent increase in the use of violence by the police show an almost incredible lack of human and moral qualities...The only solution, I can see, to this revolting situation, which sullies the honor of the entire German people, is that all police formations together with their senior commanders… should be dismissed in a body and the units disbanded."

In his concluding report, Blackowitz wrote to Hitler: "Every soldier feels disgusted and repelled by the crimes committed in Poland."

Unlike Blaskowitz, most of the *Wehrmacht* officers during the Polish campaign resigned themselves to the role of "spectators" of the crimes committed by the SS.

After Dad's return from the prison, his presence at home was a source of great consolation to us. Once again, the responsibility for our household was on his shoulders, although he could not assure us of any real protection.

The persistent stories of continuing persecution and intensified Nazi efforts to destroy every trace of Polish culture were shaking even Dad's stubborn will to endure. Since summer, I had not seen any of my schoolmates or neighborhood friends. Yet it was not the dreary November weather with its damp, grim days declining into early darkness that dampened our spirits, but the thickening gloom of Occupation and fear of Germans.

The Christmas season was approaching. In past years, it was a very busy and exciting time of preparation and anticipation for the most joyous event of the year. However, the rejoicing, the glory, and the ecstasy of Christmas were now totally elusive. Nevertheless, Yanush and I decided to build a Christmas crèche. I suggested that the characters should be movable so we could arrange them in different scenes. The angel turned out to be beautiful, but our project did not progress any further because new events took our attention away from it.

It was the end of November when we received a police order to stay away from the windows that night. Anyone seen looking out a window would be shot! We had been given a similar warning once before, in early October, and expected that another party rally was going to be held on the Town Square. Evening had fallen with a cold wind sweeping across the street. Yet there was still no sign of any preparation—no posting of swastika flags, no testing of microphones installed on the balcony of the building just across the street from us. We stayed longer than usual in the dining room. Its windows overlooked Holy Ghost Street. The heavy drapes were drawn, and the lights were lowered. Not one of us went to sleep, but there wasn't much comfort in being together. We were immersed in a dead silence.

Lord God! What are we waiting for? a thought flashed through my mind.

It was late at night when the sounds of some commotion outside started to reach our ears. Milek couldn't wait any longer. He sneaked into Dad's bedroom, hoping to somehow get a glimpse of the Town Square. He returned deeply shocked.

"There are a lot of people…families with children," his voice broke for a moment, "cordoned off by police."

It was all so terrifying that I got goose bumps brooding over what lay ahead for the captured families. Dad's presence had a somehow calming effect, but he himself was unsettled, pacing back and forth with his fists clenched. This was a tough night for all of us. The event, taken on such a massive scale, couldn't escape the attention of the town. Within hours the next morning, news spread that the dreaded all-powerful

SS police had staged that late-night massive round up of some of Ino's Polish families. They were directed to the Town Square and, from there, rushed in columns to the station, loaded into rail cars, and taken to an unknown destination.

This was a portent of what might come. There was no relief in sight, no escape.

As far as I can recall, I ventured into the chilly, spooky darkness of the cellar of our large apartment building on only a few occasions, and then firmly holding the hand of our maid while she went in the winter to fetch coal or potatoes for our table. The entrance to our cellar was secured by a heavy door with an old lock. The wrought-iron key to this lock caught my particular attention because it was long and roughly ornamented.

It was with this key in his hand, Daddy summoned all three of us to the entry hall. To my surprise, he included Rozalia. "Follow me quickly," he said, descending the stairs leading to the cellar. "I want to show you something very important."

He opened the cellar door. The darkness and specific smell of a long closed-in space only increased my apprehension. Whatever was Dad going to do? The flickering flame of a single candle feebly pierced the semidarkness. In total silence, we formed a circle around a freshly dug hole in the cement floor. Daddy reached into the hole and brought out a securely sealed glass jar.

"My children," he solemnly addressed us, "this jar contains your mother's jewelry and the last letter she wrote to you before her operation."

I noticed that he was speaking in an unusually somber tone.

"Whoever of us will return after the war is over must come down here and reclaim them."

Is it possible some of us will not return? A cold shiver ran down my spine.

"The floor will be cemented and covered with a pile of coal," Dad's voice snapped me out of my musings. "Only you will know the jar is here. Now let's go back."

I was part way up the cellar stairs when I realized that by burying Mommy's jewelry and the letter, he was trying to preserve the memory of her for those of us who would survive the war. For that, I was very grateful to him.

8

It was an early December evening. Strangely quiet, we were seated at the supper table, absorbed in our thoughts. Uncertainty was hanging heavily in the air. Rozalia had just cleared the last dishes. Somewhere in the midst of this tension, the grandfather clock, which over the years had measured many happy hours, struck eight o'clock. It was the same sound as always, and yet there was something ominous about it.

It happened suddenly. A loud pounding on the front door made us freeze in our places. No one needed to ask who such brutal nighttime visitors might be. Rozalia must have let them in because immediately after we heard the tramp of boots, the door was flung open, and two SS policemen forced their way into the dining room. We jumped to our feet. The portentous giants, as they looked to me, were the embodiment of aggression, arrogance, and malice.

One of them immediately addressed Dad and, in harsh commanding German, was giving him some orders. The other kept us kids under his vigilant, cold fish eyes. In a single glance, starting from his high black boots, up his slick black coat, and his hand resting on the belted hip next to a holstered gun, I identified the trappings of terror.

My eyes were now fixed on Dad. Despite the duress of the situation, Dad was composed, his voice steady. He was being interrogated by the armed brute, whose voice sounded like the barking of a dog. At that very moment, the other gunman frowned, unholstered his pistol, and aimed it at Dad's temple. I was holding my breath, paralyzed with fear, but thank God, the shot didn't come. In a flash, I realized the policemen were just trying to intimidate him. Yet my fear was justified. Any SS policeman could kill any Pole on a whim!

Next, all of Dad's pockets were thoroughly searched. While the claw-like hands frisked over Dad's torso and all the way down his pants leg, my heart was beating so fast that I thought it would burst. Only instinct kept me from showing any sign of panic.

At noon that day, I had been passing the slightly ajar dining room door when I saw Dad, his left foot on a chair seat, one pants leg rolled up, preoccupied with bandaging his leg. I did not make much of it then, but now it became obvious to me that, fearing our deportation, he was securing something important under the bandage. The search disclosed nothing, and with an enormous relief, I took a deep breath. Dad collected himself after a rough experience, and now, deliberately controlling his voice, he turned to us.

"We have fifteen minutes to get ready. Put on your coats, scarves, hats, and gloves. We are allowed to take with us just the basic necessities. Rozalia has already taken care of that. Everything else will have to be left! Since I am permitted to take only 200 *zlotys* ($50) per family, we cannot take any of your savings."

Next, Dad was escorted to the study. I put on my coat, passed the dining room, and followed behind him. I wanted to have a last glance of my favorite charcoal drawing, which was overshadowed by the landscape paintings gracing the study. It was the drama and tension of that scene that had caught my imagination ever since I was seven years old. Dad told me that it depicted a group of fellow students who were confined in a dungeon-like cell of the Basilian Church in Vilno because they had refused subjugation and Russification efforts of the Tsarist regime during the time of Poland's partition. A gleam of light came from the kerosene lantern, which was held high by the robust Russian warden wrapped in a heavy sheepskin. The light lingered on the visionary face of a youthful poet, Adam Mickiewicz, whose poetry was going to be an inspiration to generations of Poles. *If I would be permitted to take one thing from our house*, a thought passed through my mind, *that drawing would be my choice.*

It didn't escape my attention that Dad was going through the drawers of his desk getting more and more papers, keys, and money. The SS policeman was selecting items of interest to him and shoving them greedily into his bulky leather case. He had just been looking over Dad's military orders and decorations.

"*Eisernes Kreuz!*" (Iron Cross), I heard his impressed voice as he saw Dad's meritorious German decoration. He added the cross to the spoils. Although I was still a child, I realized that in those few minutes, Dad's whole fortune, accumulated over years of dedicated work, was being confiscated.

As we were about to leave the house, one of the policemen went through the children's pockets. He took my expensive fountain pen and the gold watch from my wrist and put them in his pocket. This was plain looting. Of the three things I inherited from Mom, I was now left with only her prayer book. Rozalia was told that she could stay in Ino and keep all her personal belongings. They needed cooks and housekeepers who spoke German, but she declined the offer and chose to go with our family.

Our apartment was sealed, and we were hurried down the stairway. Banished from our home, with no reason given, we entered the darkness of the wintry night. The policemen escorted us to the town theater, several blocks away.

Two burly guards, standing with their legs apart, guarded the entrance to the theater. Once inside, we were led to confront yet another, this time a bespectacled villain. He fixed his gaze on us with his scrutinizing, repugnant eyes and plunged into a chair behind a desk piled up with papers. After asking Dad some questions, he turned a few pages and made a short note on one with a long row of names. We were directed to the vast theater hall. There were many other families already there, settled on the floor covered with straw. We chose a place farthest from the entrance.

Dad, trying to comfort us, spoke encouragingly, "You slept on straw pallets in September, remember? I trust you will be as resolute now as you were then." With our clothes on, Yanush and I curled under one blanket. With no pillows and no pajamas, we still said our little prayer:

My guardian angel,
You always stand by me
At morning, evening, during night and day.
Come always to my help.

Protect me from every evil
And lead me to everlasting life. Amen.

With these prayerful words on our lips, we tried to lull ourselves into an uneasy sleep. I was awakened by a crying baby. Startled, I saw a place humming with people, whole families settled on a straw-covered floor. Some of them must have been newcomers because the vast hall was now packed to capacity. At first, I wanted to shut my eyes in the hope that the scene would disappear like a bad dream, but I was too painfully aware of what had happened last night. Eh, maybe it's better to face the harsh reality than be put to the shame of giving up so easily.

Look at Rozalia, I thought. She is busy getting out the food we brought from home. We are going to have some breakfast after all.

Everywhere I turned, I saw tense, distressed faces, people worrying themselves sick over what was to become of us. The armed guards posted at the entrance to the hall were an obvious reminder that we were cut off from the outside world. The Germans have power, they can drive people from their homes, they can shoot any of them if they choose. I was bursting with indignation! From earliest childhood, we had been taught not to steal and not to do harm to other people. The Germans obviously ignored this basic commandment of God. There was nothing to do but sit on the blanket spread on the straw and wait. It was December. Christmas was just around the corner.

"Yanush!" I turned toward my brother. "I just realized that tomorrow is the sixth of December, St. Nicholas' Feast!"

"So where are the stockings?" Yanush was teasing me.

Since I was already carried away, I closed my eyes and saw this hall as it was four years ago. The words that were then shouted here echoed in my ears: "Po-ma-rancz-ka! Po-ma-rancz-ka!" (Little Orange! Little Orange!)

They were the cheerful shouts of the audience assembled for the Christmas play. For a few fleeting moments, I was standing again on that stage in my gorgeous costume, with the eyes of all the children drawn to me, as I was overwhelmed by excitement, my heart filled with gratitude. It was Mom's help that saved me from defeat.

"What is the matter?" Yanush was surprised, seeing my tear-filled eyes.

"I was thinking of Mommy," I said in a voice choked with emotion. "Wherever she is now, I am sure she is watching over us."

"Like an angel!" my little brother had no doubt.

Around noon, an announcement was made in Polish. The heads of the families were to report to the vestibule to fill out forms and questionnaires. Soon, a few names were shouted, one of them Dad's, probably because our name started with the letter *B*. After spending a long time in the vestibule, Dad and Milek returned, evidently unsettled.

"We were ordered to make a detailed inventory of my property that was confiscated last night," Dad explained.

"This is under the pretense," Milek commented mockingly in a hushed voice, "that Dad will be reimbursed by the Third Reich once the war is over. The thief is asking the victim to honestly estimate the value of the property stolen from him. Who could think of more cynical mockery?"

It was a long, uneasy day. Evening was approaching, and gloom in the hall was thickening with spirits sunk low. In the midst of this tension, Dad's name was called again. To our surprise, he was told to return home. Simple as that: return home! In minutes, we left the theater, this time with no escort. What a big relief it was to be back after such a strenuous time of confinement and to go to sleep in one's own bed!

By the next morning, the contentment of being back home was overshadowed by the uncertainty of what our release really meant. The answer came soon enough. I clearly remember that Dad was summoned to present himself at 10 a.m. at Municipal Office. We waited for his return in anxious anticipation, not daring even to guess what it was all about. He finally came back, his face somber and pale, his lips tightened, but in total control of his emotions.

"What happened, Dad?" I asked. "What did they want from you?"

"After a long and supposedly amiable talk, the mayor asked me to carefully read and consider signing a paper."

"I assume," Milek tried to guess, "he wanted you to accept a status of *Volksdeutscher*."

"What would this mean?" Yanush tried to understand.

"That we are suitable for Germanization," Dad said bitterly.

"What did you do, Daddy?" I asked.

"I declined," Dad said simply, as if there were no other option to consider.

That was all he said about the meeting. By then, we realized what would happen next. It didn't take long.

It was evening when the already familiar banging at the front door announced a *deja vu* expulsion routine. Within a few minutes, we were escorted back to the theater, carrying our meager possessions, not yet unpacked. I did not turn and look over my shoulder for a last glimpse of the house. I knew that we were leaving for good.

∞o∞

Another uncomfortable, restless night of sleeping on the floor was followed by a long frustrating day of waiting fearfully for what would happen next. It may be that I kept my eyes closed since Dad broke the silence.

"You are sad, Halinka, but consider how fortunate we are to be all together."

It was then that, with a startling suddenness, a question crossed my mind. What would have happened to Yanush and me if Dad had not been released from prison? Being too young for slave labor, we could have been sent to the Deutoche Reich as suitable for Germanization. I shivered at the thought of it.

There was another question, however, that had been weighing heavily on my mind. *Should I ask Dad, or shouldn't I?* He has so much right now to worry about. Seeing me so pensive, he gave me a shadow of a smile.

"What is it, Halinka? Something is troubling you."

Encouraged, I asked, "Daddy, why did you fight so bravely for the Germans during the World War that they awarded you the Iron Cross?" Dad was at first astonished at my question, but instinctively guessed why, in the present situation, my feelings could be hurt.

"As you know, I was born in Bogumin,[5] where some years ago, my family settled down. In the nineteenth century, Bogumin was in the Austrian Empire. When the war started in 1914, I was conscripted into the Austrian Army and served in the Medical Corps. I got that cross, not for bravery on the front line, but for saving a life."

"For saving a life?" I was impressed. "Tell me all about it."

"It was a long time ago during the battle of Gorlice."

"Gorlice? That's a town east of Cracow, isn't it?"

"That's right. It was one of the bloodiest battlefields of the World War, fought on our native soil by Poland's occupiers. Ironically, the Poles had been drafted in the hundreds of thousands by all three of them. Russians were pitted against the Austro-German Central Powers." Dad lapsed into a long silence.

"One late afternoon," he resumed in a low voice, "the stretcher bearers brought a wounded German officer into our Austrian field hospital. He was unconscious and chilled to the bone. There was no doctor around at that time. I managed to resuscitate him, but as I saw his lifeless face, I knew he had no chance to survive if the bullet lodged in his head was not promptly removed."

"And what did you do?" I could hardly contain my curiosity.

"Ah, well, you see, I had been assisting the surgeon for some time, and I was occasionally allowed, in the heat of battle, to amputate a hand or leg." Dad spoke now with animation. "The saying going around was that I had golden hands, but to drill a hole in the skull and remove the bullet— that was strictly a no-no for someone who, not only was not a surgeon, but also had no medical license."

"But it was a question of life or death, so it should have been justified."

"That's exactly what I thought. I realized that I was taking an enormous risk, not only for the life of my patient, but also for mine."

I looked at Dad admiringly and said, "That sounds like you, Daddy."

"For the next couple of weeks, I lived under the threat of court-martial," he continued, "but while the patient was delirious at times, to everyone's relief, he not only survived, but completely recovered. As it turned out, he was the scion of a distinguished German family. He was so grateful I had saved his life that he spoke in praise of me to my commander-in-chief, and because of his intercession, I was excused."

"You should have been a surgeon." I was very proud of my dad.

"That is what I wanted to be, but I fell in love in Cracow." Daddy's face lit up, his whole being comforted by memory.

I looked around, eager to share Dad's story with my brothers, but Milek and Yanush were nowhere to be seen. Then I realized I hadn't seen them for some time. Where were they? I looked for them in every corner of the hall, and so did Dad, but in vain. At last they both appeared, Yanush struggling under the weight of a large bundle.

"What is that?" Dad, Rozalia, and I asked almost in unison.

Yanush's eyes sparkled. To our surprise, in the bundle were two beautiful eiderdown covers, two eiderdown pillows, a whole cured ham, and a big tin of delicious apricot jam. The pillows and covers had been in Milek's room and Aunt Marysia had donated the food.

"My son, how did you get all these? This was a very audacious and dangerous thing to do. The guards could have shot you!"

"Daddy, Milek and I planned the whole thing very carefully. First, we found that the restroom windows here in the theater are set quite low and can be opened and closed with no trouble. They are facing the quiet side street, and we observed over a long period of time that no guards were posted there. Yesterday, when we were back at our house, Milek found out that his room on the third floor was not sealed. Obviously, the policemen were not aware that he had a separate room up there. I knew that Aunt Marysia has an extra key to it. So Milek boosted me into the restroom window, and I slid down unnoticed to the street. I hurried directly to our house."

"You are brave, Yanush!" I said with warm approval.

"For God's sake, be quiet!" Rozalia reproached me. "We'll attract the guard's attention."

"Aunt Marysia was so surprised that she almost fainted when she saw me," Yanush eagerly went on. "But after she recovered from the shock, she went with me to Milek's room and helped to choose what we might need and arranged this bundle. Bringing it here took some guts, but I figured out how to get back by following side streets. Milek was waiting at the restroom window. He helped me to get in."

Milek was strangely quiet all this time, but all our attention was centered on Yanush. It was so good to see his animated face, to hear his quiet laughter. He had played a trick on the Germans and succeeded.

The orders were given. Families were hurriedly picking up their belongings as they were pushed by guards with machine guns. The guards shouted in German, "Alles raus!" (All out!) "Shnell!" (Fast!)

A huge column of people was proceeding, as it turned out, toward the railway station, a long distance away. We were just passing the coffee house where I had such good times with Uncle Stefan six months ago. Yanush and I were carrying the big bundle with the precious eiderdown covers, pillows, and the whole cured ham, but I couldn't see how we would be able to reach the station without dropping it somewhere on the way. I noticed that some older people walking in front of us were also struggling under the weight of their luggage.

The column was moving now along Queen Yadviga Street, and soon, we reached the corner with Solankova Street, the location of a familiar droshky stand. I couldn't believe my eyes. First in line was our friendly coachman, Mr. Lewandowski, perched high atop his seat, waiting for customers.

Yanush saw him too, so we both called, "Mr. Lewandowski, come help!"

In an instant, he pulled his droshky from the curb. "Put your bundle in the back and climb up here with me," he said, as if it were the most normal thing to do. We followed his directions willingly, giving no thought how the guards might react to this audacious act, which seemed so natural to us. Dad told us later that for some time, he was paralyzed with fear. For much less insubordination, heads were being smashed with the butt of a gun or people shot on the spot. Everyone was relieved and surprised that no one interfered. Gradually, the marching people made enough room, and our droshky was fitted into the column.

Encouraged by the lack of reprisal, first one elderly lady and then other struggling people tossed a bag or suitcase on the back of the droshky until it was filled all the way to the top. Mr. Lewandowski put the carriage hood up halfway so the stuff would not fall off. Yanush and I sat on the driver's seat as the column proceeded slowly to the station.

The train was already pulled up at the platform. Screaming guards were hurriedly packing us into the antiquated rail cars, probably last used during the World War. The windows were blacked out so there was no way to see anything outside. Then the doors were noisily slammed shut and locked.

We could feel the tension mounting.

"Daddy, where are we going?" Yanush asked plaintively.

"I don't know, my son," Dad answered wearily. "I have no idea."

It was late afternoon when the train finally began moving off with a wrenching chug, and soon, it was clacking over the tracks to a measured staccato of wheels, taking us ever closer and closer to our unknown destination.

PART II

Exile

9

We had been traveling for two days, not having the faintest idea where we were going. The train moved on some miles and then came to a stop, waiting for passage. We were obviously a low priority on the railroad's schedule.

There were only a few places on the hard wooden benches so the rest of us had to sit on the floor. No food or water was provided. Each family survived on what they had managed to bring. In the dimly lit wagon, people sat silently, plunged into tremendous sadness, absorbed in their worried thoughts. The hours crept painfully by. Eventually, Yanush and I were very weary and overcome with sleep. Some passengers took pity on us and thoughtfully gave up their seats, moving to the floor, so we could lie down on the bench, head to toe, our legs stretched, trying to sleep.

The abrupt slowing down of the train woke Yanush from a fitful dozing. Rubbing his sleepy eyes, he turned to Dad. "Daddy, when we get where we are going, we will have an even nicer home than the one we had in Ino, won't we?"

♆

We lost track of how many times the train stopped and started and stopped again. The people were now worn thin. Then, after two and a half days of tedious journey, the train stopped, this time for good. The door of the coach slammed open with a bang, and guards, wielding rifles, burst in shouting their already familiar order: "Alles raus! Alles raus!" (Everyone out!)

We were all assembled on the station platform. Shivering from the cold, the rattling of the train's wheels still ringing in my ears, I read the posted sign: Lubartov. I remembered that I had heard that name recently as the guards were running up and down the platform pushing us into a column. We were escorted from the station toward the town. It was a long walk, but the weary exiles shuffling along picked up their steps when they saw the heavenward spires of a church dominating the town in the distance.

In Lubartov, we followed the main thoroughfare, later known to me as Lubelska Street. It was so different from the downtown in Ino and so much poorer. The mostly one-story houses stood shoulder to shoulder on both sides of the street, nestling tiny shops within themselves. To my relief, all the signs were in Polish. Through the deepening winter twilight, I could still make out some of them: *Czapnik* (cap maker) and under it, I read *Srul Szmul Zajdman*. The name was surely not Polish, but not German either. I repeated it to myself with delight, not knowing then that I would remember it forever.

I didn't have to crane my neck to read the shop signs on the houses just opposite: *Stanislaw Lisek* and under it, *Mieszane Towary* (mixed merchandise). What kind of merchandise would that be? This was all so puzzling, so new to me.

Our destination for the night was the local movie theater, once again with the inevitable straw-covered floor. After our strenuous journey on the train, we sank down and fell fast asleep.

The next morning, word was passed that the Germans had dropped responsibility for settlement of the exiles on the shoulders of the town's municipal council. Our transport was the third in a single week, the previous two being from Gdynia and Torun. As Dad found out, to his dismay, our family had not been assigned to Lubartov, but to the village of Niedzwiada, some eight miles northeast of the town. He had no idea how this was supposed to work.

In the meantime, a group of warm-hearted Lubartovians, organized ad hoc into the Committee of Social Welfare, was serving hot coffee (ersatz, of course) and bread. The freshly baked crusty bread tasted wonderful.

Our transport was waiting—a thin horse covered with a shaggy winter coat hitched to a primitive cart. The driver, an old peasant, was wearing a short overcoat, faded with age, and dark breeches stuffed into high boots. His face was wrinkled, his shoulders hunched together. There was a great deal of simplicity about him, but I liked the direct look of his pale blue eyes.

"Are you taking us to Niedzwiada?" Yanush wanted to be certain, obviously anxious to see the place we had been assigned.

"Yeah."

We were joined by the Polanowski family, an older couple with three daughters, two of whom were grown and one a high school student. Yanush and I were allowed to ride on the cart with our baggage. Everyone else had to walk behind. Our driver cracked his whip, the wheels squealed, and we were on our way.

Light snow blew across the ground. Yanush and I were wrapped in a provided thin cotton blanket, but we were soon almost freezing. To take my mind off our discomfort, I started studying the countryside around us and found it very peaceful. We were passing through a flat treeless country with dormant winter fields on either side of the road, their snow cover glistening. There were no people to be seen, no evidence of German brute presence. The only sounds were the frosty breathing of the old horse and the creak of the wheels on the road. I was eager to talk to our driver who, from the beginning of our journey, hadn't uttered a word.

"It feels so good not to see any Germans," I said cheerfully. "Are they around here?"

There was no answer, just the soft flap of the reins on the back of the poor horse, so I assumed that the driver had not heard me. However, just as I was going to repeat the question, he turned around and said, "They are here, but they will be gone."

I couldn't have agreed more. All of us, in our heart of hearts, believed that this would happen sooner or later.

"You say they will be gone. How can you know this?"

Again, there was a very long silence before he replied, "They are godless."

That makes sense, I thought, struck with amazement. They are godless. Their wickedness will turn against them as Milek once said. Unexpectedly, I felt greatly comforted.

✺

The snow was getting deeper, and our cart occasionally jolted right or left into a drift, causing Yanush and me to lunge to the side of the cart, and we laughed. It was late in the afternoon when we spotted a group of log huts with their pointed thatched roofs looking like so many festive *kolpaks* (fur caps) charmed into being by the abundant snow.

"Niedzwiada!" announced our driver, as the wagon drew near. The village before us was buried deep in snow, a fairyland, a kingdom of winter, I thought, stiff with cold. (*Niedzwiedz* is "bear" in English. *Niedzwiada* may mean "bear's den" or "bear's domain.")

Our driver stopped in front of one of the huts and motioned us inside. The big rough door squeaked ominously, and a haze of snowflakes fell on my head and arms. We crossed the low threshold and stepped onto the packed clay floor. The first thing I noticed was a large wooden bed that occupied much of the room. A woman, pale as the snow outside, lay in the bed, motionless amid white sheets, her head propped up by the pillows. Another middle-aged woman, wearing a large apron over an ample skirt and a foulard crossed on her chest, was attending to her. A young farmer, whom I guessed was the son of the sick woman, was adding chunks of peat to the fire burning in the big whitewashed clay stove with a chimney hood.

That fire totally captured my attention. It blazed and danced like a living thing. Enchanted, I walked straight toward it and stretched out my cold hands toward it. Thanks to this fire, I felt at home. A joyful sensation swept over me. "Greetings to my brother fire," I mumbled as St. Francis would say. Unlike our fires at home in Ino that burned black chunks of coal, this fire burning peat created an entirely different flame that jumped and danced gaily, throwing off little showers of incandescent sparks. *This is spirit fire*, I thought.

There were ten of us newcomers crowded into the rustic room along with its three occupants. The husky young man was supposed to be a host for this unusual bunch of well-dressed strangers.

"Please take off your coats and sit down," he said, pointing to the wooden benches alongside the table.

We sat. It was getting dark, and Rozalia lit the candles we had brought with us. The Polanowski girls got out some cards and began to play a card game. Dad was deep in thought. The taciturn sister-in-law conveniently disappeared into the adjacent alcove. Yanush and I did not have the inhibitions of adults. "Daddy," we said, "we're hungry. We haven't eaten anything since a piece of bread at breakfast."

Here was another crisis. How was our host to feed all these people from his obviously meager means? Dad saved the situation. "I heard that they call you Stas. Well, Stas, would you allow me to buy two of your chickens?" he asked.

Our host's face broke into a big smile, and in no time, the chickens were produced, killed, cleaned, and dropped into a pot of water. Willing hands were chopping vegetables, and soon, the aroma of chicken soup was filling the room.

Perhaps it was the smell of the chicken soup or just the excitement that comes with the arrival of strangers from far-off places, but before long, several poorly dressed village children had slipped into the crowded room. They occupied the long clay bench by the side of the stove. I saw their blue eyes darting intently in our direction every so often.

The soup would be ready in an hour or so, but Yanush and I were hungry now. Rozalia reached into her satchel and produced leftovers from the food brought from home: a few mouth-watering, thin-as-fingers sausages, called *kabanosy*, and the last slices of already dried fruit cake. She looked to Dad with an unspoken question.

"Distribute to all the children," he said, without hesitation. So we all shared the food, and the icy wall between the village children and us melted as if by magic.

By the time we finished our bowls of chicken soup, it was growing late. Stas brought in straw and fresh-smelling hay for the floor, and each of us found our own space for the night. The fire in the stove died out. I curled up as close to it as possible to keep warm. The room became quiet, the silence broken occasionally by the coughing of the sick mistress who, I found out later, was seriously ill with tuberculosis. The dog, Burek, settled for the night in his corner. Chickens were quietly clucking for a while somewhere behind the thin wall. I was almost asleep when a loud *mooo* startled me. People and animals alike were all one family wrapped up in the warmth of a friendly space.

Far above our snow-covered roof, the sky twinkled with thousands of brilliant stars.

After a lean breakfast the next morning, our host took a bucket and went to bring in some water. I decided to tag along, but I was not prepared for what was involved. Outside the sky had cleared, and the morning sun had turned the snow to a dazzling white. The drifts were deep, and Stas began shoveling a path toward the well. As he threw the shovels of snow into the air, they turned magically into clouds of glittering crystals, which was to me, a remarkable and beautiful sight. For him, it was just hard work.

My attention was now on the well. I had never before seen a well like this. A long pole was fixed on an upright post with a heavy weight on one end and the water bucket on the other. Stas lowered the bucket into the well, and when it was filled with water, the counterweight helped lift it to the surface.

I had never given any thought to how we got our water back in Ino. We simply turned a tap, and there it was. We drank it, cooked with it, bathed, and even played in it, all with perfect ease, but here, every drop was brought into the house with great effort. I was beginning to learn how precious water was and what a magnificent gift was the fire. They were more marvelous than any wonders I had ever dreamed about.

Dad and Milek were gone most of the day. In the morning, Dad had hired a buggy pulled by a bay horse, and they drove back to town without much explanation. When they returned, Dad told us that the next morning we were going back to Lubartov.

He turned to our young host and said, "Thank you for your hospitality, Stas, but there are too many of us to impose on you any further. I have made arrangements for us to stay in town."

Our stay in Niedzwiada was very short, and yet the villagers gave us a touching farewell. The small group assembled outside to bid us good-bye. An elderly woman was tracing the sign of the cross in the cold air, the traditional Polish blessing for a safe journey.

10

We were on our way back to Lubartov, a place of exile assigned for us by some ruthless Nazi official, not aware that by providential design, it would become a holy land in my memory.

The day was extremely cold, and the frosty wind was whipping around us. Since more snow had fallen overnight, the roads were fit for travel by sleigh. As we were approaching the town, our sleigh was occasionally gliding over the slick surface, causing us to bounce around. I looked at Yanush, laughing. Bundled up in layers of blankets like a cocoon, his fur cap with ear flaps pushed down to his brow, he seemed to be happy! During our first winter in Lubartov, running after the passing sleighs, grasping the back, and hanging on for a free ride turned out to be his favorite sport. We rode, but the grown- ups had to walk the eight miles.

I was thinking about Lubartov all the way. It had taken us two and a half days to reach it from Ino by train with all the long halts, but I now recalled that Mr. Skrzypinski told us last summer that Lubartov is on the River Wieprz. It was from the valley of the Wieprz that Marshal Pilsudski's legendary counter offensive against the Bolsheviks had been launched. Perhaps one could assume that Lubartov must not be so far from Warsaw. We must have reached the outskirts of the town, because on both sides of the road, small houses sat amongst gardens, side-by-side with patches of fields, now dormant under their snowy cover.

Our sled halted at the sidewalk, just opposite an impressive baroque church with twin spires raised toward the pale blue sky as in supplication. Its beauty and grandeur momentarily filled me with awe. Our driver had already sprung down from his seat, and Yanush and I followed. He was warming himself by slapping his crossed hands against his arms. After he took a deep breath and exhaled, clouds of vapor came from his mouth.

We all assembled in front of a plain building with small shops. It stood solitary at the corner of the street, just opposite the splendid church. Dad led the way to a narrow lane running along a low squat wing of the front house. The lane was bordered on the opposite side by a high wooden fence of tightly fitted planks. Dad was aiming for the third and last entrance. Following him, we found ourselves in an obscure, narrow hallway with a dirt floor. Milek pushed the first door to the left. There was no need for a key because the flat did not have any locks. As we found out, the door could only be fastened from the inside by thrusting a metal bar into a notch.

Our new dwelling consisted of a kitchen and one large room. There was an old-fashioned cooking stove in the kitchen and a tile stove in a corner of the room, which did not quite reach the ceiling. Two things came immediately to our attention. The floor, made of pine boards, was littered with broken glass, paper, and all manner of trash scattered about. It was a truly repulsive sight. Secondly, it was very cold! The flat had obviously not been heated for some time. With the heavy shutters left open, the windows were covered with frost. Yanush and I got busy creating fantastic designs on them with our fingers, which made everyone laugh.

Yanush suddenly turned around and said, "There is no running water, no plumbing, no electricity, and no gas. How can we live here?"

Rozalia was convincing in her reply. "This is where we have been placed, the only shelter we have. So let's do our best to make it home."

We knew that this was a situation in which she would thrive, so we were not surprised when she immediately took charge. With Mrs. Polanowski and her three daughters, there was a force of five women, not including me. With Rozalia as the leader, they were a formidable group, indeed. Of course, there was absolutely nothing to work with. In this situation, Dad's help was essential because he was able to dip sparingly into the German marks he had hidden under his leg bandage. Milek was delegated to buy whatever was immediately needed to heat and clean the flat. With Yanush and me in tow, Dad went to town to purchase some basic necessities for starting our new life. Merchandise was in short supply so it was not an easy task.

As we were passing through our large courtyard, I noticed that it was enclosed on three sides by buildings of uneven heights. Despite the cold weather, the courtyard was teeming with tumultuous life. People were going to and fro, and it seemed that everyone was in a great hurry. The crowd was made up mainly of men, but I was astonished and intrigued because most of them were wearing long black caftans under their overcoats. From beneath their black hats, long side curls were sometimes hanging all the way to their full bushy beards. The skinny boys, wearing skull caps with their faces framed by shoulder-length side locks, scampered around. There were no girls in sight. I have to admit that I was totally confounded at the scene, which was precisely why my new impressions became so unforgettable.

"Dad, who are these people?" I asked.

"They are our new neighbors, pious Jews. They dress and live according to Jewish law."

An older woman with a kerchief tied under her chin was passing by carrying a bucket full of water from a well that occupied a central place in the courtyard. That well was different from the one I saw in Niedzwiada. Returning home with shopping done, we passed through the courtyard again. Just before entering our murky hallway, I noticed a folded iron bed leaning against the wall. Dad also saw it, picked it up, and without a word, carried it to our flat.

How the place had changed during our absence! The floor was swept with borrowed brooms and scrubbed clean. Fires were kindled in both stoves, and water was boiling in a big black pot on the kitchen stove. The mattresses were filled with fresh straw and arranged on the floor of the room from wall to wall. By now, we were used to sleeping on the floor, so no one complained. To provide some privacy for each family, the men took down the large door leading to the kitchen and somehow managed to use the door to separate the sleeping areas.

The iron bed, after a good scrub, was dressed with beautiful sheets, a pillow, and an eiderdown cover, brought from Ino. Oh, it looked so inviting! It was going to serve Dad for several years to come.

And then Milek surprised us all, this time returning with a cartload of old furniture, including a large, much-needed sturdy table and six chairs, which he had obtained from the movie theater where we spent our first night in Lubartov.

Outside, the late afternoon shadows were deepening into an early wintry twilight, but inside, our room was glistening in the light of a large kerosene lamp that seemed to burn with a special radiance. Thank heaven, we had a home!

Thus, by the middle of December, we were settled down at Number 1 Siedlecka Street in Lubartov. A new era of our life had begun.

One of the first things I learned was that Lubartov was in Lublin district, part of a newly created General Gouvernment, usually referred to as the GG.

"What is this GG?" I asked Milek at first occasion.

"Well…" He reflected for a while. "You know that Hitler and Stalin partitioned Poland. Our western provinces were incorporated into *Deutsche* Reich (Germany), and our eastern provinces into the Soviet Union." He took a break. "Now listen! The remaining Polish territories—with Warsaw, Cracow, Lublin, and Radom—have been renamed General Gouvernment. Actually, the GG is a Nazi colony."

Ala, the youngest of the Polanowski family, joined us. "Milek, what do you think about Hans Frank, the new general governor of the GG?"

He looked at her with surprise. "What can you expect from this Nazi fanatic? As former Minister of Justice in the Nazi Reich and the GG governor, he first abolished all existing Polish laws and then declared the GG *Arbeitsbereich*, which means 'lawless work area.' Frankly speaking, this indicates that we Poles are to work as slaves for the Germans."

What I heard lowered my spirit. After all our recent nightmarish experiences in Ino, I was hopeful that Lubartov would be our safe haven until the war was over. I realized that we might well be facing a harsh future. Yet being young and full of curiosity, I looked ahead with a certain kind of anticipation. As a newcomer in Lubartov, I would be able to grasp and experience the life here, so different from the one I had known in Ino.

The frost had subsided a bit, and I was on my way to explore the town. I promised to pick up Yanush on the way. He was with his new friend, Yasio, who lived with his grandparents, the Rogatkos, at the nearby Market Square. Yanush's gift for making friends always amazed me. If only I could learn his secret. The day was bright. The sun was dancing on the silvery branches of the majestic linden trees standing guard by the church. The snow was crackling cheerfully under my feet. A horse-driven cart was just passing by. The whiskered peasant, seeing me smiling, called out, "Pochwalony!" (Praised!) I guessed that it was short for "Praised be Jesus Christ!" a traditional greeting still practiced by the country folk.

In the Market Square, the shops were open, people were moving freely, and the Polish language was openly spoken everywhere. There were no trams, no buses or cars, just the atmosphere of a quiet provincial town in winter's embrace.

This first impression, as it turned out, was an illusion. I had a long way to go to find out what was actually happening and with what terror the GG was governed.

Yasio's grandmother, Mrs. Rogatko, was a small and fragile woman but with strong principles. She received me kindly. I sensed right away that she had been overwhelmed with worries.

"After the Germans occupied Lubartov in September," she said, "they started right away to issue one decree after another. It's almost the end of the year, and all of the schools are still closed. What's more, they ordered all schoolbooks for Polish language, history, and geography to be turned over to the authorities. The sports fields and facilities are permanently shut, and all youth organizations disbanded. What are the children supposed to do, day after day?" I wondered that myself.

"All the parents in town are asking the same question. If not for the reading…"

"Is the public library open in Lubartov?" I asked with anticipation, still not quite believing my ears.

"No…but if one knows Father Aleksander Szulc, one can borrow a forbidden book directly from him. For years, he was the very popular school catechist and head of the school library, which is located in his house. The library was shut down by the Germans, but he is secretly lending the books to youths he trusts. It's illegal, of course, but greatly appreciated."

I listened politely while Ms. Rogatko continued, pondering how I could get acquainted with Father Szulc and have access to the books.

"There were several petitions sent to the German authorities asking for the reopening of the school library, even though it is understood that censorship would be in full force," said Ms. Rogatko.

At long last, the library at Mickiewicza Street was open! It was a little wooden house with a small front porch, framed by large trees and bushes. Passing a dark hallway, I entered a room made even smaller by a grand piano filling one corner. It was swarming with people. At once, I realized that this library was far too small for so many avid readers. Most of them were young, both boys and girls. They besieged the long table serving as a loan desk. Undernourished like me, with not much to do, they were eager for any chance to get engaged in great adventures they could share with a book's heroes. The two librarians were bustling around. The shelves were not full because so many books had already been checked out. They tried to find at least one book for each reader.

I was aware that they were far too busy to explain the library's rules to me so I was leafing through the pages of worn manuals filled with neatly handwritten information. So many authors, so many titles…which one to choose? Would I be lucky to get even one on my list? I held my breath as the librarian searched the shelves, then suddenly, there she was, books in her hands, extended toward me!

I left the library ecstatic, holding two books under my arm, as if they were treasures. How much more time I had now for reading. I loved to read.

Our life was hard, but I had been totally engrossed in reading the books, and sometimes, I didn't know which was more real: the story I was reading or my everyday existence. We were very poor. The marks Dad had smuggled from Ino were supposed to be seed money for his new tiny shop, but time and again, he had to take small amounts just to keep us warm and fed.

German regulations and restrictions started to govern every move and every aspect of our lives. Poland had always produced an abundance of food, but now, so many basic items were difficult to find. I was sent on my first assignment to buy sugar. On walking into our closest grocery store on Siedlecka, I got the impression that there wasn't much to buy, but undeterred, I asked for sugar.

Mr. Tarnowski, the owner, looked at me surprised. "We haven't had any sugar since September. Sugar is now for Germans only." He winked his eye. "Let me give you some fatherly advice. If you have connections in town, there is sugar somewhere under the counter, but it's expensive! For Poles, the substitute is saccharine."

It was then I noticed that the little packages on the almost empty shelves were *ersatz* coffee, *ersatz* tea…*ersatz* reigned supreme on the store shelves next to the bottles with real vinegar. For the first few months after our arrival in Lubartov, milk, cream, eggs, and butter were still available. So by next morning, the pattern was set—we had *ersatz* coffee with saccharine but with real milk!

How lucky we were to live in a small town. Its outskirts had a semi-rural atmosphere. From the gardens, vegetables of all kinds were collected. Cabbage was processed into sauerkraut for winter and packed in large barrels. Chickens, geese, and ducks shared the chicken coops, feasting during the warmer seasons on nearby meadows. Here and there the *oink* of a pig or the lowing of a cow could be heard. Self-sufficiency was in vogue, and the surplus was sold to the hungry townspeople, at least during the first months after our arrival.

On market day, peasants from the neighboring villages still brought milk from the last milking in one-liter vodka bottles, butter wrapped in horseradish leaves, and eggs secured in baskets, which were often homemade. Inflation was rampant, and prices were constantly rising while wages were restricted to their pre-war levels, and the people suffered greatly.

There was an acute shortage of meat. The farm families could keep only enough to sustain their lives. Everything else was requisitioned for shipment to Germany. Yet I heard that if one knew a farmer, one could occasionally purchase a cut of pork called *rabanka*. This was possible only because, while the Germans kept track of every single cow, attaching ear tags to them, it was more difficult to keep track of pig litters. So it would happen that while most of a litter would be accounted for, one or two piglets would be raised in secret on the farm. Such contraband food was smuggled under potatoes, hay, or wood logs and delivered to the customer's house. However, the Germans caught on to the peasant's tricks and would often set roadblocks, checking all carts and passersby with outrageous brutality. If a farmer was caught with "illegal" meat, the meat was confiscated, and the robbed farmer was beaten, arrested, or in the later years, sent to a concentration camp. It was a deadly struggle for survival.

Two days before Christmas, Anna Wrobel, from the village of Gorki Lubartovskie, set off for the market in Lubartov carrying two roosters in her basket. When she approached the wooden bridge on the River, she spotted the uniformed Germans in the distance. It became obvious to her that they had set up a roadblock there. To avoid the search, she turned around and quickened her pace. She may not have heard or understood the German order "Halt!" and continued walking. A German soldier fired a single shot, and the mother of three small children was dead on the spot. The news of the shocking murder reverberated through the county. Human life had never been cheaper than under the mounting oppression of the Nazis.

ꙮ

Christmas arrived, frosty and snowy. It was our first Christmas in exile and the first without Mommy. Hush! A tear wells up in the eye.

Because of the Nazi-enforced curfew, even the traditional, always joyous, *Pasterka* (Midnight Mass) was not permitted to be celebrated at midnight. The town was embraced in darkness, and only the occasional tramp of the boots of German police patrols broke the silence of the Holy Night.

ꙮ

Shortly after Christmas, Yasio Brzozowicz, his cheeks and nose red with cold, dropped into our home like a bomb of energy.

"How are my friends? It's time for Christmas season festivities, for a little fun…and you are sitting here idle. Because of the war, people are depressed and gloomy. What about going caroling to cheer them up a bit? We could also put up a little puppet show."

I listened to him with anticipation. It was such a wonderful idea.

"I have already made a Christmas crèche," he followed up, "large enough to be a stage for the short acts we will perform. You should see the puppet of King Herod! A truly cruel villain…with Hitler's fierce eyes and unmistakable mustache. How he will tear his chest, moaning, 'Ah! Woe to me!' when a malicious-looking, black-as-night devil will appear, with the short horns and tail, bat wings, and frightening claws to drag him on his pitchfork to hell for everlasting damnation!"

"Let's put our wits to work!" I exclaimed.

It was an old custom that only the boys were revelers. Being a girl, I offered to make a traditional eight-pointed star of colorful paper. We would have to look for an old large sieve for a frame, I thought.

"Do not forget," Yasio reminded me, "that inside the star, there has to be enough room for a candleholder with a thick candle stuck on it."

"If we are going disguised as animals, I want to be a *turon* (wild ox) with golden horns," Yanush insisted." I could borrow the sheepskin from Dick Filipowicz."

"For *turon*, we need a husky boy," Yasio said, "but you could be a stork. Their presence is considered a good omen. As for myself, I plan to be a goat. I will carry a goat's head set on the long pole. I made it in the school last year with the help of our teacher, Mr. Skaruch."

"We also need a drummer and maybe a bell ringer." Yanush got carried away.

"To make so much noise would be foolish," Yasio said. "My goat has a little bell hanging from its neck. With every movement it rings, *ding-dong*. That will suffice."

"Shut your eyes!" he commanded.

We did, puzzled as to what he was up to.

"Open now!" he said, emerging from the kitchen.

To our surprise, he was holding a pole crowned with a goat head obviously brought from his house. The head was nicely sheathed in leather and adorned with two long pointed horns. But most amusing was the clitter-clatter of its jaws when the string attached to its lower jaw was pulled.

"Watch me!" Yasio said. Standing in the middle of the room, he started to maneuver the pole with the goat head, dancing and singing.

> *Dance, little goaty, dance poor little thing*
> *One-and-a-half pierogi you'll surely earn.*
> *One-and-a-half pierogi isn't very much*
> *Jump, my little goaty, jump at once!*

"How lovely!" Yanush and I applauded him.

"You surely deserve a full plate of pierogi (dumplings)!" I exclaimed.

Yanush's face flashed with a grin. "This is all fantastic! I am sure people will reward us with sweets, nuts..."

Suddenly, it came to my mind that we should avoid attention of the German police. I shared my thought with Yasio and Yanush, and we agreed to go caroling only to nearby Zagrody.

11

Soups were always popular in our country. A dinner without soup was not considered a full meal, but in the first months in Lubartov, soups were the only dish we knew. They were as thick and nutritious as Rozalia could make them. The menu varied: one day, cabbage soup, the next, kasha soup of barley or pea soup or Ukrainian borsch. No wonder that we kids were hungry much of the time.

One cold January day, Ala, Yanush, and I had just returned from the nearby village of Skrobov with milk and butter. We were numb with cold and hungry as wolves. Entering the kitchen, we found a pot with large potatoes boiling on the stove. They were almost finished cooking.

"Just one!" Yanush exclaimed and fished out one potato, split it and, blowing on it to cool, devoured the whole thing in no time. Ala and I followed suit. It didn't seem like such a terrible thing to do because there were other potatoes in the pot.

At dinner time, ten of us gathered around the table. In front of each of us was an enamel bowl with the soup of the day, and in the middle of the table stood a solitary dish with fried potatoes, all that was left after our earlier feast. Dad looked at his very small portion of potatoes for a long time before he said quietly, "This cannot continue."

Ever since we had settled in Lubartov, he had been the main provider for a household of ten. We shared with the Polanowski family, not only the flat, but also the food. At first, it was a natural thing to do, and we got along very well. This made the misery of our life bearable. However, Mr. Polanowski exhausted his resources quickly. Days were passing by, and he did not show any initiative to restart life on his own. Finally, he and Dad agreed that he would look for work and a place for his family to live.

A few days later, an extraordinary thing happened. I was sweeping the floor in the sleeping room when suddenly I heard a loud shout from Mrs. Polanowska, who was cooking something in the kitchen. At first, I was frightened out of my wits. *The Germans*! I thought. But the voices were friendly and cheerful. Rushing into the kitchen, I saw Mrs. Polanowska embracing a man, her face flushed with joy. "My son," she kept repeating, "he is safe and here. My prayers were heard!"

The first thing I learned was that he was a priest. He brought news. Three nights he stayed with us, and each night, we gathered close to the still warm tile stove and listened to his sorrowful stories of the persecutions of Polish clergy, monks, and nuns in Pomerania, Great Poland, and Silesia, now annexed to the Deutsche Reich.

"The church has once again become a church of martyrs," he said gravely. "The clergy there are a special target of Nazi vengeance and atrocities, next to the Jews. They are educated patriotic leaders of the people. Those arrested are often executed in transit camps or deported to the various concentration camps. I've heard that almost the entire Cathedral Chapter of Pelplin was executed. Our Kuyavian diocese of Vloclavek is decimated…only a few churches remain open."

At least here the churches are still open, we reassured him, and you surely can count on the help of the local clergy.

The Nazis were running the GG with ruthless efficiency. How we missed the normalcy, safety, and comfort of our previous life. Our whole existence was temporary. Yet to survive, we had to confront the new reality head on. Gradually, absorbed in our tasks, we became accustomed to the rhythm of our new daily life. After all, we were not the only ones going through this undeserved ordeal. The Polanowskis, energized by the sudden appearance of their presumably perished son, moved to a flat of their own.

Milek, with the help of Mr. Guderian, another exilee and our neighbor from Ino, was employed as a translator in the county administrative office. I didn't have any idea that his German was so good. But then I recalled that when he was in the missionary school in Cracow, he had excelled in languages: Latin, French, and German.

Dad obtained a required concession and opened a small shop with glassware, porcelain, and household articles at the corner of Market and Parish Streets, dominated by St. Anne's church. Once a week, he would travel to Lublin, some fifteen miles away, to buy whatever he judged he could resell with a little profit and hauled the merchandise to Lubartov, usually by hired cart or by taking the train. He came back chilled to the bone and exhausted. We always awaited Dad's return with anxiety. The Nazi police sometimes conducted sudden roundups whenever they needed slave labor or as a reprisal for some act of sabotage. It was not safe to be out anywhere, at any time.

With Rozalia helping Dad in the shop and school being continuously closed, Yanush and I assumed some of her duties. It was exciting, at least at first, to be responsible for important tasks and to know that Dad and Rozalia were depending on us.

We learned how to properly kindle a fire in the tile stove, starting with very small dry sticks, adding pieces of wood and finally blocks of peat until we had created a cheerful blaze. The kitchen stove consumed lots of wood since it needed to be rekindled several times a day.

Dad finally bought a whole load of firewood from a peasant who was a trusted customer of his shop. How he managed to get and deliver the firewood we didn't know. There were large forests near Lubartov, but it was common knowledge that the Germans requisitioned all the timber. Cutting trees in the forest and selling the wood was strictly illegal, but since so many things were illegal, we didn't worry about it too much.

The wood arrived as logs, so Yanush and I decided to take our responsibility seriously and set out to learn the skills of a forester. First, we had to saw the logs into pieces using a two-person saw. This was very hard work, and we didn't make it any easier by allowing the saw to jam part way through the log. We soon figured out how to do it correctly and were sawing with vigor. The next step was to chop the cut logs into still smaller pieces, splitting them lengthwise with an axe. This was not only hard, but it was also dangerous because one slip of the axe could amputate a toe or worse. As we persevered, we sweat freely under our winter coats even though the outside temperature would be well below freezing. We took turns swinging the axe and stacking the wood, laughing, and taking great pride in our newly acquired skills. We had learned that we could do all kinds of grown-up jobs if we just applied ourselves to the task.

This was not a one-time job. The kitchen stove had to be kept going any time hot water was needed and, of course, whenever cooking was to be done. When the stove was hot and we were very hungry, we would stir some flour with milk and a dash of salt, knead it into a smooth dough, form round pancakes, and bake them on the glowing stove lids until they were a golden brown on both sides. Spread sparingly with apricot jam brought from Ino, they were gobbled up in no time.

Modern conveniences had not yet reached most of Lubartov, so electricity, gas, and running water were still luxuries. Water was especially precious, as I had already learned in Niedzwiada. I was a frequent visitor to the well in the courtyard because one of our duties was to supply our household with water, buckets and buckets of water for cooking, washing, cleaning, and laundry.

My first experience of fetching water from the well made such an impression on me that I recorded it in my diary something like this:

It is nine o'clock on a cold morning.
I am shivering even in my winter coat
On the way to fetch the water from the well.
But look! The well is atop an icy knoll...
What bad luck! Blame the previous visitors
Who carelessly spilled this precious gift of God.
I can hardly stand up on the icy slope
Even holding on to the well with both hands.
But I will not give up and return
With the empty bucket. Not I!

The drawing bucket is sheathed with a skirt of ice,
How heavy in my young hand. Wow!
I have to slowly lift it up and
Put it gently into the well's open mouth.
But what will happen if I let it drop?

Who cares? No one is watching.
Take the hand from the handle and let it go!
Such a trifling offense...

It drops! See, the chain is unwinding
With a loud metallic whirring sound.
How fast it goes!
The handle is turning...just a blur...
Should I grab it and stop?
No, it goes much too fast!
Maybe this was not such a good idea after all.
What will happen when it hits bottom?
Will the bucket break?
Then no one will get any water
And I will be blamed.
Splash!

The bucket has hit bottom!
The windlass crank has stopped.
Is the bucket still attached? Hold your breath!
Turn the crank!
The bucket feels heavy. It must be full of water.
Keep standing steady on the ice
Turning the crank. It's hard!

But has anyone seen what I did?
Be on your guard! Look around!
No one is in sight.
Oh, no!
In the second floor window, overlooking the well,
A boy…sort of my age. Tallest of them all.
Thick mane of black hair…
He is watching me and must be thinking
'What in the world is she doing there,
This girl with the wavy blond hair?'
Turn the crank! Lift the heavy bucket and fill yours!
End or beginning…who knows?

For some time, before the ration cards were introduced in February 1940, bread was in short supply in town. Our closest bakery was at the Market Square. The queue formed in front of the store when the bread was still in the oven because everyone wanted to be sure to get a loaf while the supply lasted. I had been standing near the head of the line. In front of me were two middle-aged women bundled up in heavy coats with woolen kerchiefs wrapped around their heads. They were engrossed in an animated conversation. At the repeated name "Majewski," I strained my ears.

Was it the same Majewski I had already heard about from Milek? Milek had recently started bringing home the news and gossip he heard at his office. Francis Majewski, we were told, was a prominent Volksdeutsch in town. Born in Berlin, carpenter by vocation, he had a Polish wife and five children, a daughter and four sons. The oldest son was serving in the German police. His father was generally regarded by the townspeople as an easygoing man with whom, over a glass of vodka, one could talk business and perhaps obtain a concession or other favorable decision.

The gossiping women's voices were coming at me whether I wanted to listen or not. "My dear lady, did you hear the latest news about the Majewskis?" the voice was instantly lowered to a whisper. "Adam, the oldest of the brood, has joined the Gestapo! May God have pity on us all!"

"He and his sister, Valeria, two of a kind," the other woman said, following suit, her voice reaching the proper pitch for serious insult. "This blood-sucker, this disgusting wench! They live like princes now on Lubelska Street in Benjamin Cytrynblum's1 house while he, once the wealthiest Jew in town, is starving as is his family…"

"She is far more greedy than you think," her companion broke in. "When the Germans were expelling Rabbi Goldblum and dentist Rajza Laks from the apartment house on Lubelska Street—it must have been October, if I remember correctly—Valeria was there, grabbing their best furniture. The horse-drawn cart she hired was already full, but standing on the balcony, she was still throwing bedding on top of the load, shouting, 'Finally the justice came! Now we are going to sleep on the pillows of the Jews, and they will sleep on the hard boards!'"

"People will remember her for that when the day of justice comes," her companion said vengefully.

I was walking home with my loaf of bread, struck by what I had heard standing in the queue. Here in the GG, the Germans were tearing apart the lives of the Lubartovian Jews as they had torn the lives of Poles in Ino: expulsion from home, deportation, and extreme poverty.

Hearing about the Majewskis' betrayal brought to my mind something that had occurred some days earlier. I had been at home alone. As was often the case, the door to our apartment had not been fastened. Suddenly, I heard someone's steps in the kitchen and then, to my great surprise, Joseph Majewski walked into the room.

"I have some stamps for Yanush." he said casually, "but how lucky I am that you're at home."

"I don't believe Yanush will be interested in your stamps," I responded haughtily. "I am very surprised that you didn't bother to knock."

"I did, but nobody answered," he replied, quite unfazed. He was a handsome boy, not easily discouraged. "I've wanted to talk to you for a long time. Didn't you notice that I follow you like a shadow?"

"You better leave me alone!"

He moved closer and suddenly put his arm around me, intending to steal a kiss. Deeply shocked, I moved back a step and slapped his face. Momentarily, I regretted losing my temper, but I would not apologize. Being home alone, I had to defend myself. Joseph was a stranger to me—and Volksdeutsch at that! He left without uttering a word. After hearing those outrageous things about the conduct of his brother and sister, I felt I had been touched by a devil.

I would not tell anybody what was bothering me. That evening, I slipped out of the house to see Mrs. Filipowiczowa, our close neighbor at Siedlecka Lane. Once outside, I paused for a moment to take in the beauty of the scene. The heavy snowfall had piled drifts up to the windows while icicles hung from the eaves like crystal lace. The German-enforced blackout was still mandatory. A few lanterns dimly lit the Market Square, but the rest of the town was enveloped in darkness. Yet high over my head, the three stars of Orion shone brightly and gloriously on the velvety black sky. All the power of the Nazis couldn't black them out!

A few quick steps led to S. Filipowicz's carpenter shop. He was a solitary figure with a pale face, shriveled cheeks, deeply set small eyes, and receding, disheveled hair. With a plane in his hand, he was still working and paid no attention to his visitor. He was a coffin maker, a continuous process.

"Death is unavoidable, all life on earth eventually dies to be replaced by new life," I recalled the passage from the book I had just recently read. Surely I didn't want to think about death, even though seeing Mr. Filipowicz putting the final touches to the coffin, I imagined the cold dead body lying motionless there.

That would never be my body. I was hooked on living!

I passed the shop as if it were a familiar picture on the wall, aiming for the kitchen stove with its white-washed hood, where the fire was happily burning. This narrow extension of the shop was the kingdom of Mrs. Marianna Filipowiczowa.

Mrs. Filipowiczowa was a sturdy woman, neatly dressed in simple clothes, her hair smoothly combed. She was always busy, but like my mom, she had time for her five children, four of whom were already grown-up and all the visitors who often dropped by. To me, Marianne Filipowiczowa was a living example of the gospel story of the loaves and fishes. She had very little and yet had plenty to give to others. Her warmth and friendliness were the genuine gifts of her heart.

Her kitchen became an open house. Everything here was ordinary, but everyone felt equal and special.

I loved to stop here on a snowy, frosty day and take my seat on the low wooden bench next to the stove. I sat there now and poked the glowing pieces of peat, fascinated by the dance of flames and the mysterious patterns in the heart of the fire. Helka and Danka, the daughters of Mrs. Filipowiczowa, joined us as she graciously served us some herb tea. We sipped it, sweetened with a hard candy melting slowly in our mouths, a local custom. We talked about the good old days—exaggerating the bliss of "paradise lost"—to make us feel good and about the bright future just around the corner.

Wrapped up in the warmth radiating from the stove as well as our companionship, we were able, for a while, to forget about the war.

12

Yanush and I were busy shoveling snow, clearing the path in front of our Siedlecka Lane home, when we heard a friendly voice say, "Working hard, *nu?*"

I raised my eyes and saw the tall broad-shouldered figure of Mr. Aron-Ber Sztatman. He was standing in front of his door, shaking snow from his thick eyebrows and coat collar. He looked very tired and subdued, obviously returning from some exhausting job. All able-bodied Jewish men and boys, from age fourteen to sixty, were forced to toil for the *Wehrmacht*. Mr. Sztatman was a craftsman painter. Since he had proven himself a skillful worker, his German masters didn't hesitate to keep using him, ignoring the fact that he was over sixty years old.

Yanush's and my acquaintance with the Sztatman family was quite natural since they were our closest neighbors. Their tiny flat at Siedlecka Lane was between Filipowicz's carpenter workshop and our dwelling. In Lubartov, Jews had never lived in separate quarters. Our contact with the Sztatmans was possible since they spoke Polish as fluently as Yiddish. I noticed that Mr. Sztatman pronounced some Polish sounds in a slightly peculiar way, but this didn't bother me at all.

The Sztatmans were simple, unpretentious people. They settled on Siedlecka Street years before and were blessed with six children, all of whom were now grown-up. Only the two youngest daughters—I guessed them to be in their early twenties—still lived with their elderly parents. Mr. Aron, as Yanush called him, was not like most of our Jewish neighbors at that time. I had never seen him wearing a bushy beard or sidelocks. It was from his older daughter, Machla, that I soon found out that he was a deeply pious and observant Jew.

"Oh, my father has a habit to rise fairly early and recite his prayers," she spoke softly and kindly as usual. That didn't satisfy my curiosity, so she continued.

"He reads verses from Scriptures, usually from *Gemara*, *Mishnah*, and Psalms. He used to go to synagogue every Saturday and pray and chant with his close-knit congregation of fellow Jews."

"What do you mean he used to go to synagogue? I believe that in this present grave time, praying in the synagogue with the faithful would be very helpful."

"Don't you know," Machla was surprised, "that after Germans occupied Lubartov, they took over the synagogue and desecrated it? That was very painful to my dad and hardened his rage against them."

"The Germans are crueler than wild beasts. They are blinded by their malice." I reverted to my own heart-rending experiences of the past months. "Shortly after the *Wehrmacht* entered Inovrotslav, they not only shut all the Catholic churches but one, but also blew up the impressive synagogue."

∽o∾

The weeks were flying by, and since Yanush and I had nothing much to do, we were learning more and more about our neighbors through daily contact with them. All this was a revelation to me, a totally new experience.

The most striking was our Jewish neighbors' otherness from the Jews we knew in Ino. I recalled from our Ino days, the familiar figures of Mr. Fisher and Mr. Paswolski who used to come from Lodz to take orders for textile goods for Dad's store from the firms they represented. I particularly liked Mr. Paswolski. He was a thick-set man of short stature, and with his receding hair, his face looked like a full moon. Always elegantly dressed, he had impeccable manners and exuded a warm vivacity. Just before last Easter, he presented us with a huge chocolate egg wrapped in colorful ribbons and filled with a cornucopia of delicious chocolates. He spoke fluent Polish, occasionally exchanging with Dad some pleasantries in German. They were Jews, but they looked and spoke like everybody else.

In Lubartov, our Jewish neighbors spoke Yiddish, their mother tongue, and most of them spoke little Polish. They dressed and looked differently and seemed to have no social contact outside their own circles.[1] The Jewish presence there was far more evident than it had been in Ino.

Ever since the Germans entered the town in September, Zenek Filipowicz told me, they were taking every opportunity to harass and humiliate the Jews. Now all Jews in the town, from age ten and up were are stigmatized, obliged to wear on their left sleeve a white band with a blue Star of David. Oh yes, the Jews learned quickly that when they saw an approaching German, they should immediately step off the sidewalk into the street and, in a show of submission, bow, and take off one's hat. Nonetheless, some Germans were hard to please, and pretending that this was not done quickly and humbly enough, they would beat the innocent man unmercifully. If he happened to be a Hasid, they would cut off his ritual beard and sidelocks. That was a common occurrence, done in plain daylight with bold impunity. We were appalled at this treatment of our Jewish neighbors, but we were unable to help, knowing that this would bring even harsher retribution down on any "Jew sympathizer."

The swaying body of Jew Finkelsztajn, mutilated from beating, was left hanging in the center of town for days to strike fear in all town inhabitants. It was to leave a lasting scar in the memory of Lubartovians for years to come.

Even the children were not spared from German barbarity. One afternoon, passing through our courtyard, I was stunned to see a uniformed German conducting an impromptu chorus of very young Jewish boys. I noticed that his baton was the handle of a whip. When displeased with the boys' performance, he would unfurl the whip. Oh! I closed my eyes and covered my ears with both hands to keep from hearing the shrieks that followed. This German soldier appeared in the courtyard for a few weeks, forcibly assembling the chorus to satisfy his perverted love of music. Our whole neighborhood was relieved when his unit finally left the town.

With our Hasidic neighbors, we just lived next to each other, but with the Sztatmans, we could talk since they spoke Polish. At first, I thought Mr. Aron must be tongue-tied, and yet with time and maybe out of sympathy for our shared hardships, he began to engage in bits of chitchat with me. It was from him and Machla that I learned a great many things about the Jewish way of life and their religion.

Mr. Aron thought himself fortunate because his skills were needed, so he and his family continued to live in their flat while hundreds of Jewish families had been driven on foot from Lubartov to nearby little towns and hamlets. Only a few rich expellees could afford to hire a horse-drawn wagon to take at least some possessions with them.

"They are evicting them by simply withdrawing the permission to continue to live at the place of their residence, a cruel way to uproot and impoverish them," Mr. Sztatman's voice broke in disgust.

Most tragic was the fate of Polish prisoners of war who, being Jewish, were excluded by the Germans from the protection of international law. For a short time, they were held as hostages in the synagogue. Mrs. Filipowiczowa, moved by compassion, took some food and hot coffee to them. They were soon driven in freezing weather toward Parchev. In this death march, many of them collapsed and died from exhaustion and some were shot.

On the first occasion after they left, Mr. Sztatman told me, his voice trembling with pain and indignation, that the Germans had turned his synagogue, a holy place, into a stable for their horses. "Scoundrels!" he exclaimed. "Horses where, for years and years, the peace of Sabbath had reigned!" Yes, I had no doubt that the Sztatmans were deeply religious people.

"The hand of Providence is in everything," I heard Mr. Aron saying on one of the rare occasions I visited in their home.

"Our people were oppressed in Egypt," Mrs. Sztatman recalled, "but God delivered them from captivity."

I saw Mrs. Sztatman probably only a few times, since she didn't venture outside, and we usually talked standing on the steps leading to their flat or, on warmer days, seated on a wooden bench beneath a window. Mrs. Sztatman was a small person, and her husband towered over her. In her matron's wig, she looked fragile and sickly. I still recall that when she noticed my eyes centered on her wig, she said, "The Jewish married women wear wigs, being careful not to look too attractive to strangers."

I had heard she was a good cook. Her kitchen, of course, was kosher. In her youth, she had been considered a beauty. This didn't surprise me, knowing Machla and admiring her delicate features and large dark dreamy eyes. At first, I was impressed by the Sztatmans' fervent devotion and total confidence in the righteousness of God in times when grim and ugly realities were lurking dangerously outside the window. Then I asked myself, "Why am I surprised by their deep faith? Didn't faith sustain me during the trials of the past several months? Didn't my piety become more intense?"

One Saturday morning, I heard a gentle knocking on our door. When I opened it, I was face-to-face with a middle-aged woman in a blue satin dress. Her face was flushed with embarrassment. She spoke little Polish, but I understood that she was asking me to come with her to kindle the fire in her kitchen stove.

Of course, I thought, *she is the wife of the glazier!* They lived on the other end of our hallway. Sometimes, while walking on my way to fetch water, I brushed against him, rushing to his job. He always wore his patched caftan under the winter *capota* (outer garment).

That day, I entered the house of a Hasidic family for the first time. The kitchen was small and dark. The peculiar smell of garlic, onion, and wood burning permeated the air. The yellow sand sprinkled over the scrubbed clean floor reminded me that this was the Sabbath. By then, I knew that for the Jews, Sabbath is a day of repose and total dedication to God. So they would ask a trusted Gentile girl to do a job forbidden for a Jewess.

I kindled the fire in the old-fashioned wood burning stove with my recently acquired skill. My neighbor's face broke into a faint smile of gratitude. She was saying something in Yiddish. Her *a'dank!* sounded like German *danke* (thank you).

In the meantime, my eyes were fixed on the figure in the adjacent room. I had been struck dumb with amazement. It was the glazier, yet how he was changed! His full dark beard was already familiar, but now the side curls fell from beneath the round, fur-trimmed hat. The white woolen shawl, with black strips at the ends beautifully fringed, covered the back of his head and flowed down his arms and over the long, silk caftan. The most intriguing, however, were two little round boxes—one attached to his forehead and another strapped over his arm. Turned toward the wall, he was swaying rhythmically back and forth, reciting with earnest dedication and accompanying gestures, some magic incantations in a language totally incomprehensible to me other than one single word, "Israel."

"A sorcerer!" was my first impression. I quickly came to my senses and realized that, dressed in his ritual garments, he was praying. The rest of the day, I kept thinking about the scene and confided my confusion to Daddy.

"Halinka," he said, "imagine that a Hasid child would for the first time see our priest in his liturgical vestments, chanting in Latin. He would be as bewitched as you were this morning."

It was Mr. Aron who explained to me that the little box that so stunned me, was a *phylactery*, called by the Polish Jews, *cyces*. "The *cyces*," he said, "contains the text of the Ten Commandments given to Moses by God. They are, by the way, also the cornerstone of your Christian faith. *Hasid* means 'one who is pious.' Obviously, he was chanting 'Hear, O Israel, the Lord our God, the Lord is One!'"

Listening attentively to Mr. Sztatman, I was reminded that we shared in common the belief in one God, creator, and ruler of all. Back home, I opened my diary, and without delay, I recorded my impressions. My diary burned with the house during the Warsaw Uprising, but despite the passage of time, the concluding stanza came back.

> *For you candles are burning*
> *In Sabbath menorah*
> *For me the bells are ringing*
> *Every Sunday morn,*
> *But the One God is praised*
> *Tho different name*
> *Is on my lips and yours.*

When I closed my diary that chilly evening, I suddenly realized that the solemn bell that once rang from nearby St. Ann's Church was heard no more, and that on Friday nights, the flickering lights of Sabbath candles were no longer dancing on the windowpanes of Jewish homes.

Several days after my experience in the Hasidic household, Yanush and I were surprised with a visit from Yasio, who had finally recovered from a bad case of the flu that had kept him at home for several days. Upon his arrival, Yasio announced with a bright smile on his face, "My grandma is inviting you for a treat Sunday afternoon. Be sure that Milek comes with you."

How kind of her! What a surprise! We were both thrilled. This was going to be our first party in months.

Yasio's grandparents lived at 16 Market Square, where they had settled years ago. "People are still talking about Casimir Rogatko's butcher shop and fine beerhouse," Rozalia said, readily sharing information with the customers of Dad's nearby store.

"Casimir's wife, Anna," she continued, "always keeps her head high. She was determined to be a model wife and mother as she brought up their six children."

Benia Kurzawska, a frequent visitor in our store, listened politely. "I have heard," she said, "that her oldest son, a cavalry captain who fought bravely in the September campaign, was captured and is now in the prisoner-of-war camp in Germany."

"Hmm, hmm…" Rozalia was impressed. Yet nobody could out-perform her in the thoroughness of gathered information. She winked at Benia, who as I noticed, seemed a bit incredulous and, with her eyes glinting, tried to impress her with a climax to the story.

"The older daughter, Yadviga," she continued, "well-educated as she was, wed a merchant from Chenstohova. Local gossip has it that something went awfully wrong there, since she left him soon after Yasio was born and, with the baby in her arms, returned to her parents in Lubartov. To everyone's surprise, she remarried in the Catholic church, but Yasio remained with his grandparents."

∽o∾

The Sunday we awaited with such anticipation finally arrived. For the special occasion, I wore my nice dress brought from Ino, a sapphire-blue with white-ribbed collar and pleated skirt. How exasperated I was when I found that my dressy shoes were too small for me. "They are too tight. I cannot wear them…I need a new pair," I implored, sobbing.

Rozalia bent over them and tested the position of my toes. "Oh, there's still a little room there," she declared. "You will be all right. Where could we find a new pair of shoes like that? Or any new shoes? Before long, we will all be wearing wooden sabots. Be realistic!" As we were leaving, she reminded us, "Don't extend your hand first when greeting Mr. and Mrs. Rogatko. Wait for them…and don't talk first!"

A thick blanket of snow covered the town, but the Rogatko's house was not far. Once there, I felt a little constrained, but Mrs. Rogatko's warm reception soon put me at ease. The room we entered was spacious and nicely furnished, bringing back memories of "good homes" I knew in Ino, and for a moment, I was overcome by sadness and nostalgia for the comforts we had been accustomed to throughout our childhood.

"Taking tea or cocoa?" Mrs. Rogatko asked and disappeared into the kitchen. Mr. Rogatko was preoccupied talking to Milek while Yasio led Yanush and me to his room to show us his latest sketches. Turning one by one his portfolio pages with caricatures mocking Hitler and Nazis, we laughed and giggled with delight.

When we returned to the living room, Mrs. Rogatko presided over the table laid lavishly with dishes we hadn't seen for a few months. While sipping my Dutch cocoa, I wondered how Grandpa Rogatko and Milek could overlook those tempting goodies and talk about such an unpleasant topic as the war.

"The Nazis are turning the *Wehrmacht Blitzkrieg* into myth and trumpet that the German army is invincible," Mr. Rogato remarked resentfully.

Milek, careful not to contradict him, was pointing out that the *Wehrmacht* still had to face a formidable military force. "The French divisions are deployed on the Franco-German border, not to mention the presence of the strong British Expeditionary Force."

Mr. Rogatko was not so convinced. "The two hostile armies are facing each other, but nothing, absolutely *nothing*, has happened. In the meantime, the Nazis will decimate our elite, terrorize our people, and annihilate the Jews."

"Our neighbors here are mostly Jews," I said, and in an instant, I regretted my daring statement. Mrs. Rogatko, aware of my confusion, changed the subject of conversation. "For centuries, there has been a large and thriving Jewish community in Lubartov," she admitted. "At the Market Square, all but two or three houses—ours and a nearby druggist—were in Jewish hands. On New Year's Day, our Jewish neighbors, and always the affluent merchant, Mr. Finkelsztajn, would come with greetings."

Carried by memories of the time past, she recalled that out of reverence for God, the stores in town were open only five days a week—Saturday being the Jewish Sabbath and Sunday, the Catholic Sabbath.

Seeing me glancing at the plate of delicious looking *paczki*, Polish-style doughnuts, she passed it to me with an encouraging smile.

"They are my favorites," I said with appreciation.

While Yasio and Yanush played a great war with tin soldiers and toy cannons on the floor, I remained at the table, listening attentively to the grown-ups' conversation.

"Ah, our Jewish neighbors!" Mr. Rogatko warmed up. "They were born entrepreneurs, masters of bargaining. They loved to buy and sell for profit."

"In the office where I work," Milek's voice was elaborately polite, "I have heard that as soon as the Germans occupied Lubartov, they took over from the wealthy Jews all enterprises without redress. Being an exile myself, I understand their pain."

Mr. Rogatko was well aware of German ruthlessness. "We lived here side by side for years and years," he said. "Everyone needed everyone else."

He stared at Milek and continued, "It's far from me to deny there have been some problems."

At this moment, I noticed that his face was moved with emotion. "When Christian businesses started to bud in the thirties, Jewish competition was formidable. Government jobs were hard to come by for the Jews, so one could hear a lot of fuss on both sides." He paused and then asked, "Do you know who was president of Cracow before the war? It was Kaplicki, a Jew, remembered for his brave fighting in Pilsudski's Legion!"

"This much is certain," Mrs. Rogatko sighed. "What is going on now is unthinkable."

Her husband couldn't have agreed more. "These are dark times for us all," he said bitterly. "Nonetheless, we will not give up."

When we were leaving, Mrs. Rogatko stroked my hair and said reassuringly, "Maybe God will grant us peace soon so that by next Christmas, you will be back home in Inovrotslav."

Shortly before curfew time, not long after our memorable visit to Rogatko's home, we heard a nervous knock on the door. I rushed to open it. The late visitor turned out to be Milek's friend, Zenek. They conversed in the kitchen for a long while. When Zenek left, Milek was unsettled when he returned to the room.

"What is wrong, my son?" Dad asked, alerted.

"Zenek just returned from Lublin and brought gruesome news. Tadeusz Illukowicz, former head of Lubartov county, was shot in a mass execution on Christmas Eve."[2] He was known in town as a man above reproach. We listened petrified.

Milek paused, then spoke through clenched teeth. "The SS and Gestapo raided Lublin Catholic University, Seminary, the Bishop's Curia… scores of professors, students, clergy, were hauled to the prison in the Castle." Dad moved impatiently, evidently shocked.

"Zenek also has heard that they are now plundering the Bishop Palace and Cathedral with total impunity. People are so outraged," he said, "that they refer to the Germans as a pack of rabid wolves falling on the things most sacred to us."

The news was crushing, and intense silence followed. Finally, Dad stood up, his brows drawn together, and spoke. "All this defies comprehension. The Nazi terror is reaching every corner of our country. Nothing is sacred to them. Yet we will never give up. We have to keep our spirits up."

13

It was the beginning of March 1940 when exhilarating news swept through the town. One swallow does not make a summer, but this was extraordinary news. After a long eight months of leisure, the children were going back to school!

I had been counting the hours to the school's opening, imagining myself sharing a bench in the bright classroom with the nicest girl in town. Meanwhile, Yanush dashed off to collect some more detailed information. He returned, bursting with vigor. "The first thing I found out was that the large school building on Legionow Street, with the nice bright classrooms, is occupied by the German police."

"Do you know where our school is located?" I asked, my hopes diminished.

"At Number 10 Cemetery Street in our own neighborhood!" Yanush announced excitedly. I sighed, disappointed.

He grasped my hand. "Let's go see. I believe we've never had it better," Yanush insisted. "What good fortune to have school so close."

We crossed our courtyard, slipped through a hole in the fence, and in no time at all found ourselves in the courtyard of a small unimpressive building. I wondered how it could accommodate all the grade students of the town.

"I've been hearing," Yanush boasted, "that before the war, it was a neighborhood *cheder* run by teacher Federbusz."

"What is a *cheder*?" I asked, puzzled.

"You seem to know so much, and you don't know what a *cheder* is? Well, it's a Jewish school where the boys in skullcaps are reading verses from Talmud all day, studying for just one year. Can you believe it? One year only? That's life!"

The first day of school arrived. I was assigned, as expected, to the sixth grade and directed to a classroom on the second floor. How dismayed I felt seeing it was so small and dull with the benches packed as close as possible and filled with girls, not one of whom I knew. We all sat silently, as if spellbound. To make things worse, the odor of turpentine wafting from the wooden floor, obviously recently treated to keep the bugs away, annoyed my nostrils.

Ah, to be back in my classroom in Ino—bright, cheerful, and familiar. The vivid memory of happy years there only intensified my feeling of dismay.

The door opened, and with the entering teacher, a wave of energy burst into the classroom. We sprang to our feet. This was Ms. Yadviga Kecikowna, the principal of our new school. She was small in stature but had the bearing of a leader. Her face was beaming with vitality and determination.

She spoke out and said to us, "Welcome after a long vacation. At last, we have a school. Yet this interim building is so small that the girls and boys will be studying separately on alternate days."

"By order of the German authorities, Polish children in the GG are only permitted to complete seven years of elementary school. In this situation, we should consider ourselves lucky to have dedicated teachers whom you'll find very supportive. I expect each and every one of you to do your very best to learn."

This was a powerful message that enhanced my motivation. I promised myself to study hard and with total dedication, right from the start. I was so encouraged by what I heard that as soon as school was out, I went straight to our grocery store.

"How can I help you today?" Mr. Tarnowski asked, noticing my glowing cheeks.

"We've just started school today, and I need a writing desk."

"But, Halinka, how do you expect to find a desk in a grocery store?"

"Well, I thought that you might spare one of those used wooden cases without a lid, big enough so I could use it as my desk."

He thought for a while, disappeared, and returned with the case I had dreamed about.

"Put it with the shorter side down, and hopefully, it will work."

I was delighted. With the small allowance I got from Dad the previous day, I bought four sheets of dark blue cardboard and used them to cover three sides and the top of the case. To make my desk more cheerful and inspiring, I painted birds and flowers on the sides.

This was not a Chippendale piece, but it served me well until Milek presented Yanush and me with an old, long, and sturdy office table with two deep drawers. They could be locked with a key to keep our treasured possessions undisturbed.

∞o∞

It was so good to be a student again! The first classroom assignment was to write a short story about our summer vacation. Several of us were selected to read our stories aloud, and mine was declared the best. After that, I enjoyed star status. I still remember the first line of what I wrote: "It was a memorable September 1939…"

I realized that the Gestapo would certainly not approve what I wrote, yet Ms. Angela Miduchowna, the stately matron-like teacher of Polish language, seemed very pleased. So how astonished I was when Martha Wisniewska, with whom I shared a bench, whispered, "What did you copy that from?" I wasn't sure if she meant it as an insult or a compliment.

"My own experience," I retorted, imitating the grown-ups. We both laughed.

I quickly got accustomed to my new school and loved it. The five years in the excellent Preparatory School at the Maria Konopnicka Gymnasium in Ino had been a very valuable experience and boosted confidence in my ability to succeed. My report card was the best "from top down." I have to admit that I enjoyed the status of the best student in the class. Faced with competition, I studied even harder to keep my reputation intact.

Then one day, torn by doubts, I pondered: Was it a quest for accomplishment, or was I driven by prideful ambition to prove myself better than my classmates?

I needed to face that question squarely.

⌘

I was just entering the school on a bright icy cold day when I ran into Ms. Kecikowna.

"Maiden with a wet head!" she exclaimed, quoting the title of a popular book by Kornel Makuszynski. "I always thought you were a reasonable girl."

I blushed and passed her in a hurry, feeling exasperated and sorry that I disappointed my most respected teacher. Nevertheless, I would rather have died than explain to her that my hair was not wet but greasy, although I had washed it several times with hot soapy water. During the weekend, Dad had treated it with a homemade concoction to kill the lice I brought from school. He said he learned how to fight them during the World War.

"There are body lice which live in clothing and head lice living only in the hair of the head," Dad explained to me.

Once alerted, some days later, I noticed a louse crawling out of the braid of a pupil sitting just in front of me. It was moving freely over her neck. Well, lice don't stick to one host but love to venture out to find new victims. They feast on blood.

How lucky I was to have a knowledgeable dad. With his help, I got rid of them, and the disgusting experience was not repeated. "Just be vigilant," he told me.

The worst nuisances, however, were the fleas. They had a habit of jumping on our legs as soon as we stepped into the hallway with its dirt floor or walked in the courtyard to fetch the water. As the days became warmer, the fleas thrived. Our flat was always kept clean, but since insecticide sprays were not available to keep them at bay, they went right on feasting on our dear blood. This was particularly annoying when we were asleep. I learned the exact knack of catching and annihilating them in pitch darkness. Yet there were always more of them to attack us until we moved out to our new dwelling at the Market Square, next to the Rogatkos.

The days were flying by now. With school in full swing, our lives took on new meaning. Following a daily routine diverted our attention from the hardships brought on by the war. By a strict order of German authority, Polish literature, history, and geography were removed from the school's curriculum. Therefore, on free alternate days, we studied the forbidden subjects, using books secretly provided by our thoughtful teachers.

In late March, the severe winter of 1939–40 came to an abrupt end. A dazzling sun was rapidly melting the accumulated masses of snow and ice. The days were longer now, and after school, I would go with my friend, Martha, to look for signs of spring. One of our favorite destinations was the vast park just past St. Ann's Church. Like the church, it was enclosed by a fancy white wall, capped with red tile. We would skirt the burned-out palace, aiming for the grand alley lined on both sides with old majestic poplars and continue toward the lovely lake. When I saw it for the first time in early spring, its depth was dark and mysterious. Thin sheets of ice still floated here and there, like shattered fragments of a broken mirror unable to reflect the splendor of bygone times. The lake was supplied with crystal-clear water from two springs. Formed into a little stream, the water was rushing through a canal spanned by little foot bridges, which had lost their former charm.

Once beyond the park, we found ourselves in the wide expanse of an unbroken meadow, spreading as far as the eye could see, all the way down to the river. It was now swollen with the wetness of spring and gloriously interwoven with up-springing marsh marigolds. The strong fragrance of the moist earth was invigorating and almost intoxicating.

I was about to pick another marigold when I heard Martha's voice, "Look over there!" She was stretching out her hand, pointing to the graceful silhouette of a long-legged stork in the distance.

"They've obviously returned to their nests all the way from Africa!" I was euphoric.

The stork was wading slowly in the glory of his white plumage, once in a while lowering his head with its long red beak. Noticing us approaching, it turned and flew away. I stared up to follow his flight and was suddenly dazzled by the vast vault of the sky, splashed with floating white clouds. It was not only a feast for my eyes, but for all of my being.

Oh, dear Lubartov of my youth! An elation of being part of something far greater than myself overcame me. The world around me was so lovely, so innocent, and sweet. Life is now so unpredictable, I thought, but still a worthy adventure.

We were walking back, our shoes heavy with wetness and mud, but our spirits were uplifted, overflowing with unbounded gladness. What a fine time we had! I was reciting a recently memorized poem[1], a rapturous praise of the Creator and the beauty of his creation:

> *What wilt thou from us, O Lord,*
> *For Thy generous gifts?*
> *What for Thy blessings which know no bounds?*
> *The Church will not contain Thee;*
> *Everywhere is full of Thee…*

I raised my hand with a bouquet of flowers I had just picked in the meadow and recited:

For Thee, Spring brings forth various flowers;
For Thee, Summer walks out in a garland of corn stalks…

Martha, who had been listening courteously, now exclaimed, "I know, I know…this is Jan Kochanowski… remember what Ms. Miduchowna told us just days ago… he showed the beauty of Polish language like nobody else before him."

"Do you realize, Martha," a thought struck me all of a sudden, "that we might be following right now in the footsteps of Jan Kochanowski? He was a frequent guest in the palace here."

Seeing her startled glance, I went on to explain that when studying in Italy, Jan Kochanowski befriended Nicholas Firlej, son of Peter Firlej, the founder of Lubartov, then known as Levartov. It was actually Nicholas Firlej who built a splendid family residence here and laid out an Italian-style park and the vast garden.

"And how do you know all that?" She was curious.

"From the book, one of those banned by the Nazis, which I borrowed from Father Szulc," I whispered, confident that Martha could be trusted. "If you would like, I could introduce you to him."

As we were crossing Siedlecka Street on the way home, I started to worry about what Rozalia was going to say, seeing the miserable condition of my wet, muddy shoes.

Sometime at the beginning of spring, one of the expellees from Ino had died, and although neither Martha nor I knew him, we decided to attend the funeral service as a gesture of solidarity. Martha's family, like mine, had been deported from Ino, though I met and befriended her at school in Lubartov. Her long face, framed by two blonde braids, was animated by a pair of pale blue eyes. Martha was a practical, quiet, conscientious student. We got along just fine. Our differences in disposition didn't prevent us from becoming good friends. She would listen patiently to my chattering and seemed to like my stories and the poems I could recite on any occasion.

We were standing in the graveyard, close to the coffin still resting on heavy ropes over the freshly dug grave. The priest raised his voice in a long solemn prayer.

"May his soul rest eternally in peace, O Lord," responded the tightly packed mourners. This was the last I heard, engrossed in my own thoughts. It was only a year ago that I was standing in the cemetery in Ino by the coffin taking away our mom. I was still a child then. Since the war broke out, I had been growing up in a hurry, a little girl caught up in the trap of a hostile Occupation.

I realized how lucky I was to be cared for, fed, and dressed. I was grateful to have Dad, who truly loved us. Concentrating on making a living, he was giving us space to grow on our own, interfering only in special cases. I was starved for guidance more than ever. Deprived of Mom's presence, her warmth, and love, I so often felt tremendously lonely and lost. Without her, not our crude dwelling in Lubartov, nor even our lovely house in Ino, were true homes. Ah, how painfully my mother had been missed! Where is she now? Does she see us? Intercede for us?

All of a sudden, I felt Martha gently pinching my arm. Roused from a deep reverie, I quickly returned to reality. She had been pointing with her eyes at something to my right. I turned my head in that direction and in an instant was struck dumb. Standing just behind me, his arm pressing against mine, was Joseph Majewski! Aware of a tender expression on his face, I shot him an indignant glance.

Why did he drop in here out of the blue? Disgusted by his daring, I wanted to shoo him out, to address him in words showing my deepest contempt. However, the people were standing in a tight ring, shoulder to shoulder. Most of them were exilees, victims of German hate and greed. How could they miss seeing Joseph, son of well-known *Volksdeutsch*, making sweet eyes at me? In a flash, I recalled the rumors that Majewski's younger sons were now in the *Hitlerjungend* school in Radom. My face turned scarlet in outrage. Yet I could do nothing but endure my shame with a heavy heart to the end of the service.

Finally, the coffin was lowered into the grave, and two men started to fill it with dirt. Slowly, the mourners began to disperse. I took Martha by the hand, and we slipped past Joseph and his friend, on our way to the graves of Polish soldiers who had perished in the last battle of the war, at nearby Kock, and only recently reburied here.

Joseph didn't dare to follow us there and, as we were told later, waited by the cemetery gate for us to pass on our way out. Yet Martha and I remained, praying at the graves for a very long time.

∽o∾

That night, I had a dream that I attribute to my experience in the cemetery. I dreamt I was in a manor that was unknown to me. I entered a spacious, empty room. I moved a few steps ahead and stopped, spellbound. That room was separated from the adjacent room by a wall of glass or perhaps a thin ice sheet, bulky and uneven at the edges, but perfectly transparent.

As soon as I entered the room, I saw a person standing there. Instantly, I recognized my mom. She was motionless, unaware of my presence, facing not me but a door in front of her, obviously awaiting somebody. Her lovely, sweet face, which I saw in profile, was illuminated by subtle, joyous anticipation. It was obvious to me that whomever she had been expecting must be very dear to her. She seemed to be so real, and yet…she was unapproachable. In deep silence, I kept staring at her, hypnotized by her presence but unable to move closer to her or to say a word. I cannot tell how long it lasted, but I felt my heart beating faster and faster, so furiously that I thought it might burst at any moment.

I awoke with my face bathed in tears.

So many years have passed, and still I wonder: Was it a dream-like wishful fantasy, spun from the images stored in my subconscious or a blissful glimpse into another world, the one we try in vain to grasp when awake?

14

Our wartime school was not a place we liked, tolerated, or disliked, but rather a process of learning under the guidance of committed, courageous teachers in an atmosphere of mutual trust. School for us was also an opportunity to meet and befriend our peers—friendships that would outlast the war and separation and often became life-long bonds.

Through my and Yanush's friends, school was for me an open window from which I could see far beyond the narrow limits of our neighborhood and feel the pulse of the town. Lubartov was changing before my eyes.

∽o∽

I befriended Martha, and when Dad or Rozalia asked for Yanush's whereabouts, I would respond without hesitation, "He must be with one of his friends."

Having friends is always a life-enhancing experience, but during the war, having a trusted friend could be a lifesaver.

My brother's facility for making friends was a great blessing, not only for him, but also for me. Much to my amazement, many of our new friends were not native Lubartovians. For instance, Marys arrived with his family in early 1940. He became Yanush's classmate and closest friend throughout the Occupation. I remember him as a boy of good appearance and polished manners, indicating that he had been well brought up. His steadfastness and well-tempered disposition was in stark contrast to my beloved brother's vibrant vitality and lively face, animated by the excitement that shone most of the time in his cheerful, trusting eyes.

We didn't know much about Marys's family. He was the only son of Mr. and Mrs. Louis Bialy. They settled at 17 Lubelska Street, keeping secret their family connection in town. Quiet gossip making the rounds in our circle suggested that Mr. Bialy opened his kitchenware and household goods store with help from his relatives. Soon, we found out that Marys was definitely not a bearer of tales. He never uttered a word about his family's past. His evident discomfort, and even prickliness when someone asked, didn't surprise me. All through the war, we children were constantly warned not to talk or ask questions about personal matters or family backgrounds. Now it may seem like an unrealistic demand considering children's natural curiosity, but during the Occupation, careless talk or even the slightest slip of the tongue could bring disastrous or even deadly consequences.

Only later, we learned that Marys's family's real name was not Bialy, but Maciejewski. Before the war, Marys's father, Mr. Louis Maciejewski, was not a small merchant but a senator from Katovice in Silesia. The prewar skirmishes started early there. If the Germans were to occupy Silesia, this alone would have been enough to put him on the Gestapo's wanted list.

He had even more reason to fear the Nazis. Mr. Maciejewski's participation in the Silesian Risings[1] foretold his doom if the Nazi could get their hands on him.

Aware of the pending danger, Mr. Maciejewski decided to leave Katovice. Flying east, the family reached Lvov. There, the senator had some connections and managed to get false identification papers in the name of Bialy (White). On September 17, 1939, in the third week of the war, the Red Army, cooperating with the Nazis in the dismemberment of Poland, occupied its eastern provinces. The Poles were now caught in a trap. Stalinist terror raged in Lvov as the elimination of Polish leadership became the Soviet's foremost goal. Counting on the strained relations between Polish, Ukrainian, and Jewish populations there, the *NKVD* (Soviet secret police) was encouraging inhabitants to denounce any "*bourgeois,*" any "class enemy."[2] The senator's family fell into the Soviet trap. With providencial help, they somehow managed to cross the illegal "green border" of the GG and reach Lubartov.

It's no wonder that once settled in Lubartov, Marys's family lived in constant fear of being denounced.

Everyday life struggled on. With the arrival of Bohdan Bogdanowicz, known in school as Bogdan, we got some idea of what was going on in the part of Poland, forcefully annexed into the Soviet Union. Bogdan became my lifetime friend. Well read, bright, and eloquent, he engaged me in long disputes on subjects that preoccupied teenagers at that time. The family came to Lubartov, to Bogdan's grandparents, from the small town of Macieyovitse, near Kovel in Volhynia, where his father had been a railroad worker. In Lubartov, Mr. Bogdanowicz ran a little grocery store on Lubelska Street.

Bogdan didn't hide the fact that they had escaped Macieyovitse for fear of deportation to Siberia or Kazakhstan.[3] "It was Mr. Tuler, a Jewish acquaintance of my father," Bogdan openly admitted, who alerted him, saying, "Mr. Bogdanowicz, you must escape. I did see your name on the list of people scheduled to be deported…you to one place, your family to another. You fought as a volunteer in the Bolshevik War in 1920, and they know that."

"How did Mr. Tuler happen to find out that secret information?" I eyed Bogan with a bit of scepticism.

He reflected for a long while. "You see, there are Jewish officers and soldiers in the Red Army. Yiddish is the mother tongue of many Russian and Polish Jews. The position of the Jews there is very different from here, under German occupation." I instinctively knew that the danger was real and listened intently while Bogdan continued.

"My father amassed 2,000 zlotys to pay the smugglers to help our family of four to cross the river Bug. It was heavily patrolled and blockaded by wire entanglements. The night was biting cold," he shivered. "After we crossed the river, we had to deal with snow. We struggled through snow up to my knees."

"Thank God, you reached your grandparents here safely," I whispered.

He fell into a silence. Struggling to control his voice, he looked straight into my eyes and said very quietly, "In many ways, our existence here is more bearable than under the terror raging in our eastern provinces in the Soviets' grip."

Slowly, gradually, I had been learning that Marys's and Bogdan's families were only two of many escapees from the threat of Nazi or Soviet terror. They were hoping to find in this small, remote town, a temporary shelter. In the meantime, the transports from Pomerania and Great Poland, incorporated into Greater Germany, continued to dump forcibly deported3 Poles at the station.

The town's carpenters were busy making dozens and dozens of beds of pinewood. Instead of springs, they had wooden planks on which the straw mattresses were fitted. We waited several weeks for ours. Dad stained them a warm brown to look more like real furniture.

Life was tough with so many immediate needs and no other resources but personal skills and a stubborn resolve to persevere. Meager food and cold homes were common. There was often no money for shoe repairs or desperately needed doctors or medicines.

It was in the school that I heard that dedicated town's volunteers had been collecting money, food, bedding, and clothing for dozens and dozens of the most destitute families. However, the town was not wealthy and had its own share of families impoverished by the war. They were the wives and children of soldiers who went off to war and were killed, wounded, or captured and sent to the prisoners-of-war camps in Germany or Soviet detention camps in Russia. Scores of people had lost their jobs.

The Nazis, trying to obscure their crimes, referred to us as "resettled people." The Lubartovians called us *wygnancy* (exilees). This was, for me, a deeply touching word. One evening, I was at home alone. Suddenly, a painting, which I had seen in the art book my mom brought from Italy, was before my eyes so amazingly vivid as though I had closed the book only moments before. The painting depicted two nudes walking side by side, each caught in despair—Adam and Eve, just being banished from Paradise. I didn't know then that it was Masaccio's vibrant masterpiece. What I retained in my memory was a powerful image of exiles, an image I imposed on countless Adams and Eves who were being banished by the SS police from their homes and livelihoods. Even though not literally naked, they were stripped of even the basic possessions needed for a normal life. I was one of them myself. In the "blind" wagons, they were transported into the bleak unknown.

This piercing feeling was somehow soothed when I joined people in the Capuchin church singing the heart-wrenching Marian song, long-known, but now felt more deeply than ever:

> *O most loving Mother,*
> *Guardian of your people,*
> *May weeping of orphans*
> *Awake your compassion*
> *Exiles of Eve to you we call,*
> *Behold our sorrows*
> *Let us not to wander…*

It was Mary's humanity, her suffering and grace as Mother of the Son of God, that made her the perfect Mother Dolorosa of all the faithful. In a world of trouble, she could intercede for us, present to God our heartfelt prayers to grant us strength and wisdom to bear what was now and what was yet to come.

Thinking back now, how well I remember that evening. There were four of us: Romek, Yanush, Ziho, and me. In our dark spooky hallway, we huddled together in a circle. Someone struck a match. A hand reached out into the wavering light. It was my hand, and in it were two of Dad's cigarettes. They were lighted and passed around the circle. A few moments later, we were wrapped in our first halo of smoke, sharing the excitement and guilt, choking and giggling quietly.

Of course, we realized that we were doing a very foolish thing, but this was so irresistible and thrilling in a time when scores of oppressive regulations undermined our budding lives. The liberating feeling of breaking a rule swept over us. Ah, we would never admit that we were imitating the grown-ups. After what we had recently gone through, we thought ourselves quite grown-up. And what a good time we had together.

Ziho was Yanush's and my fellow student. We called him Ziho, short for Zdzislaw. Yes, he was the lad who had witnessed my foolish playfulness at the well that memorable frosty morning. Tall with long legs and slim hips, he exuded youthful vigor. His head was crowned by dark fiery hair. In Lubartov, the lilacs were in full bloom in May and the hackberry in June. In a romantic gesture, he would stack fragrant sheaves of them in our entrance door.

15

There were shortages of every conceivable kind in our lives, but for growing kids, the shortage of food was the one that was hardest to bear. It seemed our stomachs were constantly empty, and the tightening of our belts was commonplace.

The voracious Germans were insatiable. At first, they looted the storehouses and brutally requisitioned all the food they could find in the countryside. Later, they instituted rigorous quotas on every agricultural product. In 1940, food rationing was imposed on the whole population: bread, meat, butter, eggs, sugar, and marmalade. The Poles were expected to survive on famine rations. How could I ever forget the appalling lack of fairness? Jokes were the best remedy for our bitterness.

In early 1940, eggs were still openly available in the town market. The confiscation of food by the Germans was common, so when two gendarmes suddenly appeared in the market looking for eggs, the countrywomen, alerted to their presence, hid the eggs they had brought to sell. The sharp eye of the gendarme, however, spotted the eggs in a distant stall. He quickly approached and was about to snatch them.

The peasant woman tried to prevent him, insisting in Polish dialect, the only language she knew, "They are *kace* (duck's) eggs." Now in German, *katze* means a cat. The gendarme was furious, believing she dared to mock him. It was a tense moment. He had a gun and might not hesitate to use it. An alert woman in the next stall recognized the danger. Pointing to the eggs, she began calling, "Quack, quack." The danger was defused, and the appeased German left the stall.

Eggs in their shells were rationed, but in later years, *stluczki* (cracked eggs) were sometimes available. One wing of the burned-out palace of Prince Sanguszko was rebuilt as a large creamery for the exclusive use of the Germans. Here, eggs were also sorted, packed, and sent to Germany. The contents of cracked eggs were tossed into a large container and sold to Poles by the scoop. Since the sorting crew was Polish, the quantity of cracked eggs increased considerably during the process. Yanush loved to grab a jug and go try his luck. When Yanush's luck was good, he returned with a jug full of cracked eggs, and the whole family enjoyed a scrambled egg feast. Never mind that sometimes you had to pick out a piece of eggshell or other minor contaminant. The flavor was not harmed in the least.

While grown-ups worried about proper nutrition, we kids missed the sweets. Sugar rations were so small that Rozalia kept the precious commodity locked in a cupboard to which only she had the key, and that key was always on her person. We knew there was sugar in there; we could almost taste it, but how to unlock the door?

Finally, one of our pals solved the problem when Rozalia was out of the house. He taught himself how to pick the lock. When the door flew open, we were surprised to find not only rationed sugar and a jar of honey, but also a small box of sugar cubes. The temptation was irresistible! Each of us took one cube. The taste was heavenly, but of course, one cube was hardly enough. So we took another. We had enough self-control to leave a few sugar cubes behind when we closed and locked the cupboard door.

Unfortunately for our scheme, we did not leave enough. Some days later, when Rozalia was serving tea to some unexpected guests, she opened the box of sugar cubes and found most of them gone. She was understandably furious at the loss of the precious sugar, and since we were the only likely suspects, she demanded that Dad punish us severely. I don't remember our punishment, so it must not have been too bad. However, I will never forget that on the next occasion when Rozalia opened the cupboard, to her dismay, she found it infested with ants. Apparently, they prized the sweets as much as we did.

"Better the children should have the sugar than the ants," Dad said with a barely perceptible smile.

The fact that there were any food supplies at all in that secured cupboard was a tribute to the shrewdness and foraging skills of Rozalia. She was our secret weapon. Thanks to her, we were still better off than some others. She cultivated connections with the peasant women, and working through Dad's store as a contact, she was able to illegally acquire butter, cheese, cream, milk, and eggs. Later, when we moved to the Market Square, a back room of Dad's store often served as a parlor. The frequent visits of our acquaintances, who came to claim their "orders" of butter or cottage cheese available through Rozalia's connections, greatly animated our social life and boosted our spirits through companionship.

❧

As the war went on, people grew hungrier and hungrier. Every possible piece of ground in town was being turned into a vegetable plot. In the gardens that once held flowers, onions were now in bloom.

At the corner of our Siedlecka Lane was a paved area adjacent to the fenced orchard. We had heard that the peasants delivering provisions to the Presbytery across the street once used it to park their horse carts; now, it was vacant. After a consultation with the Filipowicz family and permission from the Town Council, we decided to turn the place into a garden and grow our own food. It was hard work moving each heavy paving stone, and pushing a spade into the unyielding ground was just as difficult. But the work was made easier by the knowledge that we would soon enjoy the product of our hard labor.

Once the ground was prepared, the area was divided into small plots and seeded. I don't know how Dad acquired the seeds. It seemed that in no time at all, a miracle happened. I was fascinated, watching the seedlings shooting up, springing to life. But gosh, they not only needed to be weeded, but watered as well! The water had to be carried in heavy buckets from the well in the courtyard, a long, tedious job.

I was carrying a bucket full of water when I met Ziho on his way to see Yanush.

"Let me help you," he courteously offered, with a warm smile.

"How nice of you, but I am used to doing this," I replied, passing him and holding tightly to the bucket to make sure not a single drop of the precious water spilled.

The garden, of course, needed more than one bucket of water. Ziho was stronger than me and eager to help. He called again and again. One day, he surprised me with a small bouquet of lilies of the valley, so fresh and fragrant. I loved those delicate trumpet-shaped white blossoms more than all the flowers on earth. How had he guessed that? Life still was sometimes sweet as honey.

The bountiful earth, warmed by the sun, was yielding lettuce and peas, carrots, beets, onions, potatoes, and mouth-watering tomatoes. These precious vegetables greatly improved our wartime diet.

The plants I loved the most were the sunflowers when they shot up and opened the glory of their disks, crowned by daisy-like, golden bright petals. They provided shade and attracted the birds from the orchard. Our vegetable garden turned out to be a place of refuge for me, a peaceful retreat where I could read, study, and dream.

∽o∾

In that spring of 1940, the momentum of the war quickened. At work, in the stores, or an occasional encounter on the street, Lubartovians were sharing the hottest news. Friends gathered at homes to discuss the situation. Yanush and I strained our ears to catch trickles of those exchanges: "German tanks are rolling over the Danish border. Holland surrendered."

Ania and *Frania*, the diminutive (and crypto) names for *Anglia* (England) and *Francja* (France) were often on people's lips. "Just wait," one would hear the hopeful wish, "Hitler will surely break his teeth on the Maginot Line."

Then, one day, Milek dropped by. "People are jumping to their feet in disbelief," his voice was choked with emotion. "Thousands and thousands of Allied troops are encircled at Dunkirk by the Germans! The British are sending every type of vessel to rescue them." He told us that hundreds and hundreds of Polish soldiers who had enlisted in the Polish army in France and fought the Germans bravely as Poles usually do were now in England. The fast defeat of France followed, striking a devastating blow to hope for a quick end of the war.

Even Dad, at first, was downhearted. "I can't imagine Nazi boots tramping down the Champs Elysees. Adolf Hitler dictating his armistice terms, so humiliating to the French people. In just months, he has mopped up a great part of Europe." The bewildering questions were now hanging in the air. What is to come next? How will it all end?

Summer came. There were no vacation plans. In town, all youth organizations, scouting included, had been forbidden. From past September, all sport facilities were permanently closed. No cultural activities of any kind were allowed, and even group singing was prohibited. We knew all of that was part of the occupiers' scheme to prevent the Polish children and youth from developing normally. Therefore, we had to use our ingenuity to find ways to have a good time, once our daily chores at home were done. We wanted to get everything we could out of life in a time when even the nearest future was unpredictable and every day was a gift.

We read voraciously. We tapped our creative skills. Yasio drew, Teresa painted, Yanush collected stamps, and

I wrote my short stories. Ziho played violin, and Bogdan learned to type on an old typewriter, even though owning a typewriter was strictly prohibited. We were preoccupied with gardening, learning firsthand the intricacies of life. This led to a multitude of questions: How did life begin? How did it achieve its astounding diversity?

All through the war, one of our favorite places was the vast park behind the burned-out palace. Martha and I loved to stroll there, sharing secrets, our arms around each other's waist. We solemnly promised that we would be friends for all time.

I particularly loved the park's lake. Sun, wind, and cloud shadows played across the water's surface, constantly altering its appearance and mood as though it were some beautiful and capricious maiden. One day, strolling with Martha, we found a rowboat hidden in a thicket at the lake's edge. There were no paddles. Two very long, sturdy branches would have to substitute for them. Or so we thought.

We boarded the boat and pushed it out from the shore. Delighted, I was standing in the middle of it. Only recently, I had memorized a nostalgic poem by Slowacki, and a rowboat gliding over the water was the ideal setting to recite it:

> *Strayed today on the vast sea*
> *Hundreds of miles from shore,*
> *And hundreds of miles before*
> *I saw the storks flying overhead*
> *In a long row…*

Carried away by my imagination, I hadn't noticed that Martha no longer had control of the boat. The stick she was holding in her hand could not reach the bottom of the lake.

"We're stranded!" she said desperately. Now our adventure did not seem like such a good idea. What could we do? Float in the boat for who knew how long or jump in the water and try to get to the shore in our best Sunday dresses?

Fortunately, the boys had been spying on us without our knowledge. After much laughter at our predicament, they gallantly came to the rescue and pulled our stranded craft to shore. I knew that the boys loved the park as much as we girls did. This was a great place for our many adventures. The ruined palace was a perfect setting for their war games. The Germans had blown up some walls and had been using the rubble for their projects. There was plenty of rubble to "shell" enemy positions from the recesses and nooks. The overheard tales of a secret underground passage leading all the way to St. Ann's Church provided extra thrills.

However, playing in the park demanded certain precautions. After the snow covering the ground had melted, some irregularities of the terrain had led the Germans to come upon buried weapons, ammunition, and military equipment of all sorts. It had been hidden the past September by the retreating Polish troops. After that find, the Germans intensified their search for presumably hidden weapons. Houses were raided, and men were arrested. One of them was Feliks Jezior, Lubartov's former vice mayor. The SS police ordered his garden to be thoroughly excavated. Nothing was found, but he was shot anyway.

Our favorite activity during the summer was swimming in the River Wieprz. It bypasses the town and broadly and swiftly flows north to Kock and west toward Deblin to eventually fall into the arms of the Vistula River. Yanush and I were on our way to swim on a beautiful hot day. It was a long walk as we passed gardens and crossed through meadows. We talked as we went.

"I have never seen Dad or anybody else reading *Lublin New Voice*.[1] Poles don't have radios. So where do people get such detailed information about war?"

"From London," Yanush said, with the air of a well-informed person. "The programs are broadcast in Polish."

"But having and listening to radio is strictly forbidden," I said. "All the radios were ordered to be turned in. To be caught listening to radio must be like being caught with weapons. Did you read the new decree plastered all over town? The Germans are trying to turn us against each other by offering a reward of 1,000 zlotys to informers."

Yanush was exasperated. "You talk like a girl. Now listen, some people turned in their old radio and are keeping a new one in hiding. I heard there are some courageous Poles who are listening to those broadcasts because we have to know what is going on with the war and in our occupied country.[2] They pass the news, which is then spread by word of mouth."

"How do you know all this so well?" I was truly impressed. "That must be a lot like playing the gossip game. You pass information to the next person in a circle, and by the time it gets to the last player, it is distorted. Information spread by mouth may often be unreliable."

"Still, it is better than being kept in the dark," Yanush said, "but we shouldn't be talking about this. Keep your mouth shut tight. Promise!"

We were approaching our usual place by the river and found three of our friends already there enjoying the water. The current was swift, creating small dangerous whirlpools here and there. Though never mind—we had prudently learned to swim. The water was wonderfully cool, clear, and so refreshing! We were swimming and splashing to our heart's content. Shaking the water off like doggies, we laughed cheerfully. Within minutes, all five of us were resting with our faces exposed to the bright sun.

The daily ordeals of life along with the disheartening news from the front had been easier to take, knowing that we were all in it together. One of us once had said, "God had brought us together in Lubartov to be friends."

Our best shield against adversity was youthful optimism, something the Germans could not take away from us. The solidarity against the invaders and the bond of love of our country brought us closer together, made us more open with each other. We were learning quickly how to adjust and survive.

We are far from perfect, I thought on our way back home. *Nobody is perfect. We have faults of character as any other kids our age.* I was glad, though, that we were growing up with our religious and patriotic values firmly set.

The sound of distant thunder caught my attention.

"The storm is coming," Yanush said. We both picked up our steps.

16

The year went on, and I was in the seventh grade, the last year of primary school. I still had the reputation of being a good student, but my peace of mind was gone. If the war had not intervened, I would already have been in the prestigious gymnasium in Ino. In the GG, run with an iron fist by the Nazis, all Polish youth were forbidden any higher education past the seventh grade. I often deliberated why the occupiers, wild with menace, would deprive us of the noble pursuit of knowledge. Hadn't we always been taught how important learning was? I was not the only one who was worrying about what would happen to us after graduation from the primary school.

"The problem is the Nazi's lust for power and domination of the world," Bogdan was convinced. "They want to grab our land and doom us to hard manual labor for their Reich. The less education we have, the better..."

"This is preposterous," I protested. "Man has a mind and should have an opportunity to learn."

"That is exactly why we are going to challenge this sinister order to our last breath," Bogdan said.

We were young and idealistic and our spirit was unbroken, but the reality was harsh and bleak. Since the beginning of the Occupation, the despised *Arbeitsamt* (Labor Office) in Lubartov had been drawing up lists of names of young people to be deported for compulsory slave labor in the Reich. We had heard that many of those called had not shown up before the Commission and had gone into hiding, despite the fear of reprisal. The Germans promptly appointed a gang of thugs to hunt down the fugitives and hand them over to the authorities. "People call them *lapacze* (catchers)," I was told in confidence by one of my classmates. "They are habitually drunk and rowdy."

The most hated of the catchers was their leader, a tall, blond *Volksdeutsch,* Jablonowsky. One could spot him from a distance in his black leather jacket, with a whip in his hand or a rifle slung over his shoulder.

The catchers were a particular scourge in the county villages as they swept through looking for healthy young people. In Lubartov, hair-raising stories circulated about their horrid conduct. Yet the inhabitants of the county could do little to oppose them. It took a long time, but eventually, they were punished. On order from the underground court, they were all shot.

Yanush and I were walking with Dad along the shoulder of a long wide road planted with large trees. It must have been Linden Street, leading west toward nearby Kozlovka with its splendid palace and deep forests sheltering escapees and partisans. The day was grey and obviously cold since Dad was wearing his hat and a fur-lined coat with a beaver collar. I do not remember where we were going or why.

Then suddenly, he stopped abruptly, and with his arms clasped tightly over our shoulders, he pulled us behind the wide trunk of a large linden tree. Alarmed, I still managed a glimpse of German policemen in the far distance and a truck parked along the side of the road. My head spun. The thoughts were flashing through my mind like bullets: German roundup, did they see us? Tense, anxious minutes crawled past one by one. Oh! Better to forget once and for all this humiliating feeling of a hunted animal.

This time, thank God, we were safe. What had happened to those who were not so lucky?

No wonder that, after that experience, I was in fear of being caught and forcibly deported to the Reich.[1] Fear hung over me like Damocles's sword. Fortunately, something unexpected happened that took all my attention and gave my life a direction for years to come.

That evening stands out vividly in my memory. After closing his store, Dad returned home, his face beaming with a warm smile. After entering the door, he reached inside his briefcase and handed me a book.

"I had a visit from a gentleman[2] just an hour ago, and he asked me to give you this book with congratulations. It's a school award," Dad explained.

The book was beautifully bound and a great surprise and joy to me. I found out at once that it was on Arctic explorers who tried to brave a sea route from the Atlantic to the Pacific Ocean through a torturous Arctic passage. Dad waited patiently until I satisfied my curiosity and then told me that the unexpected visitor had a far more important reason to see him.

"I have been told," Dad said, "that in reaction to the German's ruthless policy forbidding Polish youth to pursue secondary education, the underground gymnasium classes are being organized in town."

"Underground gymnasium?" I repeated, almost breathless.

"Yes," Dad confirmed reassuringly. "What extraordinary initiative and courage! Now, listen to me carefully, Halinka. I agreed that you will pursue, in secrecy, the gymnasium program, starting in January. You will, of course, continue attending the seventh grade in your official school at the same time."

I threw my arms around my daddy. "This is the best news I have had for many months!"

"Wait, hear me out! You still need to decide if you would like a program with French or German as a foreign language."

That night, I couldn't sleep, overwhelmed with excitement. In January, my dreams would come true. I would be a student in the gymnasium, the underground gymnasium, something I assumed was truly unusual in the history of education. I closed my eyes and tried to imagine what I might discover in that fabulous realm of learning.

I was on my knees scrubbing the kitchen floor when the front door opened, and Dad and Ms. Lewandowska walked in. I leaped to my feet and greeted her with respect, slightly embarrassed by their unexpected arrival, my disheveled appearance, and wet hands. Ms. Lewandowska was an exilee from Ino and an acquaintance of my parents there. Dignified, she was elegantly but soberly dressed. Her somewhat heavy walk and movements made her look older than she was. From her appearance, one would have thought her harsh, but she greeted me warmly. Suddenly, her eyes moistened and a few tears ran down her face.

"My child," she said softly, staring at me with compassion, "what would your mother think seeing you scrubbing the floor?"

It occurred to me that she was seeing me as some kind of Cinderella. How could I tell her that I didn't feel that way at all?

"I would rather do something else," I said, "but it has been snowing since yesterday and the floor got dirty. Somebody has to scrub it."

In minutes, we were chatting, seated in our warm and clean but humbly furnished room. Ms. Lewandowska had just come back from Warsaw, where she visited relatives and friends. To my surprise, she presented me with a totally unexpected, but greatly appreciated gift, a pair of brand-new, patent leather, dressy shoes. They fit my feet perfectly, beautiful slippers for Cinderella.

"It is impossible to find shoes like these here," I mumbled. "How can I thank you?"

"In Warsaw," she promptly replied, "the black market is flourishing. If one has money, one can buy almost anything."

I was serving cookies I had baked just days before under the watchful eye of Rozalia and listening eagerly to the news from Warsaw.

"How different is wartime Warsaw from the city I used to visit," Ms. Lewandowska began. "Then it was the vibrant capital of reborn Poland, pulsating with life and blessed with a flair all of its own. Now the German presence is ubiquitous and stifling."

She told us that Schuch Avenue had become a despised and feared police district of the Gestapo who were ruling Warsaw with unspeakable brutality and viciousness. Many hundreds of Varsovians, our best, were massacred in nearby Palmiry forest. The Jewish population was forcefully isolated in the newly created, overcrowded ghetto.

Ms. Lewandowska uttered a sigh and then continued. "I have heard that special detachments of German experts, under the eyes of helpless Poles, are shamelessly ransacking Warsaw's museums, galleries, palaces, libraries and private collections, shipping our treasures to the Reich. It is a rape of our country."

"Actions like these," Dad remarked, "only encourage fierce opposition. No wonder Warsaw is despised by the occupiers as a hot-bed of resistance."

"Warsaw is exactly that," she confirmed. "What a spirit, what defiance. Even though the university, colleges, and secondary schools are officially closed, teaching continues on a conspiratorial basis…papers, books, and poetry are written, clandestinely printed, and widely read."

"Warsaw, in the eyes of all Poles, is still our capital, the heart and brain of our country," Dad said with utmost conviction.

I noticed that Ms. Lewandowska's eyes unexpectedly sparkled with merriment. "What is most amazing," she said, "is the courage and sense of humor in this defiance. One day, the Germans plastered posters all over Warsaw advertising conscription for labor in the Reich, saying:"

Jedzcie Z Nami Do Niemiec
Ride With Us to Germany

"Overnight, someone made a 'slight' alteration to the posters, and the next morning Poles read the 'touched-up' message and roared with laughter:"

Jedzcie Sami Do Niemiec
Ride Yourselves to Germany

We all had a good laugh, oblivious for a while to the ordeal of Occupation.

I have to acknowledge that I had been truly impressed with Ms. Lewandowska's visit and her account of life in wartime Warsaw. It didn't come as a surprise to me when she invited Dad and all three of us, but not Rozalia, to a lunch on Sunday. I could only guess the reason for it.

The lunch was lavishly served. The mood was cordial and the conversation animated. What I best remember about that occasion was a scene shortly after we left Ms. Lewandowska's apartment. Dad stopped, looked straightforwardly into the face of each of us, and asked the simple but ominous question, "Would you like to have Ms. Lewandowska as your mother?"

Without the slightest hesitation, all three of us answered with one accord, "No."

Who could, who would ever be able to replace our mom?

Sometime later, we learned that Ms. Lewandowska had left Lubartov for good and settled in Warsaw. By a quirk of fortune, Milek moved into the apartment she had vacated.

17

I was on the way to my first lesson with Maria Perczynska, professor of the underground gymnasium. I wore no gymnasium uniform, carried no books, and tried to be as inconspicuous as possible.

Prof. Perczynska lived in the house Number 1 Winding Street. I climbed a steep flight of stairs and knocked on the door of a place where forbidden knowledge was to be secretly dispensed and pursued.

The door opened, and I was standing face-to-face with Professor Perczynska, my new teacher. She was of average height, but so slender and delicate that she seemed almost fragile. Her long face was framed with neatly arranged hair. Her large eyes reflected an inner goodness and integrity. However, I was even more captivated by her reserved and subtle yet encouraging smile. I realized at once that I had found the place I belonged.

The room was small and modestly furnished. The large window offered a view of the quiet residential street, permitting her to observe any movement there. Next to the high tile stove stood a little table with two chairs facing each other. On this table were piled the schoolbooks. The teachers had hidden them just before the Germans occupied the town. This way, they had been saved from destruction and now were available to us students pursuing gymnasium courses.

The danger of being caught with those books was always present. To possess them was criminal evidence of not complying with a strict German order to turn them over to the authorities. The utmost caution was necessary. Thus, the appearance of Germans on the street below was a signal to spirit them away into a nook in the recesses of a cubbyhole adjoining the room. At the same time, needlework would appear on the table.

Professor Perczynska was a graduate of the prestigious Jagiellonian University in Cracow and held the title of Master of Art, with majors in Latin and French. She taught French in the gymnasium in Lubartov until the war. She was one of the professors who had lost their jobs when all the schools were closed. Now they were ready to serve with courage and dedication as underground educators, defying the German order that forbid any teaching not approved by them.

"I am so glad that I decided to choose a program with the French language," I said, entranced. "My dad suggested that in the present situation, it would be more useful to learn German. He could help me with my homework."

Ms. Perczynska had been listening with attention, her face illuminated by a gentle smile. Oh, I knew at once that she was a kindred spirit. Encouraged, I continued.

"My mind was made up. I would rather follow my dreams. German language, as I know it now, is brutal—the language of despised Nazis. I have been thinking recently," I sighed, "of Mrs. Michalina Kniazieucka. In Ino, she lived in a spacious apartment above our own. During the World War, she left her vast estate in Polish Ukraine and, with her daughter, managed to escape the terror and violence of the Bolshevik revolution."

"Was it she who inspired you to study French?" Ms. Perczynska asked sympathetically.

"Yes. One day, when I was recovering from an illness, she came to visit me. She told me the story of Joan of Arc, a peasant girl, who saved France in a time of great trouble and is still to this day France's national heroine. I felt a thrill running through my body as I looked at the pages of a beautifully illustrated book while Mrs. Kniazieucka read to me some passages in a melodious, enchanting French."

"Someday," she told me then, "you will go to France, so you shall study French. The knowledge of the French language may be very helpful."

Aware of my genuine enthusiasm, Professor Perczynska said cheerfully, "Then let's start our class today with French." She opened the book and read: *Maman entre dans la chambre, elle ouvre la porte et dit…* (Mother enters the room, she opens the door and says…) *Maman!* (Mother) This was the first French word I learned in my underground gymnasium.

These were my happy months in Lubartov. I continued the seventh grade at the primary school and at the same time pursued the program of the first year of gymnasium. It included Polish language, ancient history, algebra, zoology, geography, French as a secondary language, and Latin. The classes were held in Professor Perczynska's room, Monday through Saturday, one hour each day. The program was self-paced. Professor Perczynska dedicated more time to the languages. Otherwise, she gave an introduction and assignment, which she checked in her spare time. So I was studying very much on my own. She still guided me in a most helpful way, never pushing, but always encouraging.

Oh, I was in love in those days, a love that was going to last forever. However, the object of my love was not a handsome boy, real or imagined. I was in love with knowledge!

What is knowledge anyway? I was asking myself one day. I couldn't find the definition in the encyclopedia because we did not have one. So I asked Dad, and he told me that it is a fruit of human thought and experience. In my assignments, I occasionally quoted Shakespeare, of course, in Polish. Looking back now, I believe that I would have loved what he thought of knowledge: *Ignorance is a curse of God, knowledge the wings wherewith we fly to heaven.*

How much there was to learn! How exciting it was! Let's take algebra. It was so different from the math we had in the primary school. Professor Perczynska told me that in the Middle Ages, the Islamic scientists took elementary algebra from the Greek and Hindus and developed it to a high level of sophistication. The Europeans soon adopted this Arabic algebra. It was like solving mathematical puzzles. I enjoyed the "game" so much that I was solving not only the assigned problems but also all the problems for that particular lesson in the textbook.

My world those days was expanding with giant strides; eventful happenings were unfolding before my eyes. With Homer, I witnessed the vicissitudes of the Trojan War. After reading required Parandowski's *Olympic Disc,* I wrote an inspired paper admiring beauty, skill, and strength, which

Greek athletes strove to attain in the contests at the Olympic Festivals. I was standing on the Athenian Acropolis when the temple of Parthenon, a splendid and noble structure, was being built during the leadership of Pericles, whom I enthroned in my mind as my forever hero. I spoke the language of the ancient Romans and followed Rome's rise and fall.

Nothing puzzled me more, touched me more deeply, or instilled more love than ancient Egypt. In the room on Winding Street, I recall reciting with Prof. Perczynska the ancient hymn to the Nile:

> *Hail, to you, O Nile*
> *Sprang from earth.*
> *Come to nourish Egypt…*
> *Food provider, bounty maker*
> *Who creates all that is good…*

One day, I promised myself, I will ride on a camel from the fertile fringe of the valley to the pyramids rising from the sandy desert. They were built in the hope of enabling the pharaohs to attain life everlasting. I will sail the Nile in a *felucca* to encounter and touch the awesome grandeur of the most ancient of the ancient civilizations on earth.

It was as if I, a thirteen-year-old girl, stranded by the war in a remote, provincial town in the iron grip of the Nazis, had been snatched up over the grim existence of Occupation to witness the centuries parading by before my very eyes. One of my textbooks bore the title *Mowia Wieki* (Centuries Speak). I was listening with the utmost attention, recording what I learned in the recesses of my mind.

It seemed as if by magic the severe winter of 1940–41 came to an abrupt end. Spring was abroad. I didn't have time anymore for wandering with Martha since I was attending school and underground classes, preoccupied with serious studying and my household tasks.

It was a lovely Sunday, fresh and bright. Yet I was miserable, sorry for myself. It had all started with Rozalia the previous day. When I stopped by the store that afternoon, a woman client Rozalia knew well saw me coming in.

"Here is your daughter. She looks just like you!"

I was so shocked that for a while I stood mute. After recovering my power of speech, my face a bright red, I spoke determinedly, "Rozalia is not my mother. She is our housekeeper and helps Dad in the store."

Rozalia glanced sternly at me, and I saw contempt in her eyes. I left the store embittered, repeating to myself reassuringly, 'She will never, ever be my mother!'

Now I was trying to divert my thoughts from yesterday's unhappy incident by concentrating on my assigned homework. I had been standing next to the windowsill, with the window wide open, drawing models of foldable wings. In my zoology course, I was studying the evolution of insects. I felt the caressing warmth of the sun on my face, but the high fence separating our Siedlecka Lane from the parish orchard obscured what should have been a beautiful view. I hadn't liked that fence from the beginning.

Only days before I had written in my diary: "With a mighty word, I'll knock down those boards and open a view of the lovely garden which I have seen only in my dreams."

The trees, I thought, *must be in full blossom now.* All of a sudden, I heard the sound of wheels crunching on the lane, and in no time, a bicycle slid to a stop just below my window, and down jumped Joseph Majewski! It didn't escape my attention that his bicycle looked brand-new, shiny, and fancy—a dream come true. Momentarily, I realized how much I missed my bike. Joseph approached the window just as if we were close friends and I was expecting him, saying, "I just arrived this morning, and the first thing I wanted to do was to see you."

I hadn't seen him for months since his sudden appearance in the cemetery. My first reaction was to slam down the window, but I didn't want to give the impression of a frightened chicken. So I stayed put and laboriously continued with my drawings.

"I see you in my dreams," he tried to meet my eyes," and all I get is your cold glance."

Presently, he noticed the traces of tears on my face.

"You've been crying," he whispered softly with a tender, almost angelic expression on his face. I had not been flattered by his words, but it was then the thought passed through my mind: *He is just a regular chap, not as sinister as I assumed... maybe even decent underneath.* But instinctively, I retreated back inside, rebuilding the barrier of protection around me. *Be on guard, he is Volksdeutsch and the personification of German arrogance.*

"You are speaking foolishly," I managed to say, surprised by the strength in my voice, "and you are blocking my view."

Oh, how glad and relieved I was seeing Dad and Yanush returning from the late Mass. I went to open the door for them and stayed away from the window, not even checking to see if he had left.

"England is holding out!" The news passed by busy tongues kept our spirit uplifted. The British were not going to give up as easily as the French had done. England, separated from continental Europe by the English Channel, used to be for me a distant country. Nobody I knew spoke English, but now the Channel was a front line, and the fate of war depended on the determination and fortitude of the British.

The battle of Britain was not only fought in the air but also on the sea. I most probably would not have known about that titanic struggle on the Atlantic if not for a letter addressed to me that arrived unexpectedly sometime in the spring. As usual, I turned to Milek.

"You see, when Hitler, confident in his *Luftwaffe*, planned to bring England to submission, he also planned to deprive the inhabitants of the islands and British war machine of essential supplies," he said. "Now, the German warships and U-boats prey on the Allies' ships, inflicting considerable losses. Why do you want to know this?"

"I just got a letter from Marylka from Germany."

Marylka had been sent to Germany for compulsory labor on a farm before we were deported from Ino to Lubartov. As soon as I opened the letter, I was startled to see that it was signed *Marilla*. Why had she changed her name? Marilla did not say anything about her whereabouts in Germany or her work.

"To love and be loved," I read, not trusting my eyes, "is a wonderful experience. Hans and I firmly believe that our love will prevail," she wrote.

Who was Hans? Marilla revealed that he was a handsome young man of good reputation, son of the farmers for whom she worked, serving as a sailor on a German ship! I could imagine that his short visit home seemed like bliss. Back in his ship, he drew comfort that she was eagerly awaiting his return, a girl unlike any other, his own sweetheart. I myself was then under a spell, humming "Lili Marlene," a heart-touching German song that seemed to belong to every soldier separated from his beloved.

> *Underneath the lantern*
> *By the barrack gate,*
> *Darling, I remember*
> *The way you used to wait.*
> *T'was there that you whispered tenderly*
> *That you loved me,*
> *You'd always be…*

Nevertheless, I wondered how could they overcome a seemingly insurmountable restriction, the Nazi order of keeping a strict distance between German *Herrenfolk* (master people) and slave laborers? Would Marilla dare to accept the status of *Volksdeutsch* and renounce her Fatherland?

I could guess that Marilla was praying for Hans, for his safe conduct and return…and to think that at the same time, I was praying for the success of Poles fighting the Germans with our Allies so that Poland could be free again. I was too young and too ignorant to face that dilemma on my own. I had to seek the advice of somebody I trusted.

∽○∾

In the meantime, life went on. In May, the classes in our school were suspended, and the building was occupied by the Germans.

Lubartov was literally teeming with newly arrived young German soldiers. They were training on the vast meadows along the River Wieprz and in the fields surrounding the town. We couldn't go to Skrobov anymore because wooden barracks were built there for them. Returning from drill, they marched confidently, not to the song so popular just a year ago, "Wir Fahren Gegen Engeland" (We are going to England), but to a new one with a carefree refrain: "Hi-lee, hi-loo-hi-la."

In the town, there were severe restrictions on travel by train. The railway men saw the trains going eastward carrying German troops and armaments. It meant that something was afoot. One day, a German sergeant appeared at Mr. Filipowicz's carpenter shop. At first, Mr. Filipowicz was alarmed, but it soon turned out that the soldier had been assigned to make coffins in his shop. During training in the field skirting the Skrobov forest, an enormous explosion had killed a few dozen German troopers. They were buried in the cemetery in Lubartov, not far from the graves of Polish soldiers who perished in September 1939, at Kock.

By the beginning of summer, all the German recruits were gone. One of them, a decent young sergeant with no anti-Polish chip on his shoulder, was remembered warmly on Siedlecka Lane.

18

The Germans must have been very confident those days since a loudspeaker was installed in the Market Square through which official news was broadcast in Polish. In June, just one week after my fourteenth birthday, a ground-shaking announcement was blasted through the loudspeaker:

This morning, Germany invaded the Soviet Union!

The first lines of the Soviet defense had been smashed, and the German *panzers* were sweeping across the plains of eastern Poland, seized by the Soviets in September 1939. The broadcast news was deceitfully presenting the invasion as a new crusade against Bolshevism. Throughout the summer, we kept hearing of one German victory after another. The German armies were rapidly advancing eastward, and it seemed they were unstoppable. The GG was extended by a new district of Galizen in the southeast.

"What does it all add up to?" one could hear people asking. "Will the Germans take Moscow? Will they become all powerful?"

It took time, but the Russians started to fight back. *Szczekaczka* (a barker) in the Market Square, who meant to broadcast German propaganda, failed to mention the incidents of heavy German losses.

Fall was at the door, and winter was quickly approaching. In town, the books on Napoleon's 1812 Russian campaign and Tolstoy's *War and Peace* were the hottest reading. We all had been trying to learn a lesson from the past. Before Hitler, there was another unbeatable conqueror who took the war to Moscow to conquer Russia. In Napoleon's Grand Army were many Poles. How many of them returned from the adventure?

Looking at the map, the immensity of the Soviet Union was apparent. Thinking of the approaching winter, one could imagine the primitive roads connecting the vast, open country turned by heavy rains into muddy quagmires, later covered by heavy snow or ice-bound by freezing temperatures.

Whatever was going on in Russia and whatever the future held did not divert me from attending to my studies. After the departure of German troops, the classes at our school resumed and were extended into the summer. Sometime in July, I graduated from the seventh grade and, about the same time, completed the program of the first year of gymnasium.

I was a teenager by then. That fall, I suddenly became torn by uncertainties and doubts, asking questions to which I had no answers. I detested war with its fear, depravation, widespread suffering, and slaughter. It was no doubt in my mind that Hitler was culpable, along with his fanatic followers who brought him to power and carried out his belligerent orders. And yet I didn't know who to blame for the continuous outbreak of wars with their barbarism insulting the dignity of mankind.

I began to sense that it must be something inherently bad in human nature, but what? The word "evil" passed my lips. I nearly choked on those thoughts. I was too immature to find an explanation on my own and too timid to ask.

The thought came over me of the unfairness of life: "Why again Poland? Why me? What have I done?" At fourteen, I thought myself mature, even though what I really wanted and missed was guidance. I resented the bossing of Rozalia who, as I thought, tried to usurp the role of my mother. How unimaginative and utilitarian she was! Bringing out those feelings now reminds me how fragile are the bonds that connect people who live together. Was the tension in my relations with Rozalia a big issue, or was I just overly sensitive? Whatever I may have been thinking then of life, I always appreciated how fortunate I was to have a dad I could count on and a home where I was accepted and loved.

Growing up in the shadow of war and Occupation, I was maturing fast, gradually learning what immense courage and sacrifice it took to resist the Nazi tyranny. The Germans regarded the GG as a slave colony and its inhabitants as their prey. Then, at the height of their power, they intended to crush any opposition. New waves of arrests swept through the town, and we heard incessantly about the imprisonment, executions, and persecution of people who had the will and courage to oppose the Nazi terror. We prayed nights without fear, for dear ones and ourselves, never contemplating surrender.

❦

It was the beginning of August when, attending weekday mass at the Capuchin church, I saw Helka Jeziorowna sitting on a back bench, engrossed in a deep prayer. She was one of my favorite schoolmates through the sixth and seventh grades. I knew that her dad had been arrested in the spring and held in the feared Gestapo prison in Lublin. Her mother, on hearing of her husband's imprisonment, went through such a severe emotional shock that she was taken to the hospital, where she died a few weeks later.

Helka didn't like to talk about her tragic experiences, but I could imagine how lonesome she might feel. So after the mass was over, I waited for her in the church yard. She came over. Seeing her sorrowful face, still wet from tears, I took her hand in both of mine.

In a hushed voice, she whispered, "The worst has happened."

She had just received the feared *totenschein* from Auschwitz concentration camp, a notification written in German, about her father's death. In a flash, I realized that there was nothing she could do about it but to take it—as painful as it was. So I embraced her soothingly and wept with her.

Helka's father, Henry Jezior, had been a mailman in Lubartov. From the very beginning of the Occupation, the spirit of resistance was alive in the town and throughout the county. Conspiratorial organizations were budding everywhere. All the activities of the Resistance were shrouded in secrecy, and the members who swore an oath of secrecy operated under pseudonyms so their real names would never be mentioned. Mr. Jezior joined the KOP

(Command of Poland's Defenders). Together with his brother, Leon, he opened a store in Lublin that served as a contact point for the organization and a distribution point for the underground publications secretly smuggled from Warsaw. The underground press challenged and undermined Nazi propaganda and kept defiance and hope alive. Pedaling on his bicycle between Lubartov and Lublin, he had been distributing the forbidden press and leaflets on the way. It was an extremely risky and dangerous job, with dire consequences, should he be caught. German spies and informers were everywhere.

April of 1941 was coming to an end. On one fateful day, Helka's father had been arrested in Lublin, caught carrying a bunch of illegal newspapers. The agents had taken him straight to the most feared Gestapo interrogation place, commonly known as *Under the Clock*. In Lubartov, the name itself had such an infamous reputation that it made those arrested horror-stricken. It referred to a downtown building with a clock; the door under it led to some murky cells, an interrogation room, and the torture chamber.

The Gestapo, German security police, was a branch of the SS. Its role was not to track down ordinary crime handled by regular German police, but to pursue and capture politically divisive elements. Gestapo functionaries were skilled at obtaining information and confessions by intimidating interrogations, guile, and persuasion when they were dealing with the Germans. In order to extract confessions from the Poles, the most brutal thugs and sadists were employed, and barbaric practices, often reminiscent of medieval torture, were used.

Being elderly, sick, or a woman brought no salvation from exposure to torture. For years, the people in Lubartov remembered with deference Irene and her sister, Eve Tomasiak, a nurse known in town. When put under torture to elicit confessions, she bore it with astonishing determination, even while being mangled by a press with its screw gradually tightened. Hundreds of prisoners interrogated under torture did not survive. The purpose of applying torture was to break the prisoner's resistance, leading to confessions and in consequence, betrayal of others. It is to the Poles' credit that so many did not yield under horrific pressure.

Henry Jezior had been tortured in the cellar, *Under the Clock,* that measured hour by hour his martyrdom. Hardly alive, he was dragged from his cell and delivered by a van to the prison in the Lublin Castle to face a mock trial held in the castle's historic chapel. The "prosecutor" declared him guilty. There were no witnesses, no defense. The "judge," Nazi scum, pronounced the death verdict. He was deported to Auschwitz and soon perished there.

Mr. Jezior's death left his daughter, Helka, an orphan. As I was soon going painfully to learn, Lubartov had its share of children and teenagers orphaned during the ruthless years of German Occupation.

⚬⚬⚬

With the departure of the German troops for the Russian front, we could resume our visits to Skrobov. To follow paths separating the fields of rye, oats, buckwheat, and potatoes was far more enjoyable than taking a main road.

In the bluish-golden air of a peaceful Sunday, all grief seemed to expire, all troubles cease. I don't recall with whom I walked that day, but Yanush surely followed us with Ziho.

The fields stretched all the way up to the forest. At the edge, we stopped. There was a swing there! Someone had tied a heavy rope to a sturdy tree branch and its two ends to a plain board seat. We took turns standing on the board, holding tight to the ropes, and swinging as high as we dared, looking out over the countryside before we came hurtling down, only to go back up again. It was wonderful fun.

Climbing trees was another adventure. Usually though, I preferred to roam around picking berries or mushrooms. Hand-picking mushrooms is an art in itself, and expertise is necessary since many wild mushrooms are poisonous. It's easy to make a dreadful mistake. The most highly prized is *borowik* (*Boletus edulis*) of unique pungent flavor—a delight to the pallet.

One day, when we were approaching the barracks deserted by German soldiers, we saw workers putting up a menacing barbed-wire fence around the whole compound. At each corner of it was a tall watchtower. *What was this supposed to be?* we wondered, alarmed.

By November, the camp was swarming with Soviet prisoners of war. We knew from the official communiqués aired by a barker at the Market Square in Lubartov that hundreds of thousands of Soviet soldiers were being captured during the first months of Hitler's assault on Russia. To avoid German bullets, Russian soldiers surrendered far too easily and now were doomed, a pitiful looking lot: weary, disheveled, unshaven, and hungry.

In Lubartov, gossip had it that the camp was horribly crowded, with lice-laden bunks, and food rations so low as to border on starvation. The Germans didn't care. Cold and indifferent, they treated the Russian POWs with undisguised contempt.

At first, we would throw some bread saved from our ration over the electrified wire fence or a package of cigarettes we managed to obtain from Dad. (He had a concession for selling them.) The Russians appreciated whatever we brought them, but they prized the cigarettes the most. When catching them, the shadow of a faint smile gladdened their sunken faces.

As we returned home, stricken by their misery and our helplessness, Yanush muttered through compressed lips, "The war is inhumane." I couldn't have agreed with him more.

Some days passed, and when we returned one afternoon, we found that the guards, *Wehrmacht* soldiers, had become far stricter so that even small gestures of help were forbidden. Soon, typhus broke out inside the compound, and we heard that the prisoners were dying like flies.

When they learned about the large Kozlovka forest nearby, some of them risked escape. At first, the local peasants often helped the successful escapees, offering them some food and occasionally even clothing, though any help to Soviet POWs was officially forbidden. We learned our lesson the hard way when a blacksmith from neighboring Zagrody was arrested and sentenced to death for his humanitarian gesture.

Yet the most tragic consequence of contact with escaped POWs was an outbreak of typhus in town. In Lubartov, the number of cases began to climb alarmingly, and people were dying almost daily. The situation became so critical that the German authorities yielded and sent a request to Auschwitz for the return of Dr. Alfons Prus, Lubartov's respected physician and our neighbor. He had been arrested and deported a few months earlier. It was spring before the epidemic ran its course.

19

In late summer of 1941, we moved from Siedlecka One Street to a little house with a store at the Market Square, next to Rogatkos. Our new dwelling had two rooms and a tiny kitchen. The smaller room was windowless. It had been separated from the kitchen by a thin wall made of painted wooden boards. The larger room with whitewashed walls and two low-set windows was bright and pleasant. Those windows, to be sure, did not overlook a wooden fence nor did they offer a view of an enchanting garden. Secured with heavy shutters, which were closed at night, they opened on Klitki I, a narrow, roughly paved street lined on the opposite side with a row of low one-story sagging houses. Presently deserted, they had traditionally been teeming with large families of poorest Jewish craftsmen and small shopkeepers.

In our new home, the large room served as master bedroom, dining room, and study for Yanush and me when Dad and Rozalia were occupied in the store. Milek procured a desk for us—a used long office table with two spacious drawers. The kitchen door led to a narrow hallway with a dirt floor and outside to our own greatly appreciated *wygodka*. It was a tiny privy made of a plain wood. Its door could be latched from the inside. The only light came through a little heart-shaped opening. A cot was placed for me in the smaller room, so finally, ah, finally, I had my own place for sleeping, praying, and dreaming. Yanush was as pleased as I was, his face beaming with a cheerful smile.

"In the hallway, I will keep the cages with my rabbits," he announced. "To have Yasio, my most faithful friend just next door—it seems like a dream come true!"

The moving went smoothly since our possessions were few.

It was time to say good-bye to our neighborhood friends. To tell the truth, both Yanush and I were glad to be far away from the woman who lived across the narrow hallway from us. What a strange character she was! I felt intimidated every time I happened to run into her. To me, she looked like a witch: big, carelessly dressed, with a face crossed by wrinkles even though she was of middle age. When she peered at me with those cold eyes, I couldn't utter a greeting without a bitter taste in my mouth. There were men coming to see her—unattractive as she was—occasionally even a German soldier of low rank. The neighbors claimed that she lay with them and was paid for her service. I had not given much thought to this, but I could not imagine that anybody would enjoy being with her.

Saying good-bye to the Filipowicz family was hard, but we promised to keep in touch. The garden would surely be a magnet to bring us back. I stopped, of course, by the Sztatmans. They were still living in their dwelling. Obviously, Mr. Sztatman was continuously needed by the Germans. Mahla had been engaged to Izrael Kejsman. I promised to come to their wedding to wish them *Mazel Tov*, "good luck" in Yiddish. It seemed that they lived unaware of the precariousness of their fate. However, that was not true.

I've never forgotten the daring words of Chawa, Mahla's younger sister, "Whatever turns out, the Germans will never take me. My fiancé and I already have plans to join the partisans in the forest."

"Hold your tongue!" Mrs. Sztatman rebuked her gently.

It sounded like Chawa. With her sturdy build and square jaw, she took after her father. Her dark hair was cut short, and her burning black eyes had a determined expression. To me, Chawa looked more like a youth than a maiden. But if any girl I knew could endure the harsh conditions of partisan life, she could. Still, a great sadness came over me.

"Shalom!" they said warmly as I was leaving. That was our last visit.

It was a nice April day. I opened the window wide to let the flood of spring air pour in and greeted the day with an enthusiastic *Bonjour Printemps* (Good day, Spring)! At that very moment, I saw her. She was washing the window in the house across the street. There shouldn't have been anyone there. The houses had stood empty for weeks, after the Jews who lived there were suddenly gone.

Klitki I, and the little parallel street, Klitki II, were the core of a recently created Jewish ghetto. Since they couldn't accommodate the waves of newly arriving Jewish deportees from some other places, the ghetto encompassed adjacent streets as well. However, in Lubartov, we had never had a ghetto enclosed by a wall. Even a half-hearted attempt to put up fences to separate the Jews was abandoned since they often occupied one side of the street while the non-Jewish inhabitants the opposite. Nevertheless, the severe restrictions on movement of ghetto residents and the strict prohibition of comingling with the non-Jewish population were the order of the day.

So who was this slender attractive girl washing the window? I was puzzled. I guessed she must have been my age. What intrigued me was that she was going after her task with total dedication. *That is how I would do it*, I thought.

It didn't take long for her to notice me standing in the open window. The second time I caught her glance in my direction, I gave her a faint smile, which she returned. That afternoon, back from my lesson with Prof. Perczynska, I entered the room to find the window wide open. Yanush and Lutek Zelazny were on one side of it and a group of unknown kids on the other. Yanush was eager to introduce me to our new neighbors from across the street.

"They are from Slovakia!" he announced enthusiastically. "I told them that our dad is from Bogumin, and that his family still lives in Moravia and Slovakia, and that before the war, we went there twice for vacation."

Slovak and Polish are Slavic languages, thus many words sound similar or can be guessed. So it didn't take long before we were chatting away like old acquaintances. That is how I met Martha, the girl who was washing windows with such abandon that morning, her two younger brothers, skinny boys with freckled faces. There was little Vera and Marcel, a tall boy with a mane of black hair and olive complexion.

Only the previous day, I had overheard Rozalia chatting with a customer. "Those Slovak Jews are not like our Hassidic Jews. They look very European...the women in woolen suits or coats and hats or turbans…not a wig in sight! And the men in suits…"

So were their kids, very European.

I became fond of Martha. I liked her slender and graceful figure, the firm stride of her skinny legs. She had a small face with delicate features, yet her lovely mouth was resolute and her eyes vibrant with thoughtful expression and a hint of determination.

We had both been through painful experiences. Her situation was deplorable. Two or three families, usually just women and children, were crowded together in a cramped and dilapidated house. Men of working age were most often separated from their families and diverted to labor camps. I had no idea where the money came from for food, but it was obviously scarce. Yet the children were always taken care of, clean, and neatly dressed. The worst of all, I guessed intuitively, must have been the anguish of not knowing what was to come, a fear that undermined their everyday existence. The stories recently going around the town hinting at the extermination of Jews had been too appalling and too horrible to be believed.

The things that most impressed me about Martha were her steadfastness and the way she shared the responsibility for her younger brothers with her mother. I never heard her complain. To think that she was only thirteen years old!

Martha was frequently in our house, not as a guest, but a welcome neighbor. She sometimes washed the dishes after our dinner and returned home with a plate full of food. One day, not long after their arrival, she showed me a lovely scarf.

"I don't need it," she said, then hesitated for a long moment and continued, determined. "I wonder if you would consider buying it. We are short of money and anything you could offer would be of great help."

"Martha, I will be glad to give you my savings (for a new set of notebooks), and I can ask Dad to augment it, but keep your beautiful scarf for yourself."

She couldn't accept the money without offering something in exchange. That didn't surprise me. I would have felt the same way in her place. So with a certain reluctance, I accepted the scarf, and a fair deal was made.

It just happened that a couple of days earlier, Rozalia was approached by an older Slovak Jewess, our neighbor, begging her, out of despair, to buy the coat "she did not need." Led by compassion, Rozalia purchased the coat. We took it to a recommended tailor to be remade for me since I had outgrown my coat from Ino.

It was the evening before Easter Sunday when I went to pick it up. The tailor, a Hassidic Jew, looked frail and exhausted, his eyes reddened from lack of sleep.

"I worked almost the whole night to have it ready as promised," he mumbled in broken Polish. "During the day, I am toiling for the Germans, sewing quilted jackets for the soldiers on the Eastern Front. In the hall of the movie theater, forty sewing machines are clattering from the sunrise to the sunset."

Easter morning arrived, and we were on the way to church for the High Mass. I was wearing my "new" light coat with Martha's scarf adding a touch of chic and color. On my feet were shiny Cinderella shoes.

The interior of the Capuchin church was resounding with the solemnity of Easter. "This is a day that the Lord hath made: let us exult and take joy in Him" was followed by a triumphant "Christ has risen! Alleluia!" filling our hearts with thanksgiving and grace. The scent of spring was in the air.

We started home in high spirits, following Klitki Street, since Dad's store was closed on Sundays. As we approached our house, a small group of children gathered in front of the house next to the one occupied by Martha's family. Upon seeing me, they started to shout in Slovakian:

"Martha's scarf! Martha's scarf!"

My face turned crimson, and I withdrew as fast as I could into the entrance hallway of our house, my joyful Easter mood shattered.

Martha, after hearing about the incident, came to apologize for the unfortunate misbehavior of the children, and soon, the hurt was forgotten and the joy of Easter prevailed. However, I never wore that scarf again; it was forever Martha's.

Our friendship with Martha remained unscathed. Invited to my nameday[1] party, she was accepted as one of us by my friends from the underground gymnasium.

It was so long ago that I don't recall if I ever seriously considered the danger of associating with a Jewish girl. I had never looked at her that way. Yet the danger was real. Informers were everywhere, and a report to the German police about comingling with the Jews could result in sending, not only me, but our whole family to the concentration camp, if not worse. Dad must have understood this better than me, and yet he never disapproved of me receiving Martha and Vera in our house.

Vera! I loved that little girl with the sweet face. When she was staring at me with her big green eyes with such confidence and anticipation, my heart simply melted. She was Martha's three-year-old cousin. I pampered her with a glass of milk, a cookie, or *landrynki*, colorful hard candies. I loved to hear her laughter when Yanush let her hold and pet his white angora rabbit with the reddish eyes.

Eventually, we must have guessed that there was no salvation for the Jewish people since I recall begging my dad to let me keep Vera when the moment came for their deportation. I knew that Martha would never abandon her mother and younger brothers. But little Vera…

Lubrtov, October 11, 1942

The date must be written in burning letters in heaven.

The German authorities issued a strict order that on this Sunday, all inhabitants of Lubartov were to stay home. There were no masses. The churches were closed. Everyone worried over what horrid events the occupiers had on their minds.

It didn't take long before it became obvious that the Germans were rounding up the Jews, including our neighborhood Slovak Jews. From the Market Square, where they had been ordered to gather, along Lubelska Street, columns, or rather a sea, of Jews were being mercilessly rushed by German and Jewish police.

Slowly, painfully, I began to realize that this was a dark day of the final expulsion of the Jews from Lubartov. There was no doubt they were being hurried toward the train station. It was not so long ago—a scene from the past forever preserved in my memory—that we ourselves were driven under machine guns to the train station, exilees facing the unknown. Yet—at least for the time being—our lives had been spared.

Oh, we knew by then that those Jews were being herded to their deaths like the innocent lambs to the slaughter: despised, stripped of human dignity, people chosen by God whom Hitler was bent to wipe off the face of the earth. For the first time in my life, my trust in the faithful and inexhaustible love of God was questioned. Did all this suffering, this martyrdom, have some meaning?

For days, the town was reeling from the shock. Lubartov county was no more as we used to know it. Almost one-half of its population was forever gone. Deserted Klitki I and Klitki II, the ghetto area, was a ghostly place now. I wanted to keep the window shutters closed so I would not have to look at it. Everyone had his own horror tale to tell. The sick and the infirm were shot on the spot; those who tried to hide were dragged out and often beaten and killed. The young Jews who hoped to escape through the meadows toward the Wieprz River were shot like so many ducks. The well-known family of Szmuel Rubinsztajn, with its roots in Lubartov, refused the order to go to the Market Square. They were marched from their home to the *kirkut*, a Jewish cemetery, and shot fully dressed, holding hands with their dear ones, dying with dignity. They were buried there.

For days following that black Sunday, the Germans were still hunting for hidden Jews. The decree was posted all over town:

> For hiding Jews
> For helping Jews in hiding
> For not reporting Jews in hiding
> For giving or selling food to Jews
> DEATH PENALTY

On Monday, following the final deportation of the Jews from Lubartov, Edward Romanski was walking from his home to the nearby farmyard. Out of the blue, he heard a muffled voice calling his name, "Edek! Edek!" He turned around and saw standing before him his schoolmate from before the war, Wajsmel Szajndle, daughter of a shoemaker from Frog Street. She beseeched him to help her.

There was no time to hesitate. Deeply troubled by her plight, he led her to the barn and hid her there. Then, with help from his friend, Adolf, he obtained false identification papers for her and arranged employment with a cap maker in Lublin. Some time passed, and the employer, constantly fearing that she would be identified as a Jewess, dismissed her. Edek did not give up. He approached Teresa Pawula, prioress of the devout nuns in Lubartov. The nuns agreed to take Wajsmel under their wings. It was not only an act of compassion, but of extraordinary courage since they fully realized the mortal risk of hiding a Jewish girl. Wajsmel survived[2] the war in the convent, unscathed, along with a few dozen other Jews hidden in Lubartov county.

When we were expelled to Lubartov in December 1939, I could not foresee that I was going to be an eyewitness to the last years of a four centuries–long coexistence of Christian and Jewish communities in town and the final victimization of the Jewish inhabitants by the Nazis. Throughout the Middle Ages, persecuted in Western Europe and later, after the Partition of Poland, coming in great waves from Imperial Russia, they found refuge[3] on Polish soil. Now they were no more.

I have always been under the spell of the grandeur of Pharaohonic Egypt. The ancient Egyptians particularly excelled in the realm of esoteric wisdom. One of their thoughts, inscribed in hieroglyphs, reads:

> To speak of the dead
> Is to make him live again.

Writing about Martha, Vera, and our Jewish neighbors from Siedlecka Lane, I intended to bring them forth from my never vanished memories—so they might live again.

20

It was my agonizing doubt of God's justice that brought me to the Capuchin church that October morning seeking consolation. As the heavy door closed behind me, I entered into the semidarkness of the sanctuary. Silence and peace were only momentarily broken by the welcoming squeak of the worn wooden floor under my feet. I concealed myself on a side bench, and kneeling straight up, I embraced with a glance the familiar single nave interior, so strikingly simple and modest. The high altar, the two large candelabras, the pulpit, and the altars on both sides of the nave were all made of oak. Once varnished, they were now painted in a brown tone, contrasting with the pure whiteness of the walls. The altar paintings, dating to the eighteenth century, depicted episodes from the lives of Franciscan saints. They were not meant to be pictorial decorations attracting the eye, but as religious inspiration.

All my attention centered on a glowing red light. I was in the presence of God.

God was not immediately comprehensible or accessible to my senses. His grandeur and majesty, the mystery of his omnipotence and omnipresence was beyond my comprehension. Yet he was also love, I reminded myself. Because of his love for us, he sent his son to earth, true God, born of human flesh of the Virgin Mary.

It was through my religious upbringing, and later directly through the Scriptures, that I learned to love our Lord Jesus. He was hanging on the cross above the high altar, in the lunette of the finial. From earliest childhood, I had come to look at this cross as a sign of love and hope. Jesus surrendered himself to death to redeem our weaknesses and sins, I was told. "Every time we fall, he is there, extending his helping hand so we can rise again," Father Golczewski was reassuring us, while preparing the third-graders in Ino for the sacrament of penance.

Now, having before my eyes the lifeless faces of little Vera and of Martha—two of the legion of innocent children who were victims of mind-numbing crime—my heart was heavy with grief and repugnance and my face flushed with hatred for the Germans. How ruthless and efficient they were in their wicked deeds and how sure of themselves. Why would God permit the existence of such evil in the world; he, the Creator, who made all things good?

"O, Jesus, in your charity," I prayed fervently, "restore in me the grace of unshakeable faith."

The early morning mass had begun. It was Saturday, and only a few people were in the pews, but I noticed that one of the Fathers was hearing confession. After a short preparation, I knelt at the confessional. I realized that my confessor, happened to be Father Timothy.

I quickly ran through my faults and then—my lips close to the grating of the confessional—whispered in simple words the reason for my hatred of the Germans and acknowledged my troubling doubt of God's justice. He listened patiently to what I had to say before he offered his counsel. He told me that in the earliest years of Christianity, St. Paul, a true revolutionary of his time, took a radical leap, teaching that through grace in Christ, all persons are chosen because all persons are equal in the eyes of God.

"The merciless annihilation of innocent people that we are now witnessing," he said, "only shows how false and evil are the schemes of the Nazis. Wrong became right, injustice became justified, turning the whole moral order upside down."

I pressed my ear against the grating not to miss any of his words.

"Faced with their wickedness, we shall not surrender in the manner of cowards. It's our obligation to do everything we can to stop this flood of violence and death set in motion to elevate one group, a single race of people, through the murder of millions of others. Nonetheless, opposing the evildoers does not mean we must hate them. Hate is dangerously destructive to the person who hates," he emphasized.

This seemed beyond my comprehension. He realized that and continued, saying, "Christian love is an act of the will, not necessarily just a feeling," he told me. "We have to bear in mind that somehow, sometime, somewhere, evildoers may become human again."

Yet the most striking and moving were my wise confessor's concluding words as he said, "Man is both perpetrator and victim of evil, but God's charity is evil's final measure. God's true dwelling is in the heart of each human person. He yearns to be inwardly present in all of us. May we live in such a way that others see him in our lives: *Spiritus ubi vult spirat* (Spirit blows where it wants). May God grant you grace to understand this. Now let's pray."

Since that very Saturday, Father Timothy became my spiritual guide.

One day, Henry Wroblewski, known for his gentleness and piety, came to see me. He handed me a little book that looked very much like a prayer book, saying simply, "This is for you."

It was *The Imitation of Christ* by Thomas a' Kempis. I wasn't much surprised seeing the book's title. So I thanked him for his kindness and asked, "When should I return it?"

His answer was point blank, "When you will no more need it."

Henry knew the book well. When we were walking up Lubelska Street, he told me that the actual name of the author is Thomas Hemerken von Kempen. He was an Augustinian monk who lived in Holland. The book was printed and reprinted over the centuries in different languages.

I had no doubt that this unusual gift came from Father Timothy. I have it to this day—not ready by far to return it.

❧

Prof. Perczynska had a new pupil, and her name was Elizabeth Derecka. Ely, as we called her, became my bosom friend. She was an orphan and lived with her aunt and two cousins, Chris and Jean, on Cemetery Street, not far from the Market Square.

The summer of 1942 was remembered as being very hot. Ely was just crossing the Market Square carrying a pan of cookies to be baked in the nearby bakery since there was not a suitable oven at her home. Hearing the sound of footsteps behind her, she looked over her shoulder to see Yanush, hot on her heels and running as fast as he could.

Out of breath, he gasped out his message, "Leave this at once and hurry to the park! Marius has climbed up on top of the crumbling palace wall and says he wants to declare his undying love for you. If you will not come, it means that you don't care for him, and we are concerned what he might do!"

When one is fourteen, such things are taken seriously. Ely didn't have any idea about Marius's feelings for her, but being too nice a girl to cause anyone distress, she dropped the pan at our store and ran, following Yanush to the park. Sure enough, there was Marius, teetering on top of the unsafe wall, with a group of friends on the ground trying to talk him out of any foolishness. Seeing Ely, he nimbly climbed down, and content that she now knew how much he felt for her, he ran off with his buddies.

Picking up her cookie pan, she shared with me her feelings. "I'm pleased," she said, "that perhaps I prevented some irresponsible act by an over-romantic friend."

It was about this time that I realized the boys from our gymnasium circle were up to their ears "in love." The epidemic of romantic feelings was probably affecting the girls too, but they were more circumspect and secretive about their attractions. Not so, the boys.

Bogdan insisted that his first love was Helka Jeziorowna, so charmingly feminine, but soon he was "really in love" with dark-eyed, graceful Teresa Romanowska. He was so smitten with her that he carved her initials, TR, on his forearm. When the cut became infected, Dr. Prus had to deal with the problem. Yet this incident didn't cool Bogdan's passion for Teresa until he took a great fancy to Ziutka.

Love was in the air! Falling in love was like springtime, like light in the shadow of solitude. In the park, under a tree with its branches spreading over the mirrored surface of the lake, Yatsek Dumalo, with his heart throbbing, whispered to Danka, "I love you, my dearest one," words that she would remember with tenderness years after their happy marriage.

Yanush and Marys, best friends, were both infatuated with Wanda. At least that's what Yanush told me, seeking advice on how to convince her of his deep love. Yet it became evident to me that Marys had been secretly in love with Teresa, who at that time, had many admirers.

On Sundays, after the mass in the Capuchin church, one could see Ely with Rick, totally dedicated to her, and Ely's older cousin, Chris with Stenio, loafing along Lubelska Street. Obviously more than just friends, they always maintained the proper prescribed behavior.

There was no such thing as dating, and all of the teenage angst was strictly love in its most romantic manifestation, if we were to believe Vitek. Vitek, one of the youngest of our group, was the son of well-respected teachers. Years later, when he enjoyed the status of a stage and screen actor, he recalled that one of his youthful adventures in Lubartoc was lying on top of a pretty girl on a bench.

"Well," he said, "nothing much happened, just the thrill of being close."

One of the most steadfast in his love and surely the most quixotic was Ziho. The passing years have romanticized the memory, but it seemed that his passionate love for me had its beginning on that frosty morning as he watched me drawing water from the well. A chance encounter with time became a rapturous revelation. The scent of lilacs, which he stacked in our door on Siedlecka Lane, will always bring back a memory of him.

Ziho didn't talk about his love, but I could read it in his dazzled eyes. He had another love, his violin. His bow, alive with magic, drew from the strings a yearning melody from the opera *Halka*.

> *Oh, Halina,*
> *You my only girl…*

"He is obsessed with you like Romeo with Juliet," Yada laughed when on some occasion, we had been talking about the boys.

Ziho indeed surprised and sometimes amused me with his romantic gestures. On a gloomy fall day, he sent, through Yanush, a message on a folded slip of paper with the verse in which the violin strings were sobbing, and he, instead of enjoying the sweet song, had to sigh and lament, being so desperately in love.

I remember well that spring day. Totally out of the blue, Yanush presented me with a little bundle. "Ziho asked me to give it to you," he said, blinking his eye.

When I unwrapped the bundle, I was enthralled to see a silver ring with a white eagle on a red enamel background— the emblem of Poland. The Nazis specifically prohibited displaying the Polish national emblem in any way, but we did not consider the Nazi rules morally valid. I slipped the ring on my finger; it fit perfectly. To wear it was a sign of devotion to my country.

Yet I could not accept this precious ring from Ziho. He was obviously in love with me, a love that I did not reciprocate. I cannot deny that I felt deeply grateful and honored. I wanted Ziho to know how much I appreciated the ring. On second thought, I had been puzzled how he had found a ring like that. "Would his father, our well-liked teacher, have helped him?" I tried to guess. After much deliberation, I decided to accept the ring, realizing that returning it would hurt Ziho's feelings.

I liked him. He had been one of Yanush's and my best friends for a long time now. He was a tall, good-looking youth. I liked his dark hair, his blue dreamy eyes, and particularly his chivalrous, dashing ways. But I had never understood the intensity and torment of his adolescent love, the gap between reality and the fantasy of his vivid imagination. Much, much later, in the winter of our lives, he wrote to me, "I was like a thirsty pilgrim, lost in the desert with a jug empty of water."

I had been the heroine of his romantic life while I was overwhelmed with an equally romanticized quest for knowledge. Besides, the sincerity of my friendship with Ely Derecka and Teresa Romanowska, with whom I could share my thoughts and feelings, was so delightful!

It was only through the distance of time that I fully realized how precious and uplifting the awareness of being loved and respected by Ziho had meant to me—without encouragement on my part and without any demand of reciprocity on his. Then I took his devotion for granted, but I probably would have been hurt if he had suddenly changed the object of his love.

The wall of separation was very hard for him to bear. Sometime after our graduation from the grade school, the German authorities permitted us to attend an evening business course. The classes were held in the school at Cemetery Street. Ziho was sitting on a bench just behind me. One evening, he snipped off a curly lock of my hair. I was startled and vexed to find myself blushing.

With this curly lock next to his heart, I was later told that he won the athletic contest improvised by a team of colleagues. As far as I remember, it included running, jumping, and swimming. There were no spectators, no cheerleaders, and no blaring megaphones. It was held as far as possible from the eyes of the Nazis, who were intent on breaking the spirit of Polish youth and undermining their physical development.

Ziho exuded youthful vigor and fitness. "One day," I heard someone predict, "the girls will be wild about him!" Indeed, they were, but the memory of his first love outlasted all his later conquests.

∾∘∾

Looking back from the perspective of years, I can now recognize this explosion of feelings as a need for affection and consolation as well as the budding of sexual awakening. The hardship of Nazi Occupation could not stop the usual rhythm of life. Precisely because life had been so trying and uncertain, the need to love and to be loved became more intense than ever and sometimes tremendously serious. I am sure we realized then that just beneath the veneer of proper moral behavior beat the pulse of selfish desire and passion.

The secret gymnasium and the Capuchin church held our group together. It was in the church that we looked for guidance. We trusted those wise fathers and kind-hearted friars with their clear eyes and calm faces in their brown habits fastened with white cords—the true followers of the Poverello, St. Francis of Assissi. Their piety, poverty, modesty, and courage—to say nothing of their good works—touched our hearts and inspired confidence.

Being in love, we were told, is a feeling without commitment. Genuine youthful love shouldn't look for fulfillment of the senses and imagination. However, it can be creative and transforming so one can become a new person changed for the better, becoming more mature and accomplished, with greater respect for the beloved.

"You want your love to be beautiful, don't you?" Father Agripin, the guardian of the Capuchin church, simply asked one of our youth.

The Capuchin church was a choice of our heart. Here we found guidance and solace. I remember it as a beacon of light, piercing the gloom of years of war.

21

The door flew open, and a man strode into the shop in a cloud of snow, stomping his high peasant boots on the floor and shaking more snow from his short overcoat. It didn't take long before I realized that this apparition from the winter storm outside was Lutek's father with a freshly cut Christmas tree in his hand!

What a surprise! This was going to be our first Christmas tree since the outbreak of the war. Christmas trees in our house in Ino were always tall and lavishly decorated. But this tree was far more precious than its size would indicate—it was a gift from the heart. Yanush took it to the room and placed it on our table-desk. In minutes, the fresh scent of pine filled the house.

The next day was Christmas Eve. Rozalia gave us some blushed red apples that we rubbed with butter to make them shine before we hung them on the tree. Next came brownish walnuts we touched up with bits of gold paint and then a few gorgeous pinecones from Yanush's collection. Finally, the tree was wrapped with a string interspersed with golden eight-pointed stars. Yasio came over and, seeing the tree, gave us his approval. Then he said, "You have spread the hay under it, but what's missing is a Nativity scene." In no time, Mary was tenderly bending over her Baby Jesus while Joseph stood guard. Christmas Eve, the shortest day of the year, was quickly turning to dusk. Yanush went outside looking for the appearance of the Evening Star.

"Now!" he cried, storming into the room.

The candles were lit, and the light brightened the darkness. The Christmas festivities could begin. We sat around the table that had been covered with a snow-white cloth. In the center was a plate with *oplatki*, thin rectangular wafers, baked in the church of the finest flour, especially for the *Wigilia*. Father Agripin had blessed them himself.

Dad broke one of them with each of us, and then we broke them with each other, exchanging warmest greetings. *Oplatek* is a bread of love. Sharing it with dear ones is a very moving moment, a unique Polish tradition. All past wrongs are forgiven, and love triumphs.

The meatless supper followed: borsch (red beet soup), fried fish (how did Rozalia manage to get fish?), pierogi filled with cabbage cooked with mushrooms, followed by traditional poppy-seed cake.

"Why the poppy seeds?" Yanush asked, puzzled.

Daddy smiled. "Because our forefathers had believed that poppy seeds contributed to a feeling of well-being and contentment."

Our celebration culminated with lighting the candles on the tree and singing Christmas carols. The tender memories of my childhood were revived. It seemed that Mom was again with us.

It was on Christmas Day that my heart was bursting with joy when in the church, sparkling with candlelight, we joined the monks and the faithful, overflowing the sanctuary in caroling that flared up in *Gloria in excelsis Deo* and continued with a prayerful supplication for "Peace on Earth."

The winter of 1942–43 arrived on schedule. We knew how the Germans dreaded it. Their soldiers on the Eastern Front were not properly provided with adequate winter clothes and were freezing. It became common for gendarmes to burst into people's homes and ransack their wardrobes looking for furs and fur-lined coats. In the villages, clothing trunks were plundered. A farmer coming into town wearing a sheepskin coat risked having it jerked off his back, leaving him shivering in the cold.

Living now at the Market Square where the news had been broadcast through a loudspeaker, it became clear that the German media had been manipulated. The Nazi broadcaster would not admit the defeats, justifying the retreats as "straightening out of the front line."

"They must be bleeding white," Dad's customers commented. The Polish railway workers saw trains after train going westward, loaded with wounded German soldiers. At the beginning of 1943, the echoes of fierce fighting for Stalingrad rang in our ears, and then one day, news came that took our breath away.

"The Russians encircled the overextended German divisions, taking them in a gigantic armored pincer," Mr. Grodzki, Benia's husband, described the situation, bringing together his interlocking hands.

Then the unthinkable happened—hard-pressed Marshal von Paulus, forgetting German pride, surrendered to the Russians!

∽o∾

I couldn't know then that with the Moscow and Stalingrad defeats, the tide of war had turned against the invaders. The Nazis learned the costly lesson while the Polish Underground was heartened.

One afternoon, Yanush, coming back home, rushed into the room almost breathless.

"Calm down," I said, "and tell us what happened!"

"The Germans in Warsaw are bursting with rage, while the Varsovians have had their day!" he announced with starry eyes. "The Underground has pulled off a prank right in the faces of the Germans!"

The Germans always claimed Mikolaj Kopernik as their own. At the beginning of the Occupation, most of Warsaw's historic monuments were blown up or sent to the scrap heap, but the Kopernik monument was still standing in the center of the city with a new plaque commemorating "A famous German astronomer, Nicholaus Koppernick." That, of course, aroused tremendous resentment among the Varsovians. The Resistance, known for its courage and wit, decided that this winter was the time to recall Kopernik's loyalty. The heavy plaque was unscrewed from the monument, spirited away, and hidden. All of this was done under the noses of German police.

"But that's not all! Just wait!" Yanush said, beaming with excitement. "In place of the plaque, an announcement was posted." He laughed enjoying every word.

I extend the winter by three months
Mikolaj Kopernik

I was truly fascinated by the Warsaw Underground action, so daringly undermining and mocking the hated German authority, but I wondered how on earth Yanush got this news. The answer came in days. Walking down Lubelska Street, I ran into Bogdan. We were chatting for a couple of minutes when I noticed that his face had turned serious, and he seemed somehow embarrassed.

"I have something to tell you in confidence," he murmured. "Just yesterday, Yanush gave me *Biuletyn Informacyjny* (Information Bulletin). I showed it to my dad, thinking he would be thrilled to read it. But he rebuked me, evidently alarmed, and warned me about the danger of possessing forbidden underground press."

I wasn't sure how to react, but it became clear to me that Bogdan was concerned about Yanush distributing the illegal press. I assured him that I would discuss this with my dad.

Lutek Zelazny moved in with us sometime at the end of the summer of 1942. He wanted to continue his education, and Dad, after a long consultation with Rozalia, agreed to provide him bed and board in our tiny flat. Lutek was a stout country youth, lacking some of the more refined manners. Never mind! We all accepted him as a member of the family.

More youths were graduating from the primary school, and some were eager to pursue the underground gymnasium courses. While those of us who were first enrolled in the program often studied on an individual basis, now small groups of pupils, known as *komplety,* were common. The classes were held in private homes, frequently changing locations to avoid attracting attention. Yanush's group included Marys, Lutek, Chris, and Renia. They were, like myself, students of Prof. Perczynska.

We were lucky to have several dedicated gymnasium educators in Lubartov. They were called professors to distinguish them from the grade-school teachers. I knew a few of them, some others by names only. For security reasons, we were never brought together.

One of the most distinguished professors was Maria Fryczowa, who held master's degrees in Polish and German languages. I vividly recall that when her class—including Bogdan, Ziho, and Zbig Krzyk—was in progress in her home, the maid stood at the window to warn of any suspicious persons or activity in the street. The boys were well instructed on what to do then. German textbooks would quickly appear on the table; all others would just as quickly disappear into hiding places.

How supportive and dedicated our professors had been! They were resolved to give us the best education so we would be well prepared for our new lives in a free Poland. In this atmosphere, learning became not only the fulfillment of each student's aspirations, but also foremost, a noble motive of our patriotic duty. No wonder we applied ourselves earnestly to our studies. In June of 1943, I took my final yearly examination with the assigned professors. This is how I met Prof. Maria Fryczowa and Prof. Francis Traczyk.

Prof. Traczyk lived with his wife, so full of spirit and vivacity, in a tiny apartment on New Cemetery Street. I smoothly passed the tests in math and geography. Prof. Traczyk was particularly pleased with my elaborate maps, which I brought with me in a large folder. Some weeks later,

Rick Borowski brought me crushing news that Prof. Traczyk had been arrested!

"I was having a lesson there," Rick said in a trembling voice, "when two German agents accompanied by a gendarme burst in, grabbed him by the arms, and took him away, leaving Mrs. Traczyk frozen in shock, utterly helpless."

The arrest of Prof. Traczyk had not only been painful, but also puzzling. His wife, Mrs. Traczyk, was professor of biology and the forbidden books had been on the table. A young student was sitting near him, and yet, the agents didn't pay any attention to them.

Years later, I was walking down Lubelska Street, absorbed in conversation with my friend, when a person passing us exclaimed heartedly, "Halinka!" It was no one else but Mrs. Traczyk, all radiant to see me, but also sad. She told me that Prof. Traczyk had perished in the Gestapo's prison in Lublin and that they both were Jews. No one seemed to know why only he had been arrested.

Prof. and Mrs. Traczyk had come to Lubartov from Lodz in 1942 with only the clothes on their backs. Before the war, Lodz, the second largest city in Poland, was a Jewish "Promised Land." During the Occupation, it had the best organized and longest-lasting ghetto. Not knowing a soul in Lubartov, the Traczyks appealed to Mr. Dumalo for help. His son, Yatsek, and Bogdan were Prof. Traczyk's first students. After the war, Mrs. Traczyk resumed her true identity and was known as Elwira Lula. She taught biology in the gymnasium in Lubartov until retirement, well-liked by her pupils and faculty.

22

At the beginning of 1943, the German authorities replaced the town's mayor, Alexander Lalka, with *Volksdeutsch* Joseph Müller. Joseph Muller was a gardener by profession, an old heavyset man with one leg bowed. I can still sense the disgust we felt when Rozalia related the tales about his arrogance. Vicious and ill tempered, he moved quickly, snooping around, supporting himself with a heavy wooden stick with which he showered blows on coworkers and anyone else who didn't please him. One of his close relatives was a captain in the Gestapo, reason enough to fear him.

We gymnasium students tried to stay out of his way when going to classes, hiding assignments under our blouses or shirts or in high top boots. Seeing him approaching one day, Chris, on her way to a morning class with Prof. Perczynska, tried to pass as inconspicuously as possible, but he grabbed her arm and, demanding the obligatory bow, shook her violently. She was scared that the forbidden book hidden under her coat might drop out, but she managed to hang on until he eventually let her go.

Under the pressure of war operations, the Germans needed more and more slave laborers for the Reich, and sudden roundups were conducted on the street, in the market, or train station. The names of my youth group must have already been on the list in the *Arbeitsamt*. Since I might be called to present myself before the Commission when I turned sixteen, I desperately needed to find an officially approved job.

Through some connection, I was introduced to Alexander Lalka, who had just been reassigned as chief administrator of Commun Lucka, a position he held before the war. Commun Lucka was one of the largest of Lubartov's county, with eighteen villages and over 8,000 inhabitants. Mr. Lalka was a fair and honest man who knew how to govern skillfully. Somehow, he managed to carry out the orders of the occupiers in the least painful manner possible.

He offered me a position as a clerk, being responsible, among other things, for the distribution of food ration cards. Commun Lucka's office building was within easy walking distance from the Market Square. In Lubartov, everything was close. I was very fortunate indeed! A couple of days passed, and I was called to Mr. Lalka's office for a face-to-face talk. Aware that I was pursuing underground gymnasium courses, he gave me official permission to leave an hour or two earlier every afternoon on the excuse that I was attending evening business classes that were approved by the German authority. None of my coworkers knew the real reason for this favor.

To be eligible for the ration, all villagers of Commun Lucka were required to register in our office.

While a *Reichesdeuschter* in the GG received equivalent to 4,000 calories per day, working Poles had to survive on 900. The bureaucracy involved was overwhelming. The occupiers kept a vigilant eye on food distributed to the Poles.

I was now up to my neck with a new daily routine. My day began at 5:00 a.m. with some study, then off to Mass, followed by a fast walk across town to my job starting at 8:00 a.m. Since I was leaving the office early, I managed to stop off at home for a quick meal and hurried on to my gymnasium class. I was lucky if I had enough time to do some of my homework for the next day before leaving again for the evening business course.

One of the first assignments given to me by Mr. Lalka was to handwrite the list of assigned quotas for each farmer in Commun Lucka. There were separate sheets with carbon copies for each village. Typewriters were scarce because the Germans were afraid they could be used for Underground activities. By order of Nazi authorities, the peasants in GG were permitted to keep their farms, but every crop, anything they produced, was declared to belong to the Reich and had to be dutifully delivered to the collection location. Farmers were allowed to keep only the minimum to sustain their lives. Severe penalties were imposed on those who didn't strictly follow the rules.

I thought I was certainly capable of accomplishing this simple task entrusted to me personally by Mr. Lalka. I just needed to know a few German words. Unfortunately, I made a mistake in spelling *Zussammen* (Total) and had to rewrite every single list. It was a terribly embarrassing beginning. My humiliation at failing—me, a gymnasium student—seemed at first unbearable. It took me some time to reassure myself that I was studying French, not German. But it was more than that! When I came to the list with village Brzeziny clearly printed on it, I realized at once that I had heard the name before. Of course! The farmers sentenced to death for not delivering their assigned quotas on time were indeed from Brzeziny. This extremely harsh verdict was meant to warn all farmers in Lublin district to strictly follow the imposed order.

A great sadness came over me. The words of a song I heard not long after the Brzeziny tragedy brought that memory back unbidden:

If I not return,
Let my brother sow the seeds next spring
As the moss shroud my bones
So I will enrich the earth...

"What are you saying, Halinka?" my boss asked, looking up at me over his desk.

"Nothing, nothing at all," I replied, trying very hard to conceal my emotions.

Nonetheless, snatches of the song continued to press silently on my lips:

One morning go into the field
And take a rye-stalk into your hand
Kiss it as you would your beloved
I will live in the sheaves of grain.

It was a lovely morning in May when I came to work to find that the Underground had broken into our office and took two typewriters, the official seals, and files. It was a great blow to the soul of bureaucratic efficiency of the German authorities, who had a well-known habit of accumulating detailed records on all ongoing activities.

What a brave lot those partisans are, how daring! I thought. Looking at the faces around me in the office, it seemed that all my coworkers shared my feelings. *But why was it happening now?* I wondered. At the first appropriate moment, I turned to Tad, whom I trusted.

"At the beginning of the Occupation," he told me, lowering his voice to a whisper, "the Underground tried to keep the spirit of resistance alive, but now it's strong enough to take action."

So they did! At that time, only a few people knew its scope, but the wagging tongues of Lubartovians had field days anyway. The news kept coming: the telephone lines near Lubartov were cut, the *Arbeitsamt* raided, and the lists of persons designated for forced labor in Germany destroyed. One night, a barrel of butter ready for shipment to Germany had been spirited away from the creamery in the Sanguszko palace and a receipt stamped with the Underground seal was left behind. Then, in July, the most staggering rumor reverberated through the town.

"Did you hear the latest? Near Trzciniec, a mine exploded under a train loaded with German tanks and armaments."

Oh, how Yanush and I were hoping that the hour of retribution would soon arrive, bringing with it long-awaited freedom! Lutek saw the situation in a more realistic light.

"Do you believe," he said, "that the Germans are now more accommodating because they are getting a beating on the Russian Front? Quite the opposite! I've heard some very disturbing news recently, and I'm afraid of what I will find when I return home. You may not know, but the Nazis are now not only fighting the partisans, but have begun a systematic cruel pacification of the villages."

June was coming to an end, and school vacation was fast approaching. The following Sunday, all three of us decided to go for the walk together up to the river. The weather was splendid. Passing small fields of rye, sprinkled with star-like heads of bluecorns and red poppies, I was picking the flowers and making a wreath. Yanush was unusually silent, obviously pondering something. Then, out of the blue, he turned to Lutek and said, "We know that in the forests of Kozlovka and Parchev, there are many partisans, but have you ever met a real partisan?"

Lutek grinned at him. "You may sometimes rub elbows with someone, not knowing that he is a partisan. One thing I can assure you is that it takes courage and daring to be one," he said. He paused and then continued, "The partisan has to look death in the eyes all the time, but I've heard that after a few months, you get used to it and don't mind anymore."

As Lutek went on, another question was on my mind, a question that captured my attention since our talk yesterday. What does "pacification" really mean? I had heard this word uttered with horror in my office. When I asked Lutek about it, his face turned grave, and he lapsed into silence. We were walking quietly for some time, and I assumed that for one reason or another, he didn't want to talk about it.

But obviously, he had been thinking hard how to answer me since he suddenly faced me and spoke, "You see, food is the most pressing problem to the partisans. They have to eat!"

With Yanush, we both listened attentively when Lutek went on explaining that the peasants were trying to help us much as they could, knowing that otherwise, the partisans would be forced to live by looting.

"Often, they are close relatives or friends," he said. "This is why the peasants became scapegoats for the Nazi's brutal repression. Just recently," he continued, "the German SS police raided Tarlo and Niedzwiada. Dozens of villagers were arrested and hauled to Majdanek concentration camp."

"Niedzwiada?" I shuddered, deeply shocked. "That was the village where we had been sent in December 1939." The bitter answer of what the "rural pacification" was really like was to come soon enough.

⚬

Zamost, a remarkably pretty little town in the fertile, forested region south of Lubartov, was part of Lublin district. The disturbing news about the evictions of peasants from the villages there started to reach us early. Yet it was in the summer of 1943 that the massive brutally enforced deportations of peasants from the Zamost region[1] began to fuel an overwhelming outrage in town. The most moving and heart-wrenching stories going around were about Nazi barbaric treatment of Zamost children, forcibly separated from their parents. The railway workers were talking of passing freight trains, now loaded with starved, often sick, frightened little victims. In Lubartov, a spontaneous rescue action had been organized.

It was from Ely's aunt, Mrs. Filipkowa, that I heard a touching story of rescue from the transport of a little boy by a courageous railway worker.

"Only yesterday," she said, "his new mom brought little Henry to my store. She made up her mind to adopt him and bring him up as her own son. He is fortunate indeed!" Mrs. Filipkowa sighed.

Flaxen-haired and blue-eyed Adelka Czata was another of the some two dozen children from the Zamost region saved from the transports and sheltered by Lubartov's families. She had been adopted by our dentist and neighbor, Antony Mantejewski, and his wife, Gertrude, a childless couple, expellees from Naklo.

When it came to Ninka, I had heard two different versions of her rescue. She was a dark-haired darling, adopted by my dad's friends, Mr. and Mrs. Teofil Czarnecki. They operated a buffet at the train station. Even though a long time has passed since then, I still recall how anxious Ninka had been that her new mommy might abandon her. Walking with me and holding tightly to my hand, she kept looking back, afraid to lose sight of her mommy, who followed us, talking with my dad. Ninka and Adelka were for some time my pupils. Both were about six years old when I taught them beginning reading.

I had heard that after the war, Adelka's mother returned from forced labor in Germany and managed to trace the whereabouts of her daughter. Their reunion was joyous, but Mr. and Mrs. Mantejewski, who had adopted her as their own, were left brokenhearted.

23

Where is Milek? We had not seen him for some time. Rozalia was passing to Dad some rumor afloat in her circle that Milek was living with a young woman. Her words were harsh and judgmental, and I was deeply hurt. If that were going to be our attitude, it would surely drive him away from any contact with home and family. He was twenty-one years old now, and he didn't need to be told what he ought or ought not to do, especially by Rozalia.

We were in the kitchen that evening.

"Surely, he needs a feminine touch, somebody to love him, believe in him," I tried to persuade Rozalia. "Life is so hard now, so uncertain." She did not look at all persuaded.

"Maybe she is just his perfect friend. If you only knew Greek mythology..."

She looked baffled.

"One of the Greek myths held that man was created with two heads, four hands, and four legs. But humans offended the gods, and as punishment, they were split down the middle. Ever since, they have had to struggle, searching for their other halves so that they can be whole again. This is how the idea of soul mate was born. Maybe he has just found his soul mate."

Rozalia looked at me with total incomprehension and resumed her work.

As it turned out, the reason for Milek's disappearance was by far more serious and frightening. One afternoon, unexpectedly, he came home and told Dad that he had been recently "investigated" by the Gestapo. Later, Yanush confessed to me that he overheard Milek reassuring Dad in whispers, not to worry, that he had a contact with the Underground. But since that afternoon, we didn't know about Milek's whereabouts and were filled with unrest.

After a while, Zenon, Milek's chum, told me that his sister was inviting me for lunch on Sunday. I hoped that I would learn something about my brother.

Zenek's sister—I don't remember her name—was an attractive young person in her latter twenties. Her thick blonde hair was rolled up on the back and sides of her head—the style of hairdressing popular during the Occupation. She welcomed me warmly. Obviously, I was pleased to meet such a lovely person.

The room we entered was bright. Although simply furnished, it seemed to reflect her personality. How plain our home was by comparison! A handwoven *kilim* was hanging over the couch, which during the war often served as a bed. A few small bright pillows were tossed here and there. A bouquet of fresh asters, arranged in a glass bowl, brightened the table covered by a damask cloth. An orange shawl was casually thrown over the back of a wooden armchair. Two colorful reproductions of known paintings by Wyspianski, set in wooden frames, were gracing the white wall. But what immediately caught my eye was a stack of books piled up on the shelf.

"I try to keep up with the latest books," my hostess said when we were comfortably seated, drinking tea from fine cups. To make up for real tea, her tea had been brewed from aromatic fruit leaves. The omelet served with strawberry jam was made of real eggs and—oh!—tasted so heavenly.

"Zenon has told me that you are a passionate reader, so I would like to lend you a book one cannot find in the library. It's *Gone with the Wind* by Margaret Mitchell." She pointed to a thick volume on the table.

"That book was the most popular in the summer of 1939. The thunders of an approaching war, which might determine our future, were reverberating throughout the country. Thus the story of a society devastated by war held a deep melancholy fascination for us."

"I would love to read it!" I assured her, excitedly. "Even though Rozalia complains that I am pouring over books too much."

"The heroine of the book is Scarlett O'Hara, daughter of a plantation owner in the American South." She searched her mind for a while, trying to find words to explain the sudden change in Scarlett's life. "The life Scarlett knew and was prepared to follow is abruptly erased by the war, and she—a rather impulsive girl—is challenged to make critical, life-preserving family decisions."

"How did she cope with those overwhelming events?" I was very curious. "Sometimes, life forces us to face many difficult situations." I was drawing from my own experience.

"That is what I would like you to discover," she said pointedly. Scarlett had to adjust to change. Changes in our lives are so inevitable as changes of seasons. We often have to accommodate ourselves to what is beyond our control."

Suddenly, the words Prof. Perczynska wrote in Latin in my diary came back, this time better understood: "Tempora mutantur et nos mutamus in illis." (The times are changing and we with them.) Noticing my thoughtful expression, my charming hostess, leaning forward, continued, "We have to follow our intuition to make difficult decisions but always be true to ourselves and always hold on to hope."

She didn't provide me with any hint about Milek's whereabouts, nor answer any of the questions I had in my mind. And yet, on my way back home, I felt somehow comforted and strengthened for whatever lay ahead.

She looked down at me from the large portrait in Milek's room, her dark eyes dreamy and full of melancholy. The perfect arches of her brows and the triangular chin were softened by a small sensual mouth. A tempest of dark wavy hair, evidently smoothed just before posing, was parted on the side.

"She was not only pretty, but very accomplished professionally," I recall Aunt Marysia saying, "yet she still managed to be a devoted wife and mother."

I knew that the lady in that portrait was Milek's birth mother, Sara. Yet when I look back now, I realize that my dad's first marriage had always been shrouded in an aura of mystery. Some evocative accounts of that story, however fragmentary, are still preserved in my memory. Regretfully, there is no more anyone left who could answer the questions I would like to ask.

Jan and Sara had met in Cracow, ancient capital of Poland, then a buoyant center of cultural, artistic, and patriotic activities. Years had flown by, yet Dad's reminiscences of his most beloved city remained deeply ingrained in his heart and his memories. During the First World War, Cracow was a garrison city of the Austro-Hungarian Empire. Jan, who later became my father, was a sergeant major in the Austrian army and served as a physical therapist in the military hospital there. He managed at that time to take some courses, having in mind to eventually become a surgeon. It was from him, not from Prof. Perczynska, that I learned my first words and sentences in Latin.

However, Jan's medical career was not going to be. He and Sara fell in love. I can picture them strolling along the beautiful Planty promenade lined with trees that interlaced above their heads like a green canopy, a delight created just for them. And then, looking up, their eyes would embrace in the distance the silhouette of Vavel Royal Castle and the towers of the majestic cathedral where the Polish kings were crowned and buried.

There was that Sunday they would never forget. They watched the sunset over the Vistula River, meandering its way through the limestone hills. The first ridges of the Carpathian Mountains seemed almost within arm's reach, and so too, almost in reach, was their happy life together.

Sara was Jewish. Dad mentioned her family name, and it sounded like "Stammfprugell," but I am not sure if the spelling is correct. Her parents were outraged. Yet Sara believed in their love. They got married and settled—of all places—in Inovrotslav, where they successfully ran a textile store in the Town Square, the one I came to know so well growing up. Their firstborn son was named Emil (Milek) after his dad's youngest brother, who was killed wearing an Austrian uniform while fighting the Russians during World War I. Their younger daughter, Anulka, died in early childhood. I only knew her sweet face from the photos in the family album. Every year, we used to go to light the candles and pray at her grave.

Interfaith marriages were rare then. Some worldly people today maintain that it is better for a couple of different faiths to attend the same church and to be part of the same religious community. But when Sara was instructed and encouraged to become Catholic, she listened to the priest politely, truly interested, but never renounced the faith of her forefathers. She piously attended the synagogue at the corner of Solankova and Grodzka streets, later on my daily path to school. But Ino was not Cracow. The Jewish community, present there from the Middle Ages, was prosperous yet relatively small. Jan was tolerant, but when the children were born, Sara must have worried if they would be Gentiles. It wasn't easy. It is to Jan and Sara's credit that their love prevailed.

Sara traveled extensively on business trips. In the years following the First World War, train schedules were unpredictable, and in the winter, the cars were often unheated. Her health gradually deteriorated. The spells of dry coughs became more frequent, and she was diagnosed with tuberculosis. The best specialists who treated her were reassuring; nonetheless, she was not getting better at all. Hoping against hope that the gentle mountain climate of South Tyrol and plenty of rest would help, Jan took her to Merano in Italy.

From the turn of the century onward, Merano was a fashionable spa attended by royalty and nobility, but for Jan and Sara, it meant far more than that. Dozens of years later, as I stood on the balcony of my hotel room taking in the gorgeous panorama of the imposing snow-capped Dolomites stretching higher and higher toward the sunshine painted sky, I tried to capture the drama of their last weeks together. They had prayed for Sara's recovery, but what they hoped for did not come to be. She passed away and was buried in Ino, in the Jewish cemetery.

In late spring of 1943, the Germans summoned Dad for "interrogation." It must have been a blinding flash for him since it came so shortly after Milek's "investigation" by the Gestapo. It's not difficult to imagine the tense mood we were in awaiting Dad's return. I had no notion whether there was any connection between the two because Dad had been silent on how it all came about. He obviously wanted to protect Yanush and me from any distress. I sensed there was a reason things were hushed up.

When he eventually returned home, it became evident that something had gone awfully wrong. I could tell he was devastated, although he tried not to show it. All we were told was that his concession to operate the shop had been revoked. The merchandise was to be cleared out and the shop closed within a few days.

How much I understood about the consequences of this ruthless order for our family, it is hard to tell. I had been so preoccupied with my busy schedule. But for Dad, it must have been a terrible blow. How was he going to support his family? How were we going to go on living?

Nevertheless, there was no sound of complaint from him. He even pretended that nothing much was amiss, just the usual German nastiness. When we were dining that night, I noticed that when he lifted the fork to his mouth, his hand was trembling.

The next afternoon, I stopped by home between work and class and saw him packing the pots and pans and fragile glassware in wooden boxes, which were then piled up in our narrow entrance hallway. Later on, when faithful customers occasionally came by to clandestinely purchase some article, it had to be found with much effort and lots of lifting. The whole thing greatly upset Yanush, who had to give away most of his cages with the rabbits to make room for stored merchandise. He, who had been so proud that, though only fourteen, he was able to provide our household with scarcely available meat.

I recall those rabbits, which he skinned and gutted, hanging head down waiting for Rozalia's skilled hand. After my experience in Lubartov, I didn't need to live in Alsace to appreciate the taste of a rabbit meat dish. Rozalia marinated and cooked it following traditional Polish recipes for dishes of wild game. The dried juniper berries or rose hip, easily available, and thick sour cream were added to the natural juices during cooking to enhance the flavor and aroma.

How we were going to miss this nutritious main course enriching our simple everyday fare!

By that time, I was also contributing to our table. Every month, some food ration cards were not picked up by the peasants, and instead of returning them to the German authorities, I was permitted to use them for the benefit of my family. I would ride to the nearby village of Lisov on a borrowed bicycle to collect a precious allotment of sugar and not-so-good marmalade. The coupons for dark heavy bread, I occasionally bartered for small loaves of bread made of fine wheat flour at a bakery operated by Mr. Litwicki, an expellee from Ino, who had a license to bake them just for the Germans. This was my contribution to Dad's diet.

Now that our shop was closed, Yanush and I took turns going to Skrobov, bringing home milk and heavy cream. The cream was laboriously shaken in a bottle until the yellow curds of butter were formed. We separated them from the buttermilk, washed them with cold water, and pressed them, yielding fresh tasty butter for Dad.

But Dad was not hungry.

His health was quickly deteriorating. I had never seen him sick in bed. When I asked what was the matter with him, no one seemed to clearly know. The doctor was not of much help. I still couldn't believe that Dad was seriously ill. We needed him so desperately.

I remember that afternoon vividly. I came back home from work later than usual and was in a hurry to be on time for my lesson with Prof. Perczynska. I had been tidying my hair, looking up in a small mirror that hung so high between the windows that I could scarcely see my whole face. I was totally absorbed in my thoughts until I felt that Dad was staring at me. I gave a brief sideways look in his direction. He was lying quietly, his eyes fixed on me with intensity. I walked over and sat on the edge of the bed. The pallor of his hollowed cheeks, his hand aimlessly stretched over the cover, tore at my heart.

Looking straight into my eyes, he said, "I know you are brave." The tenderness in his voice touched me. Still, that was all he said—words retained in memory forever. But I did not feel brave at all. I had been feeling truly sorry for myself, and he was the only person to whom I could confide my misery.

"Rozalia," I lowered my voice, "doesn't give us enough to eat. Both Yanush and I are often hungry."

Just as the words left my mouth, I realized that what I'd just said would disturb him. How foolish of me to complain when he needed all the support he could get! He must have been worrying about our future. I would rather have bitten my tongue if I could have taken those selfish words back. To make up for my thoughtlessness, I turned all my attention to him.

"Daddy, I will pray," I promised, "I will pray with all my heart so a merciful God will give back your health."

It was late evening. The house was unusually still. Rozalia was busy in the kitchen; Yanush was in the other room, working on his school assignments.

I had been engrossed in my reading, checking on Dad from time to time. He was lying quietly in his bed. Then suddenly, it struck me that his eyes seemed strangely dull. I checked his pulse—it was very weak. Worse than that, he seemed hardly aware of my presence. The feeling that a heavy stone was headed straight for me and was about to crush me at any moment was beyond enduring. A premonition came over me that Death was approaching to claim him.

I managed to call Yanush and Rozalia, but she did not take command as I expected, so swallowing my tears, I told myself, "I will worry later...but not now...not now." In the lowest drawer of the closet, I found what I was looking for—the large candle blessed during the Candlemas service in February. With trembling fingers, I lit it.

The life was being taken from our daddy before my very eyes. I didn't want him to go—to leave us alone. It was so excruciatingly painful.

All three of us dropped to our knees by Dad's bed and on first impulse prayed for Mary's intercession:

Hail Mary, Mother of God,
pray for us sinners
now and at the hour of our death.

What next? What next? I thought feverishly, my eyes brimming over with tears.

Heartbroken, I struggled to my feet, gently pressed my lips to Dad's forehead and lovingly closed his eyes, which I knew would never see again.

He died peacefully at home. It was October 17, 1943.

24

My recollection of the day after Daddy's passing is fragmentary and blurred. There was a time when Yanush and I needed a warm hug, but Rozalia was no help at all. It must have been Mr. Stanislav Guderian, a family acquaintance from Ino, who arranged the funeral. We were told that Dad had appointed him to be our guardian. The Guderians were childless, and he was well respected in town. I had no idea what having a guardian meant for our future.

I needed a black dress for the funeral. Overnight, Mrs. Czarnecka ripped out the stitches of her old black dress, and Ziutka's mom used those pieces to sew a dress for me. The custom at that time required that I wear black for a year. Yanush was given a black armband to wear on the sleeve of his jacket. The day of the funeral arrived. A stream of friends came by the house to offer their love and support.

Mr. Lalka and my boss from the office stopped by to offer their formal condolences. They brought me a hard-to-get coupon for dress fabric.

Prof. Perczynska's words didn't come readily, but they were subtle and comforting, and Father Timothy sent me rosary beads through Henry.

Stunned by grief and fighting back tears, I saw Ziho in his altar boy surplice, carrying a large cross at the head of the funeral procession and crowd of mourners. Holding tightly to Yanush's hand, I watched helplessly as Dad was swallowed up beneath layers and layers of earth.

Oh, I tried. I tried to listen politely to all those supportive words offered with genuine good intentions while all I wanted was to have our dad back with us. It was the next day that Yanush and I had to face the challenge of a dreary future. The worst that could happen to us had happened, and we were not prepared for it. How were we going to go on with our lives? It was obvious right from the beginning that we could not count much on Rozalia. She still did the cooking and some housekeeping, but there was no longer any sense of family. We were simply living side-by-side in that flat, which now could hardly be called a home.

I realized how industrious and accomplished she had always been. It seemed that she was indispensable. But now, with Dad gone, she had simply lost interest in us. I thought that she would have some sense of duty toward the orphaned children. Thus, I was still hoping that Rozalia was just hard to understand.

One October day following Dad's funeral, Ely stopped by our house so we could go together to the evening service at the Capuchin church. There is a tradition in Poland that the months of May and October are dedicated to Our Lady, Mother of God. Each evening, the faithful gather in the churches or at roadside chapels lovingly decked out with flowers and lit with candles to pray and sing Marian songs.

As the service was coming to an end, one of the monks intoned a well-known song, "O Most Loving Mother," and the assembly readily joined in. *"May weeping of orphans awake your compassion…"*

Ah, surely Mary will intercede for Ely and me, I thought, leaving the church with my spirit uplifted.

We were walking down Lubelska Street on our way home when Ely said, "I feel closer to you now than ever before. I know how much you have missed your mom, and now to lose your dad must be heartbreaking. How I understand what you must be going through!"

I was deeply touched by her words. She must have trusted me completely since she suddenly said in a murmur, "May 28 was the first anniversary of my mom's execution, and it brought back painful memories."

All I had known so far about Ely's past was that she appeared in Lubartov wearing her summer coat on the cold Christmas Day of 1940. She knocked on the door of her grandfather's house and was warmly received. But the reason for Ely's sudden solo arrival from Warsaw had always been cloaked in secrecy.

"Your mom was executed?" I repeated, shaken, still not sure I had heard that dreadful word.

We were just passing the little house of her grandfather. It was a familiar place although she lived now with her aunt and cousins on Cemetery Street. We stopped but didn't go in. There was a patch of grass at the side of the house, so we sat down, backs against the wall, facing a large gorgeous tree. Ely was obviously ready to unburden herself to someone she could trust, and I was eager to hear her story.

"It all started in September 1939," Ely began. "The German dive bombings...burning towns and villages... roads clogged with unending streams of desperate people moving ahead, some by orders, most by fear. Following a cavalcade of cars, we were advancing painfully slowly toward the Romanian border when all of a sudden our car was stopped. A man unknown to me conversed briefly with Dad. He delivered an urgent new order not to proceed to Romania but to return to Warsaw."

Startled, I let the words hover for a moment in the air before I asked, "And why did he press your dad to return to Warsaw?"

Absorbed in her thoughts, Ely replied enigmatically, "It was that order that sealed the fate of our family," she hesitated for a moment and added in a whisper, "and my patriotic legacy."

By the time they reached Warsaw, Poland's capital was already in the grip of the occupiers. The determined Varsovians responded to German terror with defiance. Nobody thought of collaboration. Ely's parents, following their steadfast convictions, immersed themselves in a whirl of Underground Resistance activities.[1]

"Since I was only twelve years old," Ely said, "I was not initiated into their highly secret, clandestine work, unlike my older brother, Jan. But I knew that my dad, under an assumed name, was operating from a hiding place. The rest of my family," as she continued, "found shelter under the hospitable roof of my aunt, Josephine Giedroyc. She lived with her sons, Joseph and Vaclav, graduates of gymnasium."

"Your parents had obviously great courage to keep on fighting for freedom of our beloved country," I remarked, deeply moved.

"It's simply a question of freedom or bondage," Ely said. "August 8, 1940, a date I will never forget. Mom had received a *gryps* (secret notice) at morning that Dad was going to join us for dinner that evening. Anticipating to see my dad, I was returning home in a joyful mood. Our housekeeper opened the door. I noticed the tension on her face before she managed to whisper, 'It has happened! The Gestapo!'"

They didn't let Ely enter the room. The housekeeper took her into the kitchen and held her in a protective embrace. Deeply frightened, Ely heard German shouting as well as some commotion. It didn't take long. On three consecutive trips, they were all taken in a little unsuspicious-looking *Skoda* car to Gestapo prison on Schuch Avenue. Hearing the detested word *Schuch*, I held my breath. During the Occupation, Warsaw's Schuch Avenue was a German police district and had the same connotation as *Under the Clock* in Lublin.

Ely continued her story. "They put us in solitary cells called *trams*. At first, I shared one with my mom, but in the midst of the night, they took her away. I was sitting with my back to the door, as ordered. From a bulb down the hall, a dim light was sifting through a little barred opening in the door. I stared at the barren walls of the cell covered with names, handprints, and messages scratched there by prisoners. How desperately lonely and helpless I felt! I had been worrying myself sick over what had happened to my mom and all the rest of my family, my dearest ones."

Feeling deeply her desolation, I listened to Ely's story unable to move or utter a word as I was frozen in place.

"I was straining my ears, hoping that Mom would soon return," she murmured, "but all I could hear was the measured tramp of the boots of the prison guard and some distant scary moaning. That night, I lived out the death of my mom several times."

She paused to collect her thoughts. "All this was enough to keep me awake that night." Her voice was now faint and trembling. "And then, all of a sudden came the distant rattle of keys in a lock, the squeak of a door, and I heard the sound of approaching steps. Instinctively, I turned my head toward the opening in the door just in time to catch a glimpse of my dad in shackles, led by a group of Gestapo men. It was a crushing sight.

"It was daybreak," Ely's words were strained with emotion, "when I heard a commotion in the corridor. The door to my cell was unlocked and clanged open, and my mom fell to the floor between two rows of wooden chairs. She still managed to whisper, 'This is death,' before she fainted. Frightened, I began desperately to bang on the door with my clenched fists, crying for help and water, but no one answered. Slowly, painfully, Mom regained consciousness and composure." It took a while before Ely murmured, "What I had just witnessed was a moment of her weakness not ever repeated in the long months of our imprisonment. After that morning, she always managed to hold her head high."

Oh my god, oh my god, I thought because I had no idea what she had been through.

By the time Ely finished talking, the wind had picked up, and October's chill had crept through our light coats, but I was hardly aware of it, as I was totally engrossed with her traumatic account. Although no words had been exchanged after she finished talking, I sensed that she still wanted to share something important with me. She moved closer.

"It happened the same day. There had been no time to think what this imprisonment of my entire family really meant, when I was summoned for interrogation. The scene that followed has never left my memory."

In minutes, they brought in her dad. He could hardly stand on his own, obviously having been beaten or tortured. This was for Ely a hellish experience. The investigators sadistically had played on the child's affection to establish Captain Derecki's identity. Oh yes! She had been prepared ahead of time to deny that he was her father—for the good of the Cause and her dad's protection.

"With broken heart, I steadfastly insisted, 'I don't know that man! I have never seen him before!' But I could not bear watching him beaten in front of me, and my spirit was shattered by the lies I had just uttered about my beloved dad. I have to erase that horrid scene from my mind forever! Forever!" the tears sprang to her eyes.

I was crushed myself after what I had just heard, but I managed to control my emotions and took her hand firmly in mine. With calm reassurance, I said, "You just did so!"

It was getting late, and we both realized that at our homes, they may worry about us. I wanted to learn more about what happened to Ely's family, why she was here alone in Lubartov. But this had been such an emotional evening. I will ask her some other time.

We were parting when I said, "You have come to mean a lot to me, Ely. To think about the ordeal you went through, and yet you are always so gentle, so positive, and warm-hearted. Your parents must have loved you very much." She was deeply touched.

"I don't know why I spoke to you about my parents," she sighed, still engrossed in her thoughts. "I never speak of them anymore. Maybe it's because you're an orphan, like me." We both knew that, from that evening on, our friendship was sealed for life.

Some days passed before I learned more about Ely's family's long ordeal. On December 22, 1940, just one day before Christmas Eve—after five nightmarish months in different prisons—Ely was released from *Paviak,* the most infamous Nazi jail in Warsaw. She was a minor and sick.

"As it turned out," she said, "I was the only one of my entire family to be spared."

The most cherished memory for Ely was that of the last night she had spent with her mom, just before her release from the *Paviak* prison. The previous day, she was called out from the cell she shared with her mom and taken to the isolation ward, where some other women prisoners had already been assembled. When Ely found out the next day that the group was going to be free, she became desperate that she would not even have a chance to say farewell to her mom. That very evening, a miracle had happened. The Polish prison workers, "those good spirits of *Paviak,*" smuggled Ely back to her mom's cell, so that the two of them could spend that night together.

With all that I have heard from Ely in my mind, one November evening, a verse came from under my pen, a poeticized image of those last hours of Ely's farewell night with her mom. I gave it to Ely, and that is how it survived the war.[2]

To Ely

That dreary autumnal dusk I remember well—
The reflections and shadows creeping in the cell
A scrap of sky heavy with tormented clouds
And that gloom of hopelessness spreading in my heart—

And you, I remember, Mom!

The hair of your temples threaded with sneaky grey
Ghastly specter of prison mirrored in your face—
Only those beloved eyes glittering with strength
And the steadfast wholeness of your inner self.

You enfolded me closely within your soft arms
I nestled securely my head on your heart
And soon in my enchanted fairy-land of dreams—
I was oblivious to your pearl-like tears.

Now when I face the world, young and free
I remember that evening with eyes full of tears—
And, Mom! All I wish is to be with you
Surrounded by your great love, love of motherhood.

Halina
Lubartov, November 11, 1943

Someday, before her release, Ely was called to report to *Paviak's* dentist, a prisoner himself. Under her "filling" was concealed the *gryps* from her father, who was still being held in an isolated prison cell on Schuch Avenue. It was bordering on a miracle that this scrap of paper, with his note scribbled on it, was smuggled from his heavily guarded cell on Schuch Avenue to the *Paviak* prison on distant Pavia Street by daring Polish personnel.

Eventually, Ely lost all of her beloved family. In January 1941, her dad, brother Jan, and cousins, Joseph and Vaclav, were all deported from the prison in Warsaw to the concentration camp in *Aushwitz*. They all were executed there in the early spring of that year. The family members were notified of their deaths by successive totenscheins sent directly from the Administrative Office of *Konzentrationslager Aushwitz*.

As for her mom, she had been deported in September 1941 from the Gestapo's *Paviak* to the concentration camp in *Ravensbruck*. After four months there, she was brought back to *Paviak* for trial. Sentenced to death on May 28, 1942, she was shot in a summary execution along with some 200 other prisoners in the forest near Magdalenka not far from Warsaw.

The last *gryps* from her, a farewell letter written the day before her execution, reached Ely in Lubartov. She knew this letter by heart. Below is a large fragment of it in my English translation.

Dearest Little Daughter of mine! Ely beloved! I think that you already know, my Only One, that this is my last letter, that this is farewell. Only Love, I cannot leave without saying good-bye to you and I think that you also want that—although I realize that you are going to cry…Cry, My Little One, in great suffering the tears bring relief. But when you stop crying, calm down a little, think, My Only One, with gratitude, and be thankful to God that He gave your Loved Ones the most beautiful death—that they could give their lives for the Great Cause—for the Fatherland. Cry, my Beloved, but do not despair. Ely beloved! Ah, how much I love you! And know that always, always I will love you. Always, always will be with you…be brave…

Your Mommy
Paviak, May 1942

Resistance to terror was a necessity of the Occupation. The road to Poland's freedom was long and rocky. It took great courage and sacrifice to follow it, but Ely always remembered what her mom wrote to her:

"Beloved, never be sorry for what has happened. It was necessary, although God is witness how much we loved you."

25

It was after Christmas that Rozalia began leaving the house for long hours, always carrying her bag. The situation came to a head one day as I arrived home to find her coming out the door.

"Where are you going, Rozalia?" I asked, casting a sharp glance at her bag.

"To friends to do some baking," she said, brushing past me and walking quickly ahead. I could guess that Rozalia was headed to see a plump and jolly man who had a fondness for good food and had taken a liking to Rozalia or her cooking, in what order I could not tell.

It became evident that we would have to part. I delayed the bitter decision from day to day, but eventually, I asked her how much of Dad's savings we still had and offered her half of it. Rozalia left the next day. We did not exchange any bitter words, but I was deeply disappointed. We had all endured so much together, and now we were in the midst of mourning. It seemed that Yanush and I should have meant something to her, but in a way, I was relieved to see her go. There was no bond between us.

As soon as Rozalia left, I realized there was no use feeling sorry for myself. The sense of family and security that Dad had provided was gone forever. Here I am, four years after our exile from Ino, facing a future as uncertain as it could be. Yanush is the only one left, and I am determined to look after him as best as I can. All of a sudden, a thought snapped my mind to attention. *We have a guardian!* At least we had been told that the day before Dad's funeral.

I knew Mr. Stanislav Guderian from Ino. He had a drug store on our block of Holy Ghost Street, and his wife was a member of St. Vincent de Paul Society, chaired by my mom. I recalled that in Lubartov, he helped Milek to get a job as translator. I had seen him on rare occasions. Portly, always composed, he spoke fluent German. The German officials treated him with respect. It was not difficult to figure out why. His name was Guderian! Who of the expellees from western Poland had not heard of General Heinz Guderian, commander of *Wehrmacht* armored divisions of *Panzers*, fast-moving German tanks sweeping all before them? One could also hear that Heinz Guderian's family roots were in Chelmno, Pomerania, north of Inovrotslav, so he and Mr. Stanislav Guderian may be related. However, it was certain that Stanislav Guderian had not accepted the status of *Volksdeutsch* (German national), and he and his wife had been exiled to Lubartov.

In Lubartov, Mr. Guderian held a prestigious position as a manager of a subsidiary wholesale store of the German company, C. F. Corsen, from Bremen. The far too rare shipments of merchandise, such as household goods, tools, fabrics, and shoes were distributed to the town stores at the direction of Mr. Guderian. I knew that so well because my dad had received his share. One year, just before Christmas, a wonderful surprise was added—a large gorgeous doll. Probably, Mr. Guderian had made sure it came my way. In ordinary time, I might have thought myself too old for such a doll, but this was not an ordinary time. For me, struggling through the hard time of Occupation, this doll became a joy. I named her Eve.

"If Mr. Guderian was a decent man," I continued to ponder, "why didn't he come to see Yanush and me since Dad's funeral?" Frustrated, I told myself, "What are you waiting for? Go ahead and do what needs to be done." The most important thing, I decided, is for Yanush and me to continue our gymnasium programs. The more I thought about it, the more I became convinced that we should not be deprived of the opportunity of learning. The big question remained: How would we get the money for tuition?

Shortly after my deliberation, I asked Yanush what he thought about continuing the lessons with Prof. Perczynska. He laughed, "I have no intention of missing the opportunity of learning something really worthwhile."

"But the money…where will it come from?"

Yanush didn't think long, but was struck, as he believed, by an ingenious idea.

"Let's reopen the store," he said. "Some of Dad's inventory is still stored in the hallway. We'll sell whatever we can and collect the money for our tuition. And I'll again have a place for my rabbit cages!" his face brightened with a smile.

"But, Yanush, how can we ever do that? Hasn't it occurred to you that we don't have a concession to operate the store?"

"The Germans took the concession from Dad, not from us," he retorted. "Besides, people are doing 'not so legal' things all the time. It's the only way to survive."

"All right," I agreed, "but the store will only be open for some hours for two or three weeks."

Audacious and risky as it was, we went ahead with Yanush's project and restocked the store with what we found in the hallway. The opening hours were not only short but varied.

We realized what a volcano we were living on and that we had to be careful not to attract any more attention than absolutely necessary. After serious deliberation, I placed my magnificent doll, Eve, in the display window holding a sign that stated:

Welcome!
We Are Open to Tell You
We Are Closing

It turned out the doll was the best advertising we could have had. People had not seen a doll like that for a long time. Thinking of the joy she would bring to a little daughter, passersby came in to buy the doll. How disappointed they were when they were politely informed that she was not for sale. They sometimes bought an item or two since the articles were reasonably priced and the clerk so young!

"Operating the store" was just one more of our new responsibilities. After the class with Prof. Perczynska, there were the chores at home to do. The house had to be cleaned, laundry had to be done, water brought in buckets from a community pump a long block away, and meals cooked every single day!

Yanush was very helpful and worked as hard as I did. There was one chore both of us occasionally enjoyed, and that was cooking. Watching Rozalia, I learned that cooking is a creative activity. Of course, you had to have something to cook. Now winter was upon us, so vegetables from our little garden were not available. We could buy some food from the farmers we knew, but that usually meant a long walk to the village. We kept our menus simple, and while we didn't always satisfy the gnawing sensation in our stomachs, we managed.

One day, I had an audacious idea. We had a small amount of Dad's savings. We could hire a maid! Our new maid, Vladka, was an eighteen-year-old peasant girl, used to hard work. She carried all those buckets of water, did the laundry and ironing, and helped with the cooking, washed dishes, and cleaned the house. She was quiet, modest, efficient, and we all got along just fine. Hiring her was the best thing I could possibly have done! I again had some time for studies after work, time for friends, and a much more normal life.

Our circle of fellow students was a great comfort to us. Most of them, like me, were by then studying and working, but in their spare time, they would drop in, and our house rang with their youthful voices and laughter. We shared the latest news. There were always books to be exchanged and commented on, poetry appreciated and enjoyed. How romantic and full of spirit we were! Looking at reality through the prism of literature and poetry, we hoped that the future Poland would not only be free and independent but also just.

One of the rare visitors in our house was Yatsek Dumalo. I remember him as a pleasant, slender youth with a long face and hair always nicely combed. His family was from Bydgosh, a city close to Inovrotslav, so we used to joke we had been neighbors before meeting in Lubartov. In our circle, Yatsek was known as a devoted yet iconic patriot. He understood military matters better than anyone of our boys. The explanation for that came to light when his father, Mr. Stefan Dumalo, who supplied the town with vinegar, had been denounced to the SS police by an informer as a Polish officer.[1]

Yanush had shared the secret with me that during the interrogation by the Captain of Schutzpolizei, they had found out that they have common friends in Vienna. Cpt. Dumalo had been released from detention. Yatsek had his father back.

After a long winter, the snow was just beginning to melt when one afternoon Yanush came back home visibly excited.

"Can you keep a secret?" he whispered.

I looked at him surprised that he needed to ask me a question like that.

"Like anybody you ever knew," I said.

From deep in the pocket of his trousers, he brought out a carefully folded paper and passed it to me.

Nasza Warta (Our Guard), I read, hardly believing my eyes. It was a copy of an illegal weekly, edited in Lubartov! Agitated, I scanned the pages. Who were the reporters, the editor, the printer? One thing was sure—they must have been people from our town. Even now, when I recall that day, I can still imagine how astonished I would have been if Ziho had told me that the decision to edit the Lubartov region's conspiratorial weekly was made during a secret meeting in his house on Winding Street. His father, Karol Skaruch, presided over a meeting of the local Home Army's Bureau of Information and Propaganda. At that meeting, Prof. Maria Fryczowa was appointed chief editor, and the secret printing was entrusted to eighteen-year-old Genia Gembala, the close neighbor of Prof. Perczynska and Skaruchs.

The printing was usually done on Sundays in a small concealed room in the attic. On that day, the entrance to the room was always covered by wet laundry hung to dry on rows of clotheslines, a normal routine in winter. While Genia and her older brother, Sigismund, were printing the sheets, the family's youngest, Henry, kept watch outside.

"One day," Vitek recalled, years later, "Ziho and I found a suspicious-looking black rectangular box smelling of printer's ink under the bed in our room. Alerted, we called our dad."

He looked straight into our eyes and said, "We are going to print the clandestine newspaper right here in our house. Are you ready to take the pledge that you will tell no one about it?"

That day, both of them became soldiers of Home Army—Ziho as *Victor* and Vitek as *Vir*. Until the end of the Occupation, they faithfully kept the secret and served at first as printers, and when the printing was moved to other locations, as distributors of *Our Guard*.

And only to think that all this editing, printing, and distributing of *Our Guard* went on during the Occupation, literally under my nose, while I knew nothing about it. What amazed me the most was learning that each week, 300 copies of Lubartov's clandestine paper came from a most unusual place, the cell of Father Agrypin in the Capuchin Monastery.

❦

What I remember about Easter of 1944 is a bucket, not a jar, but a bucket of freshly baked cookies. Any religious or spiritual recollections of that day faded away a long time ago, and the only thing clearly preserved in my memory is that bucket of sweet-scented cookies!

Yanush and I had made a hard decision. We went to Skrobov and splurged some of our precious savings on butter, lots of butter. Following Rozalia's famous recipe, we baked dozens of cookies.

Yasio contributed hard-boiled eggs, colored and gorgeously decorated. From most ancient times, the egg has been considered a symbol of new life, and nature was once again bursting back to life all around us after a long cold winter.

Our friends stopped by, bringing flowering branches of pussy willow. Their furry tufts are the first signs of spring. We shared the eggs, and we all feasted on cookies, a pure delight to the pallet after weeks of Lenten fasting and self-denial. We laughed heartily, happy to be together.

Yatsek dropped by at last. "Alleluia!" he greeted us all and looked around. "How are the cookies? Let's enjoy them because the news is good!" With his arrival, a wave of enthusiasm burst into our room. He told us that in Italy the Allies are aiming for Rome, while in the meantime, the German cities are pounded in colossal air raids. On the Eastern Front, the German armies are clearly in retreat.

"This year has indeed begun on an ominous note," Bogdan's voice sounded not of Easter joy, but of alarm. "Have you heard that Red Army units have crossed Poland's pre-war eastern border? The Red Army is in our Homeland!"

It came back to me how euphoric we had been after the German defeat at Stalingrad. Yet the vision of the Red Army entering our land aroused in me disturbing and ambivalent feelings.

"Poland has two enemies and suffered as much, if not more, under the Soviet Occupation as under the Nazi," Bogdan went on with strong conviction. "People are talking again about the crimes Soviets have committed."

Yanush voiced his opinion, "We don't want freedom as a gift from the Russians."

"It could be like a Trojan horse," I hastened to add. Yasio had not uttered a word. I noticed the worry on his face.

"All right…all right," Yatsek's voice was deliberately calm. "This is a reason the Home Army gave the order to start fighting the smaller German units behind the front lines and to assist the Soviet advancing units to fight the common enemy. So you see, we are not waiting passively to be liberated by the Red Army."

Bogdan, who had lapsed into silence for a long while, finally spoke, "The present political situation is not favorable for Poland. But this much is certain: We have to go on fighting."

That night after everyone had left, I thought of Bogdan. How skeptical and yet how pertinent his remarks had been! Coming to Lubartov from Volhynia, Poland's Eastern Borderlands, he considered the Communists as an even greater evil than the Germans. He worried because Stalin, successfully fighting the Germans, now had support of the Western Allies. Bogdan was bright, well-read, and self-confident. He fancied himself to be a mature person, but his boyishness sometimes amused me. Yet I liked talking to him. Although I was impressed by his intelligence and cool wit,

I was not in love with him. Bogdan had been the only one of our colleagues who was openly fascinated by the erotic trends in the books he read. This had been tempered by the influence of Father Timothy, whom he saw often as an altar boy and who was his confessor.

He had been then in platonic love, as he insisted, with Teresa Romanowska, who at that time was my second best friend, only after Ely. Teresa's father, a Polish reserve officer, was in Warsaw. She lived in poverty with her mother and younger sister, helping to support the family by working as a retoucher in Photo Studio *Bebe*. Teresa was an attractive, graceful girl, gentle and sensitive, gifted with an artistic talent. She painted a beautiful Madonna on a wooden board for me. I gave the painting to Mrs. Sophia Guderianowa on her nameday in May.

A few days after Easter, I received a message that Mr. Guderian wished to see me. That was unusual, for although he was our official guardian, we did not have much contact. Still, I had a great deal of respect for him and hurried to our evening meeting. He greeted me with a very serious expression. "I have received some troubling news, Halinka," he began in a formal tone, "about what is happening at your house. I was told that young people are often seen going in and out and that boys are entering and leaving through the open window. I am disappointed that you would allow such things, Halinka, and I would like an explanation."

I was deeply astonished that he had so little faith in me. I raised my head and looked straight into his eyes.

"I don't know who gave you this report," I said calmly, "but I can assure you that nothing out of the ordinary is happening in our house. Yanush and I live alone now, and being connected with our fellow students is very helpful. They sometimes drop by after work or classes, and we discuss the news, exchange books—things like that. We all are careful to not attract attention, and we avoid loud noises." Mr. Guderian listened, but the expression on his face did not change much.

"As for the window, it happened a few times," I acknowledged. "They are set low and sometimes open this time of the year. Since our store is closed now, it's easier to ask permission and come in that way rather than to bang on the latched back door, wait for it to be opened, then go through the hallway and kitchen. Maybe it's just something out of the ordinary that boys like to do. I promise it will not happen again."

Mr. Guderian maintained his formal, serious attitude, and I never knew if I had convinced him or not, but he did not raise the subject again.

On the way back home, I decided I would not hold a grudge against him. He had a right to be concerned. *He is just a distant guardian*, I thought, *a rules enforcer*. Then I remembered Dad, how supportive he was, and I missed him very much. *If only…*

"Emotions are the hardest things to deal with." the wise words of Prof. Perczynska came back to me just in time. I have to stand firmly on my two feet and not lose confidence in myself. Yanush needs me.

26

By late May, more and more people were gathering at noon in the Market Square to hear the latest official news broadcast through the loudspeaker. The German propaganda was, as usual, full of pride and lies. Everyone knew that the heroic German armies were in full retreat and yet what was reaching our ears were phrases like "tactical withdrawals" and "straightening of the front line."

With the front line closer and closer to Lublin district, the forests in the region were teeming with partisans. When Lutek went back to his home or more likely joined the partisans himself, we lost a dependable source of information about what was going on there. But echoes of open confrontations and armed skirmashes reverberated in the town. Swift and cruel reprisals followed; the Germans were still all-powerful.

The Underground requisitioned all kinds of goods and raided administration offices, more daring and bolder than ever before. How could I know then that former Polish officers, often living under assumed names, were training new conscripts for the Home Army? I had no idea that my favorite grade school teacher, Ms. Angela Miduchowna, under the pseudonym *Kama*, was a Commander of Home Army *Women's Military Service* for the region and worked hand in hand with Dr. Prus.

Sometime around Easter, a rumor made the rounds in town that Adam Majewski, oldest son of *Volksdeutsch* Francis Majewski, had been shot in an ambush and died in the hospital in Zamost. Adam joined the Gestapo in Bilgoray, where he was hated for atrocities committed against both Jews and Poles. Nonetheless, his sister, Valeria, had confiscated Marys's father's shop with all the merchandise in it and then employed Marys so the family would not starve.

Emotions ran high. Our youth were burning with a desire to drive every German invader from Polish soil.

I remember May 29, 1944, as a happy day. We had just managed to convince Mrs. Filipkowa, Ely's aunt, to permit her to spend the night in my home. Bogdan was supposed to come over that evening to perform his new puppet show, and Yanush had already hung a white sheet, which would serve as a screen. But for some reason or other, Bogdan didn't show up.

We spent the entire evening with Ely absorbed in talking and reading poetry, mostly by Cyprian Norwid, one of our greatest nineteenth century poets. We were enthralled by his vision on what the resurrected Poland should be like, something we had very much on our hearts those days. Our hopes and aspirations were as high as his. To Norwid, recreated Poland should be worthy of her best traditions.

This was a wonderful evening, and we happily settled in for the night with Yanush on a cot in the small room and Ely, our maid Vladka, and me in the bedroom.

I was rousted from my sleep by the sound of insistent pounding on the shutters of our windows. What was all this commotion about? We all sprang to our feet and hurriedly started getting dressed. I slightly opened one of the shutters and stood, stricken with shock at the sight of gendarmes at our windows and back door. Oh yes, I understood the words they were shouting: "Offen! Schnell!" (Open! Fast!)

The pounding became more threatening, and we rushed to the hallway. Yanush was most vulnerable since he was fifteen and not yet working. We desperately tried to get him to the hiding place in the attic. He was already halfway up the ladder when the door flew open, and the Germans broke in. They rushed us to the nearby Market Square Two by the movie theater. I vaguely remember that the whole area was cordoned off by the German police. It was a scene of total confusion with people, young or middle-aged, rushed around. Trucks, with engines running, were parked at the edge. Something terrible was afoot. "Lapanka!" (Seizure of hostages!) One couldn't miss the tension on the frightened faces of the captives so unexpectedly seized from their homes.

I lost track of Ely and Vladka almost immediately but held desperately to Yanush's hand. Moments later, he was separated from me, and I only managed to catch a glimpse of my brother being rushed with a group toward the trucks. In a raging chaos, I was myself directed toward a short middle-aged man, to my surprise, dressed in lederhosen. He had a Tyrolean hat on his head, but his face was of a predatory bird. With a cane in his hand, he enforced his orders.

The Tyrolean gave me a quick scrutiny. In a flash, I realized that in confusion, I didn't take my employment certificate with me. If I wanted to stay free to be able to help get Yanush back, I needed to act with complete cool.

"I work in administration of Lucka...my father and my mother dead. I support my family," I spoke in broken German, grateful this very moment to Dad for teaching me some basic German expressions. He didn't say a word, just motioned for me to stand beside him.

All my attention was now centered on Yanush. I strained my eyes to catch sight of him, but in vain. I watched, gripped by terror, as one truck after another began rolling out. It all happened so fast—with the habitual German efficiency. It was torture for me not to be able to do anything to help my little brother for whom I felt total responsibility. Why had I failed to protect him? Where were they taking him?

It seemed that in no time, the trucks, loaded with the seized "catch," were rumbling down the road...gone. There were only a few people in sight besides the lederhosen man and me. He led me toward a distant group of men. When we came closer, I saw that two of them were in German uniform, the third was a civilian. They all towered over me. The lederhosen man spoke to them briefly. One of the officers, his lips tightly compressed, shot an unfriendly glance at me and quickly addressed me in German. His voice was purposefully intimidating. I stood my ground, kept calm, and repeated exactly what I had earlier told the lederhosen man.

"She has a mouth on her," he barked back.

The moment was critical, my fate in suspension, but I was saved by the man in civilian clothes when he said, "It's all right. Let her go."

I walked slowly toward home, still not sure that a bullet would not hit me in the back on the way. Once inside, I was overcome by the most immense feeling of loneliness that I have ever experienced. To be bereft of my little brother was more than I could bear. I stood, rooted to the spot in the middle of the room, thinking all of it must be a macabre dream. This should never have happened to me! The silence was screeching, and I covered my ears with both hands.

∽ᴑᴔ

How long I was trapped in this heart of darkness I cannot tell. Finally, I managed to collect myself. How many times was I going to have to ask the same bewildering questions: Why us? Why me? And then reflection: How quickly, how easily can one succumb to the pressures of misfortune and anguish. Where was the courage, the moral strength we had been talking about with Ely just hours before?

Ely! What had happened to her, to Vladka, to Yanush, and all the other people seized in the mass sweep? I decided to go and find out. The marketplace and the streets around it were strangely empty. I talked to some neighbors, and they were all painfully aware that the trucks were going toward Lublin, no doubt to Majdanek concentration camp in its suburbs. Among those taken were Bogdan's dad and some other people I knew well.

The sweep was a terrible blow to many of the town's families, and it happened before we had recovered from a recent wave of arrests, mostly of the town's youth. I was deeply saddened when I heard that among others, our fellow student, fifteen-year-old, Marius Jarczak, who was so hopelessly in love with Ely, and Bogdan's best friend, Valdemar Materko, had been taken to Lublin Castle prison, sentenced to death, and executed.

Now a new tragedy!

"We will stand in it all together," people consoled each other.

The only good news was that Ely, with her face framed by two braids of blond hair, was released after presenting her employment certificate. She was lucky that the German who checked her paper was relatively human. Yasio was saved by Grandma Rogatko, who hid him before opening the door. Seeing an old couple living alone, the gendarmes gave up searching the house.

Within days, the news started to trickle in from Majdanek, passed in whispers to the relatives and trusted friends. Gradually, a picture of how Yanush might be faring began to emerge: They are held in Field V, a work camp administered by the *Wehrmacht*, thank God not by those evil SS-men! And then more news followed, bringing some relief and a gleam of hope: They are marched off every day in groups to different places in Lublin's outskirts to dig antitank trenches. Someone had managed to escape.

Facing their own imminent perils, the Nazis kept on terrorizing the Polish population. What would they do with the concentration camp prisoners before retreating? The vision of impending danger to Yanush was an unbearable torment to me. By day and by night, lying in bed wide awake, I tried to figure out how to get Yanush back home. *I will not submit to despair! Tomorrow I will go see Mr. Guderian and ask for his help*, I made an uneasy resolution.

"I've heard that Yanush is being held in Majdanek, in the *Wehrmacht's* work camp," I told Mr. Guderian. "I am resolved to go there and try to see what could be done to get him released. He is only fifteen years old." Mr. Guderian took a long look at me.

"I am glad you came to me before making any step in that direction," he said. "Let us consider if this would be a wise thing to do."

"First, how are you going to get to Lublin? If by train, you could easily get caught in the roundup at the station yourself. And then you intend to see someone in authority? Will you speak Polish or French to plead your case?"

Of course, Mr. Guderian was right. Not that I had not foreseen all of those problems, but I was hoping that, seeing how determined I was, he would offer to go to Lublin himself. Of all the people I knew, he was best suited to do so, and after all, he was our official guardian. But I quickly realized that as sympathetic as he seemed to be, he would not lift a finger to try to get Yanush out of the concentration camp; it would have taken a lot of determination to do so.

On my way home with my heart broken and my hope gone, I felt totally lost. What was I going to do?

"Go to him!" the inner voice was like a ray of light in total darkness. So I turned around, slackened my pace, and as usual when confronted with grief and uncertainty, went straight to the Capuchin church.

"I've tried so hard, and I've failed. Nothing is left but to put the whole thing in your hands, O Lord," I prayed.

I had already learned that relying on one's own wit and strength in deep distress is an illusion. What I needed was God's grace and charity and inspiration from the Holy Spirit.

It all began with an idea that came to my mind shortly after: Milek! He was the only one who really would care. I didn't know his situation in Warsaw or his address, but somehow, in days that followed, I managed to find a contact and sent him a note about Yanush being a prisoner in

Majdanek's Field V. I implored him to do anything he could to get Yanush back home.

In the midst of all this, the end of the school year was approaching. So many things had preoccupied me over the past months, taking priority and diverting my attention from the studies. How many hours normally dedicated to it I had missed; how often I didn't complete my assignments on time. Sometimes, it was hard for me to concentrate on the lesson at all. But other times, solving a difficult trigonometry problem, or writing a paper on a subject I was passionate about, helped take my mind off the dilemmas.

"You are going through a tough time…don't be discouraged…take heart," I had been told now and then. So I didn't totally give up on my studies.

When my nameday arrived on the first of July, just two weeks after I turned seventeen, Yanush's and my friends tried their best to cheer me up. They came to my house invited to a party with warm greetings and gifts. It was so marvelous to be together again. Our silent house reverberated once more with lively young voices. Ziho surprised me the most. Early that morning as I was leaving the church after Mass, he presented me with a bouquet of red roses, velvety soft, and so fragrant! "How nice of you to remember!" I murmured. He still managed a few words of greetings and swiftly disappeared.

Back home, I found a little card hidden in the roses. It read:

In your wonderful, wonderful, wonderful eyes
When I look the sun withholds its radiant gaze
And the flowers in the meadows are by them surprised

And charm streams from the heavenly blue skies
In your wonderful, wonderful, wonderful eyes.

It was a known verse by Tetmajer.

Feeling a prickle of excitement, I took a small mirror from the wall and looked at a pair of blue eyes full of spirit and vivacity. Putting the mirror back, I hummed a French song that has touched every adolescent girl's heart:

Un jour mon prince viendra...
(One day my prince will come...)

❦

It was a glorious sunlit morning just two days later that Mr. and Mrs. Guderian came to see me. In his usual formal manner, Mr. Guderian announced that they were leaving town and moving to Glovno. As my guardian, he had an obligation to take me with them.

"Mr. Czarnecki is already there." Mrs. Guderian said. "He accepted a position as manager of real estate not far from the town, and I am delegated by the Corsen Company to liquidate their store there. We have already rented small apartments in a new building." He seemed not to notice how utterly miserable I was, totally unprepared for the shock.

"Before we leave, somebody will come to pick up your folding bed, some linens, clothing, and a few things you would like to take with you."

"Where is Glovno?" I asked, my voice trembling.

"Not far from Lodz. We will be closer to Ino." He told me they planned to depart in two weeks. "Be ready!"

He didn't even bother to ask if I was willing to go with them. Did he give a thought that it might be very hard for me to do so? Dad had passed away, Rozalia was gone,

Yanush had been torn from me, and now I am told to leave my home and go to Glovno, where I didn't know a soul? Does he realize that it may be hard for me to part with my friends and colleagues with whom I can talk, share my doubts and hopes, and learn from our experiences in the process? Nevertheless, there was nothing I could do to oppose Mr. Guderian's decision. It would take a miracle to reverse it! Yet who knows what might happen in the next two weeks?

How bountiful is the goodness of God! Only a few days after their visit, I received, through my contact, tremendous, almost unbelievable news: Yanush was with Milek in Warsaw! And I even had their address. A great burden seemed to have been lifted from me. My heart was almost bursting with gratitude and joy. After I cooled down a little, I started to see this move to Glovno in a new light—as an opportunity given me by God. I might as well go with Mr. and Mrs. Guderian. To get to Glovno, one has to change trains in Warsaw. Now all I had to figure out was how to finish my journey there. My only wish was to be reunited with my brothers.

The Guderian and Czarnecki families were not the only ones on the move. Bohdan Jastrzebski, our gymnasium colleague, was also leaving after his mother had found the name of her husband, Jan Jastrzebski, a Polish reserve major, reported dead in the official paper issued in Polish. It was a list of thousands of Polish officers who fought the Germans but had been detained by the Soviets when the Red Army invaded Poland's Eastern provinces in September 1939. They were deported to the detention camps in Western Russia and in May 1940 were killed in a massive execution by bullets in their heads. Understandably, Mrs. Jastrzebska was not eager to see Soviet troops on Polish soil. There were other people leaving as well for various reasons.

The war that Hitler unleashed in 1939 was raging to its end. In Lubartov, preparations were being made for possible Soviet bombardment, so we were not at all sure if we would be able to get to Warsaw by train. If the Russians were bombing our towns, they surely would want to destroy the communication lines, the primary targets.

The day of our departure arrived. At nine o'clock in the morning, someone was supposed to come pick up my suitcase. I opened half of the shutter on the front door, leaving the other and the window shutter closed and stood in front of the empty store shelves, waiting for my suitcase to be picked up. Suddenly, a tall silhouette appeared in the entrance. It was Ziho! He had come to bid me farewell. He looked at me with his dazzling eyes. I don't remember anything we said. Surely it wasn't much, but my recollection of what happened next is still clear and vivid.

In the semidarkness, I noticed an intense emotion passing across his face, and next he reached out his arms and drew me to him in unexpected yearning. In seconds, his lips were on mine. They were tender and warm, and then, just as suddenly, he stepped back with chivalrous self-control. Without a word, he turned and, propelled by the rapture of his first kiss, walked quickly away. He didn't look back.

The train started to chug away. At the end of the second week of July, the Soviet offensive was approaching Lublin. That we made it to Warsaw unscathed was a gift of Providence. My eyes, besotted with tears, softened Mrs. Guderianowa's tender heart, and I was permitted to stop in Warsaw to see Yanush and Milek. I promised my guardian that I would join them in Glovno in two weeks.

The Warsaw train station was a mad house. There was no one waiting for me since Milek didn't know when I would be coming. Clasping my suitcase, I somehow managed to find a rickshaw instead of the planned droshky.

"Senatorska 8," I said, trying to steady my voice.

I couldn't know that the Warsaw Uprising was only days away.

Yanush and me on the edge of Skrobow forest in the fall of 1941

Milek in Lubartow, 1942

My special friend Ely. The photo was taken just days
after she learned that her mother had been executed
in the forest near Magdalenka in 1942.

Three friends, left to right: Yanush, Yatsek
(standing) and Bogdan, 1943.

The spirit of youth. We never gave up hope and life.

PART III

We Have Something
to Fight and Die For

27

The rickshaw stopped at one of the noble residences lining Senatorska Street. On its façade was a clearly visible Number 8.

"You are in the heart of Warsaw," my young driver said proudly, pointing toward the imposing Theater Square just in front of us. Across the street, the ruins of the palace with its semi-circular wings stood abandoned, obviously a reminder of the grim reality of the 1939 siege of Warsaw. Yet, this was only a fleeting thought since all my attention was centered on a single question: "Am I really going to see my brothers?"

I stepped down from the rickshaw and entered an open gate. Following Milek's directions, I made my way into a courtyard enclosed on three sides by tenement houses four stories high. "The one in the middle," I repeated to myself, "second floor, door to the left."

Burdened by my heavy suitcase, I climbed the flights of stairs as fast as I could and, almost out of breath, knocked on the door.

Milek opened it. "Halinka! You are here at last! Come in. Come in. I have a surprise for you." I stepped inside to find myself in Yanush's warm embrace. As I looked at his mischievous face and sparkling eyes, everything I had been through the past months—terrible worry, anxiety, loneliness—suddenly seemed irrelevant. By the grace of God, both of my brothers were safe and sound, and all three of us were reunited. Nothing would ever obliterate that joyous moment from my memory.

I glanced gratefully sideways at Milek. "Oh, what a relief it is to see Yanush out of that concentration camp," I said.

"If I had been a prisoner of the SS," Yanush hastened to explain, "those evildoers would never have let me go, even if I should have had advanced tuberculosis. We were lucky to be held in Field V, under the exclusive authority of the *Wehrmacht*. At that time, they had already started to release some inmates cleared by their work places in Lubartov."

So we began our lives together. The reality was harsh. Milek laid down the ground rules.

"You must stay at home. Don't be tempted to venture outside unless it is absolutely necessary. You are not registered here and don't have work papers."

Truth to say, I didn't take the warning of my elder brother too seriously. I'd never been to Warsaw before and yearned to see it. Milek must have sensed my attitude since the tone of his voice became more serious. He explained that the situation in the city was tense. The Red Army had unleashed a full-scale offensive and was storming ahead toward the Vistula River. The Germans were trying hard to hold them back. Meanwhile, the Underground was getting ready to start the Uprising and liberate the city before the Soviets enter it.

"Hah," Yanush's eyes flashed with exhilaration, "I've heard that the German civilian population is already fleeing in droves."

Milek glanced at his watch and calmly continued, "The occupiers are well aware of the mood in the city. We are living on top of a volcano these days, on the eve of a great event. So be prudent and stay home!"

Milek left each morning and returned late in the afternoon. I did not know where he was going or what he was doing. I revered my brother and trusted him. Back home, he would share the latest news with us. I still vividly remember that afternoon, shortly after my arrival in Warsaw when, upon entering the room, he announced pointedly, "The Red Army has taken Lublin!"

"So Lubartov must be free of Germans too!" Yanush and I exclaimed in unison.

That night, I tried to imagine how one feels suddenly back in a free Poland.

∞⚬∞

For most of the day, Yanush and I were on our own. We had to decide what to do with our time. Our meals were frugal since we hadn't been legal residents of Warsaw and hence had no ration cards. It was possible to buy food on the black market, but we had very little money.

Though we missed the routine of gymnasium courses and our circle of friends in Lubartov, we didn't complain. Thank goodness, we were not totally alone!

Prior to my arrival in Warsaw, Yanush had already befriended a teenage boy who lived with his aunt, just one floor above our flat. Yurek was of average height with a graceful bearing. The first time I looked into his shimmering blue eyes peering out from under blond hair, I felt instant sympathy for him. Yurek's maturity, astonishing for a boy so young, I thought, would tone down Yanush's spontaneity. The three of us became close friends.

Yurek had a great deal to tell us about our capital, which Yanush and I had never had a chance to visit. At first, the talking centered on the heroic defense of Warsaw in September 1939.

"We were so heavily bombed that the whole city was in smoke and flames, and yet fierce fighting stubbornly continued," he recalled. "It was the middle of September when the German attack concentrated on the Old Town's St. John's Cathedral and the Royal Castle. We lived so close that I could see the flames licking the castle's roofs and Sigismund tower already in flames. Residents from the nearby streets, battered as they were themselves, rushed to the castle's rescue."

"So the castle was saved?" Yanush asked almost breathlessly.

"That you may see for yourself."

All at once, a disturbing thought raced through my mind. After a moment of hesitation, I asked, "Yurek, why are you living with your aunt and not with your parents?"

I noticed a sorrowful expression on his face before he whispered in a hushed voice, "My mom perished under the rubble of a bombed house."

He gazed thoughtfully at me, then at Yanush, and continued reflectively, "That is why those September days remain forever imprinted in my memory."

"I am so sorry, Yurek," I said, feeling a lump in my throat. "What about your dad? What happened to him?"

"My dad is in England serving with the Polish force there. That is why I am living now with my aunt, but she is so…so callous. How glad I am to have you as my friends."

Inspired by Yurek's tale of the heroic defense of the Royal Castle, we went with Yanush to see it. Since our stretch of Senatorska Street was between the Theater Square and the Castle Square, we soon looked with dismay at the phantom of the once splendid Royal Castle we knew from school books. Some of its wings and Sigismund Tower lay in ruins, but most of the roofless walls still stood defiantly, gazing toward the July sky with empty sockets of blown-out windows.

On the way home, we stopped at the Capuchin church on Honey Street. Like our Capuchin church in Lubartov, its modest interior, in accordance with the Order's rule of poverty, was devoid of gilt and the splendor of polychrome decorations. It was a worthy and welcoming sanctuary of God. Kneeling in prayer, I implored God for the successful liberation of Warsaw from Nazi tyranny so we might again live in dignity and peace.

"I have already found out," Yanush boasted as we hastened toward Senatorska, "that it was King Sobieski who brought the Capuchins from Italy to Poland. He founded this church for them as a votive offering for the victory of Polish cavalry over the Turks besieging Vienna."

"Which saved Western civilization from the onslaught of the powerful Ottoman Empire," I said with a boast of my own.

We were back home before Milek arrived.

As days went by, the city was abuzz with news. Events that could hardly have been anticipated only months earlier followed one after another. The most encouraging news concerned the successful Allied landing on the Normandy coast, which was an enormous blow to the German army already reeling under the pressure of the Soviet offensive. Then rumors of a failed attempt on Hitler's life by a high-ranking German officer took everybody by surprise. Evidently, the once pro-Nazi German military leaders were at last openly challenging the folly of their Führer.

Throughout the last week of July, the strong drive of the advancing Red Army forces toward the Vistula River and Warsaw seemed to be evident. Milek was convinced that the Rising was about to start any day.

"Once we have control of the city, we can present ourselves to the Russians as sovereign hosts, ready to cooperate with their army to fight the Germans, the common enemy," he said.

"This is exactly what our friend, Yatsek Dumalo, has been saying," Yanush was not a bit surprised. "He always had reliable information. You see, his dad was a pre-war Polish officer. He must be up to his neck in the Resistance."

"The Germans have enormous superiority in armaments," Milek admitted. "But our strength is in commitment and determination."[1]

He reflected for a moment and added, "Mind that we have Warsaw's population on our side—more than one million strong."

I knew that. The windows of the apartments overlooking our courtyard flew wide open when the first notes of songs were played and sung by wandering musicians. They had the magic and appeal of a "golden horn" calling to the Rising. It was common knowledge that singing in public places was banned by German order, so the neighbors would shower the courageous performers with money tossed from generous hands.

Writing these words, I still have on my lips the refrain of my favorite one:

> *O willows, do not rustle*
> *With a heartbreaking sorrow*
> *O do not weep, my sweetheart*
> *Being a soldier is not bad.*

28

One Saturday, not long after my arrival in Warsaw, Milek returned home earlier than usual.

"Wait dinner for me," he said in a distracted tone as he looked for a place to put something he had brought with him. "I have some urgent business to take care of, but it shouldn't be long…one hour or two at the most."

Already on his way out the door, he turned around and, looking straight into my eyes as though he wanted to be certain that he could count on me, whispered confidentially, "The Rising is imminent. We are on alert."

Aware of emotion passing across my face, he put his hand on my arm in a fatherly gesture and said, "Keep an eye on Yanush! Where did he go? He is always ready to put his head into the wolf's mouth." Shortly after Milek left, Yanush returned, accompanied by Yurek. He brought staggering news that the Germans were blaring an order through the loudspeakers for 100,000 men of the city able to work to report for obligatory digging of anti-tank trenches around Warsaw.

"That's a ridiculous demand," I said. "I'd be surprised if anybody showed up."

Yanush nodded. "To issue an order like that when the Russians are right on the heels of the retreating German troops aiming straight for Warsaw would make a horse laugh!"

Yurek, who had been silent, clarified the situation calmly. "The Germans are jumpy and obviously want all able-bodied men out of the city."

He didn't stay long this time. His aunt worried herself sick about the possible consequences of any armed action against the Germans, insisting that they were still far too strong. And she was not sure about the intentions of the Soviets either. She seemed to be unable to share our youthful expectations and enthusiasm.

The first hour after Milek left passed quickly. The table was set for dinner. But as the hands of the clock hanging on the wall continued to move inexorably, our apprehension began to grow.

"We shouldn't worry...worries are like worms eating hope. He will be back soon," I tried to reassure Yanush as he fed his pet rabbit, Kuba, some precious carrots I had purchased the previous day.

It was close to five o'clock when, all of a sudden, we heard a knock on the door. We both jumped to our feet and raced to open it, with Milek's name on our lips. To our dismay, it was not Milek but a short, middle-aged, slightly balding gentleman we knew as Milek's friend. He had come to our apartment the previous Sunday with a couple unknown to us, supposedly for a bridge party—a common cover for a conspiratorial meeting during the Occupation. The name *Niewiarowicz* passed through my mind.

One glance at his face told me that something dreadful had happened. He entered the hallway, cautiously closing the door behind him, and turning toward us, got straight to the point.

"Emil (he referred to Milek) has been arrested. There is no time to waste. You must come with me. Grab only what you need for tonight. The Gestapo could be here at any moment."

We were rushed down to the street. If I remember correctly, we took a tram and before long found ourselves in front of one of the large apartment buildings lining the wide street of Jolibord, a suburb of Warsaw. We climbed some stairs, a door opened, and Mr. Niewiarowicz (this could be his assumed name) entrusted us to two ladies who greeted us warmly.

Before leaving, he told us that Emil and his companion had been seized carrying grenades[1] from an ammunition cache to a designated location. Noticing my questioning look, he added, "All we know," he spoke with a composed voice, "is that they were taken to the Szuch Avenue."

A thought of the Nazi infamous prison on Szuch made my legs go weak under me. I was shocked to the heart. I knew it all too well. Ely's entire family was held and interrogated under torture there, and from her accounts, I could imagine what might be awaiting Milek. Desperately, I tried to compose myself. Mr. Niewiarowicz was soon gone, leaving Yanush and me with the two ladies.

During dinner, while plunged into my thoughts, I tried to listen politely to their warm, comforting words. It was then I learned that the husband of our hostess was a pre-war Polish officer. I would not ask what had happened to him, not at that time. Yanush and I realized what a great risk our hostesses were taking. Harboring a person without proper documents was an offense against occupiers' law with dreadful consequences.

I didn't sleep much that night. It was a nightmare to imagine Milek being interrogated by those Gestapo toughs. All I could do was to pray for him. I finally dozed off, the rosary beads still clasped tightly in my hands. The next day was Sunday, but we did not go to Mass. We were caged in. Most of the day we spent sitting on the sill of a window, opened just a bit, listening to the distant roll of artillery.

This time, Yanush tried to bolster our spirits. "The Red Army must not be far. I'll bet the Uprising will be launched any hour now, and the insurgents will surely liberate the prisoners in a sweeping attack." Our gracious hostesses were very supportive.

"The eyes of all Poland are on us now," the older lady said. "Our country has a long tradition of fighting for freedom. No straits are so desperate that they cannot, with God's help, be overcome."

The events that were going to decide the fate of Warsaw and its population were just around the corner, but for us, the hours dragged on at an unbearably slow pace.

It was Tuesday, close to noon, when we heard some commotion and voices. We opened the door and stood face-to-face with a girl unknown to us.

"My name is Chris," she said. "I am going to take you home to Senatorska."

She must have been in her early twenties. Her face was beaming with youthful energy. It didn't escape me that her blouse was fastened with a leather belt and a conductor-like purse was flung over her arm. Chris was in such a hurry that we hardly had time to say a quick "good-bye" and "thank you" to our courageous hostesses.

When we got down to the street, I saw a horse-drawn carriage approaching. It stopped at the curb just in front of us. We jumped in, and in a minute, all three of us were on the way toward the Old Town.

"The Uprising is set to start today," Chris spoke in a low voice. "You might as well be home. The Germans will soon have their hands full, so you don't need to worry about the Gestapo's visit to your flat." We didn't talk much during the ride, but I clearly recall Chris's words as we stopped at Senatorska 8.

"Farewell, and see you in a free Warsaw!" she said smiling, reassuringly.

We waited on the sidewalk until the droshky disappeared around the corner of the Theater Square. The moment it was gone, I noticed our young neighbor, a dashing lad in his twenties, strolling along Senatorska, with his knee-high, black officer's boots polished to a sheen. As we were about to enter the hallway, I saw him abruptly turn around, and with decisive, measured steps walk back to the Square. It passed through my mind that he might be surveying access to the Theater Square.

That scene was to remain in my memory as a first indication of the imminent Rising.

Yanush and I were almost at the threshold of our apartment when we heard steps behind us. It was our building caretaker, an elderly man with bushy whiskers. He was trying hard to catch up with us. Still panting, he said, "A kid is waiting in the courtyard. He wants to see somebody from your apartment. I couldn't get anything more from him—obstinate as a mule that little fellow. He's been here since morning."

Intrigued, we hurried back down the stairs with the caretaker right on our heels.

The boy, no more than ten years old, was indeed sitting on the concrete pavement of the courtyard, his back against the wall of the apartment building. Seeing us approaching, he got up briskly. He looked to me like a typical city urchin. His visored cap was pulled down so low I could hardly see his eyes.

"These are the persons you are looking for," the caretaker said to the boy.

From the pocket of his short trousers, he pulled out a torn scrap of brownish paper and handed it to me without saying a word. Before I could figure out what it was and thank him, he ran off, disappearing into the shadows of the hallway that led to the street. I had only a glimpse of his bare legs and feet in strap leather sandals.

With one close look at the scrap of paper, I recognized Milek's writing. It was just a short note, obviously hurriedly scribbled. I read it feverishly.

Senatorska 8 Apartment 17
They are deporting me from the *Paviak* into unknown
Hold on
Emil

Puzzled, Yanush read the note over my shoulder and said, "No name of addressee. But at least we know he is out of Paviak alive, and as I told you, thinking of us." Preoccupied with Milek's message, we only now noticed that the caretaker was still standing by, a silent witness.

"Do not worry," he said gently. "Being out of a Warsaw prison these days, your brother may have a better chance to survive. Remember the old saying, 'Every cloud has its silver lining'."

On the way back to the apartment, we wondered, "Is this a *gryps* smuggled from the prison or a note dropped from a truck or train? Who picked it up and thought about its delivery on a day like this?" We also marveled at the remarkable spirit of solidarity of the little messenger.

29

After three nights and two long days, we were finally back home. But with Milek gone, the familiar room was strangely lifeless. For some time, we kept quiet, each of us immersed in our own thoughts.

At last, Yanush broke the silence. "It's so hard to think of Milek being deported—God knows where and what he may be going through." He sighed and for a long moment stood motionless. Then he whispered, "What will we do now, having no connection in the city and with no money?" Seeing Yanush's saddened face, I tried to control my own emotions. "We have to deal with whatever comes along, as we did before. At least we don't need to worry, as Chris assured us, about a Gestapo raid." At that very moment, it came back to me that Milek had brought something to the apartment last Saturday, something he had been hurriedly trying to hide. So we both started to nose around.

"Look here!" Yanush pulled a book from the shelf. It was a manual with illustrated instructions on the use of firearms.

Behind the row of books, he found a bundle wrapped in soft white cloth. Carefully, he began to unwrap it, and to our great surprise, in his hands were two pistols!

"They are more precious than gold!" Yanush exclaimed. "We cannot fight the Germans with our bare hands." In the closet, behind a pile of towels and bed linens, were berets, each with a Polish eagle pinned on it, and a bunch of red and white armbands. With no doubt, they were meant to be worn by the insurgents.

"We have to somehow secure all this stuff," Yanush spoke thoughtfully.

Thinking what would be the best to do, I sank down in an armchair and almost at once realized there was something unusual about it. I ran both my hands down in the spaces between the cushion and the sides of the chair, and, to my amazement, I came up with handfuls of bullets.

We put the pistols and bullets in a small pillowcase and, together with the berets and armbands, into a bag I had used once or twice for shopping. Yanush grabbed the bag, and we were about to head for the cellar when we heard a knock on the door. For a moment, we froze. But the knocking was gentle, one…two…three. This surely was not the Gestapo, but Yurek.

Yanush put the bag back in the closet and rushed to open the door.

"Where have you been?" Yurek's voice was tense with concern. "I had just heard from the caretaker that you were back home. I've been so worried."

"We just came back from Jolibord." Yanush's face was radiant seeing his friend. "From Jolibord? Then you must know about the shooting there."

"We didn't hear any shooting," I replied.

"Let's go down and find out what's going on." Yanush was excited. A group of residents had gathered in the courtyard, sharing information on the events. Someone was pointing toward the entrance hall.

I still remember the emotion I felt seeing the motionless body of a middle-aged man in a business suit lying on the pavement by the flight of stairs. His face was deathly pale. Somebody must have closed his eyelids because he looked as though he was just asleep. Seeing our puzzled expressions, an elderly man standing nearby explained, "The bullet went straight through his neck when he crossed Senatorska. He was shot by a German sniper. You kids be careful if you plan to go out."

We were still in the courtyard when shooting could be heard close by. The sounds of fierce exchanges of gunfire and explosions grew louder as the time went on. We knew what it meant. The insurgents had taken to the streets and were attacking German positions. They were putting their lives at stake to set us free.

"Barricade! Let's build a barricade!" the strong, loud voice called for action.

The empty street in no time was teeming with enthusiastic volunteers. Some came with shovels and pickaxes and immediately started to tear up flagstones from the sidewalks. We teenagers hoisted them up with our bare hands and carried each one to the fast-growing barricade, blocking access to Senatorska from the Theater Square. In a spontaneous community effort, people were filling bags with sand, bricks, and rubble. Stronger men were hauling furniture, while others struggled to dismantle an iron gate. Everyone worked with selfless, fervent dedication.

Two elderly sisters in black dresses with lace collars were each carrying a tray and serving tea, water, and cookies. Sipping my tea, I noticed that the people in front of me had been all looking up in the same direction. I raised my head, and instantly my eyes caught sight of the Polish flag hanging from the window of a residence next to ours. I had not seen the national flag during the five years of Occupation. My heart was beating with joy. The elation transcended anything I had ever experienced. This flag was a portent of freedom so close at hand.

What I remember best of the following days is Yanush standing face-to-face to me, and in a serious voice I had never heard before, saying, "Yurek and I decided yesterday to join the fighting."

I looked up at his determined face. Knowing Yanush, I wasn't surprised. He pointed to the bag slung over his shoulder and remarked casually, "I'll introduce myself by bringing the two pistols and the bullets. We all know that the insurgents are desperately short of weapons. But take my word, we will get them from the Germans themselves." Aware of concern written all over my face, he added reflectively, "I do not know how to shoot...not yet. But I will do whatever it takes to help."

Only then, I fully realized that my little brother was heading straight for the fighting.

"I will keep in touch with you," Yanush assured me. "We will come back hungry as wolves, so have a meal ready for us."

It was a tense moment of parting only days after we had been reunited.

"May God keep you in his care." I had tried to steady my voice. I stood motionless long after the echo of his footsteps faded away.

When I had calmed a little, I took my obligation to prepare a meal for the boys very seriously. That was not an easy task since our food supply was meager. Then I recalled Milek saying the Rising was planned for three days, a week at most. While taking to the cellar a couple of blankets, a first-aid kit, and bottled water, I ran upon the residents laboriously knocking a large hole in the basement wall.

"We need subterranean passages that will permit communication from building to building," they eagerly explained, "without walking above on the street."

The place was filled with rubble and dust, so I offered them some water, which they gratefully accepted. On the way up, I stopped in the courtyard and joined a little crowd of residents, who like myself came to hear and share the news. They were passing from hand to hand the Information Bulletin. It was soon plastered on the wall for everyone to read:

The Commander of Home Army issued the order to fight the enemy.

The joyful mood was reflected in the happy faces. Some overheard snatches of conversation were heart-warming. "Several Old Town and downtown streets are already under control of Home Army soldiers."

A heavyweight, elderly man spoke cautiously, "This morning, I saw German tanks still rolling freely through the Cracow Faubourg."

"Oh well, the Germans are obviously on alert trying to secure their main thoroughfare to the Eastern Front," a man standing behind me retorted. "Those tanks have no access to the side streets. They are already sealed off by the barricades that sprang up overnight, just like ours."

Back in the apartment, I immediately preoccupied myself with preparation of the dinner. The previous day, having nothing to feed his rabbit, Yanush sacrificed him and pre-cut the meat in serving pieces. It took a long time for the meat to be tender because the gas flames in our gas stove was very low. Served with lots of vegetables and a cold cherry soup with homemade macaroni, I thought, it should be a nutritious meal. Cleaning and cutting the veggies, I prayed with all my heart for Yanush, Yurek, and success of the Rising. It was early evening when both boys appeared, their faces beaming with emotion.

"The Blank Palace had been captured by storming insurgents!" I still hear Yanush's triumphant cry and see his eyes sparkling like two bright stars. "Our fighters had taken a squad of German prisoners and much needed weapons and ammunition."

For Yanush, the most emotional moment during the fighting was when a German soldier from Silesia begged in Polish for his life to be spared.

Dinner was served promptly because the boys were starved. They had eaten nothing the whole day. The meal was consumed in an atmosphere of high spirits and hope.

"It's amazing," I said, "how fast the fortune changes. Only days ago, we were passing the Blank Palace on our way to *Kanoniczki* Church. It was heavily guarded. Do you remember, Yanush, it was then Milek told us that the palace was housing the offices of the Nazi Mayor General of Warsaw?"

"This beautiful palace," Yurek hastened to explain, "until Warsaw's capitulation, had been a residence of Mayor Starzynski,[1] who so heroically led the defense of our capital in September 1939."

"And now it is back in the rightful hands!" Yanush concluded joyfully.

On August 3, the second full day of the Uprising, Yanush enlisted in the Home Army (AK) headquarters on the Long Street and chose the pseudonym *Bogdan.* He was assigned to the NSZ (National Armed Forces)–AK Support Armored Brigade. By then, the whole north side of the Theater Square—the Blank Palace, the ruins of Town Hall, bombed during the 1939 siege of Warsaw, and the adjacent St. Andrew church, known as *Kanoniczki*—were all in the hands of soldiers of the Home Army.

Since from the beginning of the Uprising, the Germans had been firmly established in the ruins of the Grand Theater on the opposite side. Theater Square became one of the hot fighting grounds in Old Town.

Facing Theater Square, Blank Palace (Senatorska 12) was separated from our Senatorska 8 by only a narrow street and corner building (Senatorska 10). Yanush would drop by sometimes with the news.

"Our boys are positioned in the windows of the Palace and the ruins of Town Hall, trigger fingers tensed, ready to shoot any German who shows himself out of the ruins of Grand Theater. In the meantime, the German sharpshooters are keeping our side of the Square under constant fire. They have plenty of ammunition."

Soon, there was far more to it than an exchange of shooting. On September 4—I recall that day clearly—the German grenadiers, under cover of tanks, attacked the Upriser positions[2] with rounds of machine gun fire. Yanush assured me later that the fighting spirit in our ranks was wonderful, and the Germans were forced to retreat. Yet there was no doubt that they would continue the attacks.

∽o∾

For me, August 4, 1944, is a day of my first experience with devastating German air raids. I was on the way to take a blanket and a pillow to the Capuchin church. Its spacious basement was filled with homeless civilians, many of them escapees from the neighboring district of Vola that had been under ferocious German attack. I was halfway down the stairs when I heard the roaring sound of approaching planes and at the same time a shout, "Down to the shelters!" coming from the courtyard.

I had barely made it to the basement when a bloodcurdling *whizzz* pierced my ears and the whole structure of the building shook to its foundation. We all panicked and huddled together in fear. Everyone of us realized that if the building would take a direct hit, we would be buried under the rubble.

"Are you already downhearted?" The sound of the firm male voice had a somewhat calming effect. Somebody started to pray aloud. The roaring of the dive-bombers continued, and we couldn't be certain if they would target our building again.

"Oh God Almighty, deliver us from peril," I sighed. "Make the bombers go somewhere else." The last words came from an instinctive impulse of self-preservation, but oh, how vain and embarrassing can be our fears in the moments of mortal danger.

It was during that bombing raid that I had realized with extreme clarity what a stupendous advantage the Germans had and how vulnerable the Varsovians have been. The Luftwaffe dive-bombers held complete control of the skies. Our Polish pilots, who had so bravely and successfully defended London during the Battle of Britain, were too far away to come to the rescue of their own capital.

Strange thoughts besieged me. For a while, I could no longer believe that there were still places in the world where the days were peaceful and quiet, where people led normal lives, woke up rested, ate breakfast, went to school or work— my daydreaming was cut short by the arrival of a small group of civilians. When they came closer, I was shocked to see their soot-covered faces, their eyes swollen from smoke. They were choking from inhaled dust. "Water…please… some water!"

With a bottle of water in my hand, I sprang to my feet. Suddenly, unexpectedly, I saw Yanush. He had obviously brought this group of bombing survivors to our shelter. What a blessing it was to see him.

"How do you feel?" he asked thoughtfully.

"Oh, I'm all right."

"Thank God, you're all unharmed. The bomb went through the top of the fourth floor of our apartment building and probably detonated in the ruins farther away."

He lowered his voice to a whisper. "There were direct hits…the house adjacent to the prison on Danilowiczowska

Street is all in flames. Our boys are trying to rescue anybody who is still alive."

Then Yanush stretched out his hand with half a loaf of bread in it. The bread, like a magnet, attracted the eyes of people nearby. With my brother's knife, I cut it into slices and passed them around, with the first one going to him.

"I'm all right for now," he said. "Let's get out of here. I prefer to be on the surface where the action is." Yanush was right. There was no safe place anywhere. On our way upstairs, I learned that the bread he brought me was his first insurgent ration. We found our apartment in a sorry state. The walls were cracked in several places, with the window panes blown in. A large glass jar that had been filled with raspberries and sugar lay smashed on the parquet floor, its sticky contents spread out like fresh blood. But in the kitchen, the pot with the remaining rabbit meat was intact.

"If our action planned on Gdansk Station tomorrow is successful," Yanush told me with his eyes on the pot, "I'll bring one of my buddies for a home-cooked meal. Most of them are totally cut off from their homes and families. Don't tell him that you are serving rabbit meat. Poor Kuba! These days, even the pets are not spared."

When we were going down, I realized what a blessing it was for me to have Yanush as my brother.

The night attack on Gdansk Railway Station, the German stronghold, ended in total defeat. Since several units from Old Town, including Yanush's unit, under the command of Captain *Dragon,* took part in it, the news spread quickly the next morning.

"There have been many casualties." The words stuck in my mind like a blazing torch.

It was already afternoon, and Yanush still hadn't shown up. The thought that he might be wounded made my heart beat alarmingly. *I'd better go to the hospital and check on the wounded there*, I said to myself. Once downstairs, on the spur of the moment, I decided to stop for a prayer before entering the basement and underground passage. On the wall of the entrance hall, someone had hung a framed picture of Our Lady, the Black Madonna with a Child. The residents gathered here imploring God, through her intercession, for protection of their loved ones and themselves.

The shelling outside seemed for a while to quiet down. Unlike Long Street, where Polish flags were posted on the buildings and Home Army soldiers in their camouflage jackets (from captured German warehouse) and black berets perched jauntily on their foreheads mixed freely with civilians, our Senatorska Street was usually empty. The Germans kept both the Grand Theater and Castle Squares under constant assault. I was on my way when I saw Yanush coming with another boy.

"I knew you would be worrying," he said warmly before introducing his pal. Relieved as I was, I didn't miss the insurgent armbands on their sleeves.

Once in our desolate apartment, I was busy reheating the meal, this time on a portable little heater. In the meantime, Yanush tried to explain the fiasco of last night's attack. "You see, it was a desperate attempt to restore a vital connection between the Jolibord and Old Town fighters."

Karol, a blond sympathetic youth, obviously older than my brother, expressed his opinion. "Gdansk Station is heavily fortified. The continuous cannon fire overcame our courage and determination."

Yanush's eyes darkened with emotion. Feeling my supportive hand on his shoulder, he declared resolutely, "Nonetheless, we will not stop fighting Germans…ah, I almost forgot to tell you that our boys stormed and took *Gesiowka*, the prison on Goose Street. And imagine, they did it with a tank previously captured from the Germans! What a surprise it was—I have been told—for the prisoners, all Jews held there by the Germans as slave labor. Most of them joined our ranks."

"You are a messenger of hope," I smiled.

The meal was served and obviously enjoyed. Karol turned toward me, his face radiant with a smile. He was telling me that last night, a long expected help finally came—a successful parachute drop of much-needed anti-tank weapons and ammunition. "Our Western Allies evidently did not totally forget us," he concluded with a sigh of relief.

The youthful optimism overcame the gloom of defeat. It was time to part.

Yanush stood up. "All we need now is a few hours' sleep." Fatigue was written all over his face.

"Where are you going to sleep?" I asked.

"Wherever there happens to be a place. Somewhere on the pallet or on somebody's couch."

"It was so great to see both of you," I smiled warmly, trying to conceal my concern for them.

"Thank you so much for the meal. The meat was delicious!" Karol assured me, as they were leaving.

30

It was late when I joined a group of residents in the cellar of our house, damaged during the air raid. By now, most of the civilians lived permanently in basements seeking protection against bombing and shelling. All I wanted was a few hours of undisturbed sleep. I just laid my blanket on the floor when I heard approaching steps. I realized how easy it would be for the Germans to come here at night uninvited. My pulse quickened. Fear stricken, I strained my eyes. To my great relief, Yanush emerged from the darkness. He was not alone. In the dim flickering light of a candle, I saw that he was accompanied by two girls I had never met. We moved to the farthest corner of the shelter.

"Eva, Hanka, messengers from Jolibord," Yanush introduced the girls briefly. "They bravely made the long stretch through the German lines and must be exhausted. Take care of them! I'll be back to pick them up shortly after dawn."

"I will go with you tomorrow too," I said to Yanush. "There is nothing more I can do here."

"All right," Yanush agreed approvingly. He gave us a friendly salute and swiftly disappeared.

"How glad I am to meet you," I turned now toward the girls. It startled me how young they were. Slender figures wearing short summer dresses. They could not have been more than fifteen years old. All three of us gathered together speaking in low voices. I offered them what little food I still had.

"You may not know," Eva told me, "that the Germans have just managed to separate Old Town from Jolibord units fighting under the same command."

Hanka stirred up. "They are shooting at anything that moves through the open terrain separating Old Town and Jolibord, making any communication between them increasingly difficult. The Citadel, Institute of Chemistry, and Gdansk station are still in their hands. Yet the worst obstacle," she shrugged her shoulders, "is the armored train, a real monster belching fire."

"For heaven's sake, so how did you manage to get through?" I was staring at them with admiration.

"Mostly by crawling—looking for any bit of rolling terrain, a tree, a clump of bushes."

"Frightened as we were," Eva broke in, "we kept pushing ahead. Yet the Germans caught us. We have been lucky they didn't shoot us on the spot."

"Then how did you get away?" I asked breathlessly.

"I am still surprised myself. After some deliberation, which we didn't understand, they gave each of us a bucket and a hoe and sent us to the potato field ahead to dig some potatoes for them. Once there," Eva continued, "we pretended to dig. But it was getting dark, so without any hesitation, we crawled under the cover of potato plants as fast as we could—toward the blazing houses just ahead."

"The Germans must be hungry there," Hanka mumbled, yawning. "They shot up some parachute flares and a rain of bullets our direction to scare us. Yet we managed to reach the insurgent barricade. The boys let us through."

With their story told, we realized how tired we were, our eyes heavy from lack of sleep. In the dark, we cautiously climbed upstairs to our apartment, hoping to find something that would make a pallet for the girls to sleep on. But anything useful had already been given away to the homeless. The broken glass, blown in from the impact of the bomb, crackled under our feet. The couch in the alcove where I used to sleep seemed irresistibly inviting. We lay down across it fully dressed, curled up next to one another, and immediately fell into a deep slumber.

∽∘∾

An urgent banging on the door! It was very early, and I struggled to open my eyes, but then came another, even more impatient knocking. Before I reached the door, I heard Yanush's alarming cry, "To the basement! Hurry! We'll meet you at the hole. The Germans are on Senatorska!"

I threw open the door but caught only a glimpse of Yanush and Yurek as they hurtled down the stairs. I could feel the strain in Yurek's voice as he called back "Hurry!"

The girls brushed past me, and we went down the stairs, literally flying. My heart was beating wildly, and I was gasping for breath as we reached the ground floor. I caught just a glimpse of Hanka running ahead of me as she disappeared into the gloom of the basement, but at the same time, the door to the outside flew open, and I found myself staring into the barrel of a gun!

He didn't fire. My eyes moved cautiously up from the gun barrel into the hostile face of a German soldier. Seeing that I was no threat to him, his trigger finger relaxed a bit.

"Haende hoch!" (Hands up!)

Oh, how I hated that German command! There were other soldiers behind him. They escorted me into the courtyard at gunpoint. Dreadfully frustrated, I realized that I was in the hands of enemies who were trying to frighten and intimidate me. More and more residents were brought in, among them Inka, whom I hadn't seen for a few days. There was uncertainty and fear on every face.

In the middle of the courtyard stood a plump woman, her neck craned toward the upper stories of the building. She was screaming, "Get out! They are setting fire!"

My attention immediately centered on the soldiers who were smashing the window of a ground level apartment with their machine guns' butts. The others were carrying tins with gasoline, which they poured through the broken window. A flame thrower was tossed, and the blast ignited a fire. Soon, tongues of flame roared inside. We all stood horrified, helpless witnesses of our homes being set ablaze.

The job done, the soldiers rushed us toward the entrance of the front residence. A few elderly men were separated and hurried up the street toward Theater Square. A wave of despair swept through captured residents. All around me, I saw the panic-stricken faces—the fearful eyes. Totally unexpected, some strong hand grasped my arm, and I was dragged out into the empty street. Next came Inka and then a young woman desperately holding the hand of her little boy. The terrified child was ripped from her and pushed back.

"Mommy! Mommy!" His pleading cry was heartbreaking.

The three of us were ordered to hold hands at arm's length, facing in the direction of Castle Square. Behind each of us crouched a soldier. With their machine guns ready, they were scanning the windows and rooftops.

"Vorwarts!" I heard a German order, followed by a hard push. I took a step ahead with utmost difficulty. Out of the corner of my eye, I still caught a glimpse of the rest of the other soldiers proceeding in single file under cover of the buildings lining both sides of the street.

What happened in the following minutes remains in my memory as a blur. All I wanted was to brush off the swarm of buzzing drones, but someone was holding my hand in a tight grip.

Suddenly, the noise stopped, and an eerie silence followed as we entered the entrance hall of a house. Pushed by gun barrels, we were directed into the courtyard that was enclosed with tenement buildings just like ours.

"Get out! They are setting the fire!" the already familiar cry pierced my ears.

But this time, the insurgents were on their positions. In one of the upper windows, I caught a glimpse of a helmet-protected head and the barrel of a gun. Our soldiers were obviously taking positions at the windows overlooking the court. I don't recall any exchange of fire, yet it must have been a reason that the German troop started cautiously withdrawing toward the street, shielded by the previously seized civilians.

I couldn't know then that setting the houses on fire was just a preparation for a planned massive offensive on the Old Town.

The soldiers crowded us at the entrance hall of the house across the street from our front residence. Just before entering the hallway, I caught a glimpse of the number 19, bathed in morning sunshine. Protected from behind by deserted buildings and from the front by the human barricade held at gunpoint, the German soldiers felt secure. Some sat down with their backs against the wall. Some smoked their cigarettes; others refreshed themselves with sips from their canteens. To my surprise, one of them closest to me, pulled out a small folding mirror, set it on the step of the stairway, and began shaving. The words on his belt buckle caught my eye: *Gott Mit Uns*. Since Dad taught me some German, I knew that it meant "God with us." How could those arsonists claim that God was on their side? They were obviously a *Wehrmacht* unit, regular German soldiers, and yet they obediently carried out this hideous order to set our houses ablaze.

All of a sudden, two soldiers approached Inka and me. They were saying something to us in German. We both pretended that we didn't understand.

"Kaffee," they insisted, pointing toward the stairway leading upstairs. They obviously wanted us to make coffee for them. This didn't make much sense to me, but one glance at Inka's tense face warned me that they might have something else in mind. We didn't budge. Noticing my clenched jaw, the German grabbed my shoulder and pushed me toward the stairway. His buddy was following with Inka. We hardly made two steps ahead when an explosion outside shook the stairway wall. The soldiers rushed downstairs to join their comrades, leaving Inka and me behind.

We found ourselves separated from the rest of the hostages, who were now being used as a human barricade. A fight flared up. Obviously, the insurgents intended to drive the enemy unit from Senatorska. Seeing that the Germans, preoccupied with shooting, paid no attention to us, Inka and I—as inconspicuously as possible—returned to the hallway. With my body pressed against the wall, I cautiously started to withdraw into the courtyard. Once there, I managed to hide behind a recess in the wall. A feverish urge to get away, to escape, overwhelmed me.

Only the width of the street separated me from our house and from Yanush and Yurek. But the street was under cross fire, and any attempt to reach the other side would be suicidal. The only possible way out would be through the underground passages that would take me further down the street, away from the battle. I turned and only then, deeply shocked, I saw several stories high buildings ahead of me ablaze with a raging fire. The flames flared up toward the gloriously blue sky. I was trapped.

A profound feeling of helplessness swept over me. In desperation, I clenched my fists and shoved them into the pockets of my jacket in an instinctive gesture of defiance. In that instant, my fingers slipped over the soft leather cover of a little book that I had carried in my pocket since the beginning of the Rising. It was Thomas a'Kempis' *Imitation of Christ*, given to me just months ago by Father Timothy. I opened it at random, as I often did in moments of indecision. Oblivious to the shooting and burning houses ahead of me, I read:

> *At that time you should not be disheartened, nor give up to despair; but with a clear mind submit to God's will and endure all that will come with humility. For the*

night is followed by day; after the winter, summer comes;
and after the storm, beautiful weather.

Faith revived my sagging spirits and renewed my strength. I wanted to live. I had hardly taken my eyes from that page when a woman, rushing past me, brushed my arm. She was part of a small group led by a man in his early thirties, his face twisted in fear. Just behind him was Inka and another man and woman. They were obviously trying to escape. Without hesitation, I joined them. We stopped at the wall of the house that was still untouched by the fire. Our leader grabbed a windowsill, pulled himself up, broke the window, and forced it open. He crawled through and, reaching back, pulled each one of us inside.

We rushed through the rooms. I had no idea where we were going. It was one of the most surreal moments of my life. Evidently, we were in a beauty parlor. There were large mirrors on the walls, and as we ran past them, I caught the reflection of frightened figures. Who was that girl with the flushed anxious face and fear-stricken eyes? I was damn sure that couldn't be me. Wasn't it just minutes ago I had been sustained with faith and hope? We reached a door leading outside, passed through it, and stopped, stupefied. We were on the enemy side of Theater Square facing the ruin of the Grand Theater! I knew only too well that this was a German stronghold dubbed the "hornet's nest" by the insurgents.

Looking for any protection, we slipped into the niche of a nearby entrance gate. I leaned against it and only then noticed a strongly built, middle-aged man with both his legs blown off. In a heart-wrenching voice, he was pleading and crying out, "In the name of Jesus Christ and his Holy Mother, help me!"

We had no stretcher to carry him and no time. Our eyes were fixed on a tank heading straight toward us from the Willow Street. At any moment, its machine gun would burst with bullets, mowing us down like so many stalks of wheat. Overwhelmed with an agonizing fear, we tore across the totally empty street and disappeared behind a still standing eastern wall of the theater.

Further down the street was lined with a row of apartment buildings. To our dismay, all the entrance gates were closed and locked. We passed the first two and stopped at the third and began pounding with our clenched fists and screaming in desperation until a frail, frightened old woman opened it just enough that we were able to shove our way through. She kept yelling, "No! Get away! You cannot be here!" But her cries were ignored; someone pushed her out of our way and slammed the gate behind us.

The house seemed totally deserted. We found the entrance to the basement and, through a hole that had been knocked in the wall, entered an unknown subterranean labyrinth. The unanswered plea of the legless man left behind pursued me in the darkness.

31

We were moving ahead in single file in total darkness. From time to time, one of our companions briefly scanned the walls with a little flashlight looking in vain for an arrow or name of the street indicating the direction. Proceeding in silence, we suddenly heard the sound of still distant footsteps. We stopped, uncertain what to do. As it turned out, it was another small group of escapees.

"The Germans are screening the underground passages," they warned us in nervous whispers.

There were too many of us, so we separated. Inka and I were now on our own. After some time, we came to a hole in the wall. We crawled through it and found ourselves at the foot of a stairway leading out of the basement. We started to go upstairs, one step at a time. The door leading outside was bolted. As noiselessly as possible, we lifted the bolt and opened the door just a bit. Dazzled by a stream of bright, blinding light, we stood motionless for a while. As my eyes adjusted to light, I was not sure if I was hallucinating. All of a sudden, we found ourselves in a different world. We stumbled out into the small courtyard of a one-story white house. It was bathed in the luminous light of a beautiful August day. After the traumatic experiences of the long morning, it seemed an oasis of peace.

Nonetheless, the whole place was teeming with life. Bright-colored birds, distracted by our sudden appearance, were hovering overhead, flapping their wings. After a while, they settled down, perching on the edges of the roof. I sat down with my back against the wall and looked spellbound into the watchful round eyes of a flock of parakeets.

"Where did they all come from?" I asked, turning to Inka.

She pointed to a sign on the door that I hadn't noticed before. Dealer in Exotic Birds, I read. The owner had obviously released the birds from their cages, hoping that they might somehow survive on their own.

"It's awfully hot here," Inka said, unbuttoning the jacket of her elegant wool suit.

One glance at her face, wet with sweat, made me realize how thirsty I was. We tried to get into the house, hoping to find something to drink, but the door was locked and bolted, and the windows were secured with shutters. The peacefulness of the place had been only an illusion.

Still hopeful of finding a way to safety, we descended the stairs, and the pitch-dark subterranean labyrinth swallowed us again.

It wasn't long before we were blinded by a powerful beam of light and struck dumb by the German command: Halt! Haende hoch! With some other seized escapees, we were led by the German patrol out of the basement.

When we emerged into a street, I staggered hearing the dreadful rumbling of a tank and the continuous rattling of the machine guns. In no time, we entered the vast hall of the Grand Theater, bombed during the air raids in September 1939. The place was seething with activity. The soldiers led us toward a large group of captured civilians further down from the entrance.

Looking uneasily ahead of me, I saw German units getting ready to leave. One was just coming back from combat. To my dismay, I recognized that they were the soldiers who not long ago set our homes ablaze and used Inka and me as human shields against insurgent snipers.

Their commander must have recognized us because he stopped his men and walked straight toward me. I had no doubt he would shoot me for escaping. But to my embarrassment, he gave me a reassuring hug and whispered some words of encouragement in German. Before I had a chance to react, he reached into his pocket, drew out something, pressed it into my hand, and hurriedly returned to his men. For some time, I stood still, feeling stigmatized by the kindness of a German soldier. When I opened my hand, I was surprised to see three hard candies wrapped in colorful paper.

Minutes later, the armed guards appeared and rushed our group through the back door to a gigantic bomb crater. Deep down, scattered all through the rubble were dead bodies of civilians and two of the German soldiers. A long board spanned the chasm and led to the blown-out window of a still-standing wall. The whole scene was traumatic, bloodcurdling. Why had they brought us here? We held our breath. The answer came soon enough.

We were ordered to run across that board, one by one. Since its far end had been positioned slightly higher, it was an uphill climb. My shoulders shook with fear. I didn't want to die. I wanted to live. "Hold on!" Milek's words came back in a flash. I had to brave this dreadful challenge.

When my turn came, I stepped out on the board and ran quickly, determined not to look down but to keep my eyes focused on the window. I knew that one misstep, and I would end up in that ghastly crater below. I had almost reached the end of the board when I barely missed slipping on a patch of someone's fresh blood. I righted myself and got to the window opening.

I pulled myself through the window into an intact part of the Grand Theater. There were about ten of us, all women, who had made the break-neck dash across the board, when the guard came and drove us through a guarded door into a large room.

The first thing that caught my attention was a big window overlooking the Theater Square. I knew that the opposite north side of the Square was in the hands of the insurgents, bravely defended against the Germans' continuous attacks. Maybe Yanush and Yurek were there at this moment, wondering if I were still alive. On the thought of Yanush, my heart quickened. Oh my god, would we ever see each other again?

As soon as I took my eyes from the window, I realized that the room was divided by a long, wooden counter. While one side was packed to capacity with the captured civilians, in the middle of the other side, sitting comfortably in an armchair, was a young German officer. One of his legs was stretched out, resting on a stool. I couldn't miss the special elegance of his black knee-high boots. The chair was positioned sideways, and from his excellent vantage point, he was looking over the Theater Square, totally ignoring the presence of the frightened people whose fate depended on his whim. There was an instant air of command about him. Two underlings scurried around carrying out his orders. He spoke briefly in a calm voice with complete detachment, holding a cigarette nonchalantly in his well-groomed hand.

What would be his verdict? The trauma we had already been through didn't bode well.

The order was given. A group of women, including Inka and me, was shoved into the theater's basement. A heavy door was slammed behind us, and we found ourselves imprisoned in a vast, murky space. There wasn't a soul in it except for three women hovering over a burning candle. To my feverish imagination, they appeared as three *Parcae*, the Roman deities endowed with the power over human fate to cut, at their whim, the thread of any person's life. Yet when we came closer, I saw three old women, doomed like us to imprisonment.

Since we were newly arrived, they assumed we came from freedom and had a better understanding about the situation outside. Inka tried wholeheartedly to encourage them. "You shouldn't worry so much, she whispered very calmly. "If we want to survive, we have to keep our wits intact."

"We do not worry so much about ourselves but for those who had been taken out from here more than one hour ago," the lady in a black elegant coat murmured, discreetly wiping her tears with a finely embroidered handkerchief.

Looking around, only now I saw the things scattered over the straw-covered floor. They had obviously been left in a hurry: a small suitcase, a leather jacket, a little further down a large doll with a porcelain-like face framed by curly blond locks.

"Where have they been taken?" I asked deeply disturbed.

"To carry the wounded and dead, or so we were told."

"Along with the children?" I felt my heart would burst at any moment.

She nodded.

It was a while before Inka's words had reached me, as if coming from a long distance.

"I'm exhausted. Let's find some place to sit down."

We proceeded in semidarkness, slim shafts of light occasionally coming from little bulbs sparingly attached to haphazardly arranged wiring. We found a nook far from the entrance, piled up some straw, and sat on the hard floor, our backs leaned against the cool wall.

Silence was crying.

Lost in my thoughts, I was suddenly alerted by the sound of approaching steps. Inka, who I believed was dozing, heard them too. Moments later, a beam of light proceeded the figure of a soldier appearing from the darkness. I shuddered, recognizing the blond German who had so embarrassed me with his friendliness in the entrance hall.

He said a few words in German. His voice was gentle. Unexpectedly, he offered me a half loaf of bread, just as Yanush had done a few days ago. I glared at him. Hungry as I was, I wouldn't take it. He must have realized that I was resenting his uniform. He left the bread on the straw, turned on his heel, and walked away. To my astonishment, he soon returned, escorting the three old ladies Inka and I had met earlier. Then he put a jar of marmalade beside the still untouched bread and encouraged me to eat. I glared at him. Realizing that I had nothing to cut the bread with, he handed me his knife.

"Essen!" (Eat!), he said, but still I stubbornly refused. He drew his pistol, pointed it at me to show he meant it, and ordered, "Essen!"

The situation became tense.

"Take it!" Inka said. "He's trying to help you." The other women nodded approvingly.

So I took the bread, sliced it into thick chunks, spread them generously with marmalade, and passed them around, keeping the last one for myself. As soon as I returned his knife, he left.

Someone lit a candle, and we were huddled around it, eating hungrily. The lady in the black coat studied my hair and eyes and said, "You must remind him of someone back home."

∽◦∾

Time was dragging on unbearable slowly. I sat close to Inka without a word, burying our misfortune and hurt deeply inside me. The past days had taught us that some of our experiences were too intensely felt, too personal to be expressed in words and shared. The silence did not seem to separate us, but on the contrary, brought us closer together.

Some time passed before the appearance of yet another German soldier. He must have been in his fifties, a droop-shouldered little fellow. With his flashlight, he screened faces of all of us, one by one. I held my breath and wished to be invisible, but his light centered on me.

"Komm mit mir!" (Come with me!) He jerked me up toward him. At that moment, Inka sprang to her feet, grabbed my free arm, and pulled me back.

"Hier!" she shouted in German with a sharp and commanding voice. The soldier blinked and let go of my arm. He turned around and staggered away. There was no doubt that he was drunk. After he was gone, my companions decided that I was drawing too much attention and that I needed a disguise. The stately-looking woman took off her black coat and put it over me. Inka stuffed my blond hair under a black beret.

In the meantime, by the late afternoon, the basement was teeming with captured civilians. The tension mounted. And then, all of a sudden, an announcement has been made in Polish through the loudspeaker:

"The persons born outside of Poland and mothers with children twelve years old or younger should report immediately with their identification papers ready to present!"

"That's a message for you!" Inka said. She knew that according to my *kennkarte* (official ID), I was born in Hohensalza, *Deutsche* Reich.

"Take off the coat and beret and go!"

"I have no intention," I said firmly. "I was born in Inovrotslaw, not in Hohensalza (Inovrotslaw was incorporated into Germany in October 1939), in Poland, not in Germany. I've always resisted this lie printed on my *kennkarte* card. I will stay here, for better or for worse."

"Listen!" Inka insisted. "We have lost so many young people. Every life saved is precious. We need you to survive, to help build a new Poland when this war is over."

Under pressure from all my companions, I finally agreed on the condition that Inka would come along as my sister, even though I didn't have any idea how this could work.

Hoping against hope, we headed for the checkpoint.

Then something so unexpected happened that I blinked my eyes in disbelief. Checking the identification papers was no one else but the blond soldier who had offered us bread! He was genuinely happy to see me.

"Where have you been?" he asked in a friendly voice. "I looked everywhere for you."

I handed him my *kennkarte*, ignoring his question.

"Meine schwester," (my sister) I spoke in German, pointing to Inka. I indicated as well as I could that we want to go together. He looked at Inka's identification card and drew in a short breath. I knew why: Inka was a native Varsovian.

"Hide this under the lining of your purse," he said in German, returning her card. "Don't let anyone see it." We understood and appreciated his sound advice.

Yet I became truly alarmed when, pointing to me, Inka, and himself, he said something like, "We are friends. You stay here, in my quarters, under my protection."

I panicked. Time was running out. I saw the last person of the departing group disappearing out of the main entrance, and I was exasperated.

With tearful eyes, I pointed to his heart. "Golden herz," (Golden heart) I murmured. He understood and let us go. Inka and I rushed to the exit.

At the entrance stood a burly German policeman. Obviously irritated by our late arrival, his shot a piercing glance at us. His small eyes were deeply set in a fat face dominated by a bulldog-like lower jaw.

"Kennkarte!" he barked.

At that moment, a voice could be heard coming from the upstairs. "Let them go, Heinrich. I've already cleared them."

Oh yes, I understood the saving words spoken in German. Looking back, I caught only a glimpse of blond hair. Reluctantly, the policeman let us go. Rushing to join the departing group, I had a last look at the Theater Square enveloped in smoke and flame.

32

Inka and I were walking down Willow Street at a cautious pace, attempting to catch up with a small group of released persons some distance ahead of us. It was extremely dangerous for civilians to be out here, so we kept close to the walls of the still-unharmed buildings. Up ahead, I could see the colonnade of the palace. I was just approaching the column when a bullet whizzed over and struck it, missing my head by a hair's breadth. I instinctively glanced over my shoulder, afraid that another bullet might be headed my way. Off in the distance, I could see the German soldiers laughing.

We had hardly joined our group when three uniformed Germans emerged from the Saxon Gardens. They walked briskly across the empty square and headed toward us. By that time, a woman standing beside me became greatly excited, babbling over and over again, "Polskie wojsko, polskie wojsko!" (Polish soldiers!) I immediately understood that some painful experience she had gone through had unhinged her mind. I can still see her slender figure, her silk blouse, and her lovely cameo brooch. With a euphoric expression on her face, she rushed straight toward the trio.

Seeing her approaching, one of the SS men pulled out his pistol and, with cold indifference, shot her in the head. Without missing a step, all three of them fell on us like rapacious vultures.

They ordered us to hold our hands high, then rushed us at gunpoint through the Saxon Gardens, a beautiful park once enjoyed by the Varsovians. After having been held for hours in the dark basement of the Grand Theatre, I was dazzled by the green foliage of the stately trees, but I didn't have time to enjoy it. Behind their trunks and under the cover of bushes were posted soldiers totally preoccupied with shooting. The whole park was obviously overrun with German troops. The rattling of machine guns was deafening.

We ran under the crossfire with hands continuously raised up, passing the decapitated statue. *How soon would we, too, be shattered to pieces?* I thought in a moment of despair. I took a last glance at the trees before we entered a large square filled with civilian population.

"Iron Gate Square," Inka said in a muffled voice.

The square was a scene of great confusion. One small group was quickly merged into the last row of frightened people. The SS men[1] paced like madmen between the rows. Their eyes flashing with malice, they were pulling out "desirable" victims and dragging them away with savage delight.

However, the worst was yet to come. Unexpectedly, tanks began creeping from the side streets. A shock wave of fear ran through the crowd. My heart quickened. This was a frightful moment, the final blow! We were painfully aware of what was about to happen. The SS men were going to tie us to the hulks of the tanks or make us run in front or behind them when attacking the insurgents' positions.

Desperation was evident in everyone's eyes. But then something unbelievable happened. Moving as one, all of us fell to our knees, and eyes raised toward the vast sky with total abandon, we joined together in supplication:

> *We fly to thy patronage*
> *O Holy Mother of God,*
> *Despise not our petition*
> *In our necessity,*
> *But from all danger*
> *Deliver us always*
> *O glorious and blessed Virgin…*

We knew this antiphon[2] by heart, and like our forefathers, we implored the Holy Mother for her intercession on our behalf:

> *With your Son you reconcile us*
> *To your Son commend us….*

In that very moment, I had a vision of the presence of the crucified Christ.

Oh Lord! my mind was taken up with a single thought. *How could I ever offend you? You, who are redeeming love and charity.* It was the most profound expiation I had ever experienced in my whole existence. Still kneeling, I noticed that an old man of patriarchal appearance just next to me was beating his breast with his fist in an apparent gesture of repentance. Strengthened by faith, I stood. Since most of the people in front of me were still on their knees, I could see, at the opposite end of the square, standing against the wall of a tall building, several rows of men, their hands tied together. My whole soul revolted.

The suddenness of our communal prayer dumbfounded the SS men, but not for long. Aroused by hatred and sure of their power, they began running wildly, rounding up groups of people, and driving them toward the tanks.

In the turmoil, Inka and I found ourselves in a disordered column being hurried out of the square.

∽∘∾

Escorted by *Wermacht* guards, we were passing streets totally deserted, the buildings lying in ruins. On a heap of rubble, I noticed a knocked-down post with the still readable street name: Ulica Graniczna (Boundary Street). For some time, the distant shooting still followed us.

Somewhere on our way, we passed a barricade blocking the entrance to a side street. As we drew closer, I could see the insurgents, three or four of them, manning it with their weapons alertly ready. The German guards seemed as watchful as the insurgents were, but no one fired. The body of a handsome youngster lay draped over the barricade. His face was ghostly white. Overwhelmed by tremendous sorrow, I raised my hand in a salute.

Thinking back, I recall the scene so painful to me. We were approaching the still standing church. Our escorted column was suddenly swallowed by a crowd of frightened people. They were coming from a church courtyard. I can still hear the continuing sound of machine gun fire dominating that of women wailing. SS men scurried hither and yon like animals gone berserk. One barreled toward me, his face contorted with hatred. Terror shuddered through me. Then

I realized his eyes were centered not on me, but on a young priest who in the elbow-to-elbow crowd happened to stand next to me. The priest, dressed in cassock and collar, had tried to conceal his fear. In a gesture of support, I reached for his hand. The SS man grabbed the priest by the collar and was pulling him roughly from the crowd. My first impulse was to go with him to whatever his fate. I must have made just a step ahead when I felt Inka grasp my belt. She held me tightly. It was obvious that the young priest would be put against a wall and shot.

The sound of machine gun fire followed our column as we were passing through the long lane of burly men in SS uniforms. They were closely screening the passersby for anyone undesirable. Bloodthirsty villains! We had to keep our hands up. Exhausted, I let my hands drop. Immediately, an SS man seized me by the arm and pulled me to the side. I shivered with fear. Luckily for me, his attention was on the narrow gold band that had slipped to my wrist when I lowered my arm. He pointed to it. Quickly, I slipped it off and handed it to him. To my great relief, he let me go. I reconnected with Inka who grinned her relief. How fortunate that I could slip the bracelet off. I had heard about hands or fingers being cut off to get a ring or bracelet.

At some point, we had been handed back over to the *Wehrmacht* guards. Under their watch, we walked through a street strewn, as from a horn of plenty, with layers of bundled GG banknotes. They must have been rescued from a burning bank. I recognized the *gorale* (mountaineers) on the 500 zloty bills. No one ducked down and picked up a bundle.

What followed next was a passage through hell. On both sides of the street, whole rows of buildings, several stories high, stood ablaze. Dark clouds of smoke from gutted houses rose high over our heads. This smoke made breathing difficult. The heat was intense. Choking, I tried to cover my hair with my hands to protect it against flying sparks.

There I was on the eighth day of the Uprising being escorted through the heart of Vola district. I felt like I was inside a nightmare. The skeletons of buildings pointed to vacant sky. Everywhere I looked, I saw Vola's ruination and marks of committed crime.[3] My reflections are so horrifying that I am reluctant to bring them back. And yet, I still have before my eyes the slim lifeless body of a young woman hanging over the upper story windowsill. Her beautiful long blond hair is streaming down in a heart-rending cascade.

As we trudged ahead leaving the scenes of the massacre, I became aware that the blasts of gunfire were gradually growing more distant. We were all at the point of exhaustion, putting what little strength we still had into forcing one foot in front of the other. We were now in some outer city district with sparsely scattered small houses bordered by patches of gardens or fields.

The residents of those houses must have seen our bedraggled column, for they came out with containers of fresh water. Not enough dippers were provided, but that did not matter. As terribly thirsty as we were, I plunged cupped hands into the water and eagerly drank from them. It was the best water I've ever tasted.

An aproned woman wearing a kerchief passed chunks of bread to a few people before she ran out. I was close enough to hear her say, "We share what we have."

The guards led us to a railroad siding. Night was falling, and we still waited. In the distance, I saw black smoke, pierced with tongues of fire. I suddenly realized that Warsaw had been cut off from the outside world. I thought of Yanush. "Do not weep for me if I am killed," he'd said. "We have something to fight and die for." Tears stung my eyes.

The short train drew nearer and stopped. The guards packed us into the cars. I was one of the last to be jammed in, crammed against the door. The train began to move. We all were exhausted. The pressure of so many bodies made breathing difficult.

As in a bad dream, I heard someone say, "At some point, they are going to stop the train and blow it up with us locked inside!"

"Why should they destroy the train?" another voice argued. "Don't we know their evil plot? They'll take us to the forest and shoot us."

I couldn't stand listening to those disembodied voices. I pushed hard to lift my hands and cover my ears. My hand found the medallion I wore under my blouse. It was a miniature of a silver breastplate with an engraved image of Holy Mary, worn for centuries by the Polish hussars. Bogdan had given me the medallion on my last nameday.

"O, Mother of God," I muttered. I thought I was going to faint. What I wanted was to get a breath of fresh air.

Suddenly, the train lurched to a stop. I was shoved hard against the door. My hand caught on something cool and metallic. It took a moment to realize I was touching the door handle. I managed to pull it and was astonished when the door opened just a crack, but wide enough to wriggle through! I jumped down into the night and took a deep breath. Fresh air at last! As my eyes adjusted, I spotted a wire-netting fencing along the rails. With my body pressed against it, I saw some shadowy figures jumping from the train.

At the same time, I heard frantic whispers from inside the train, saying, "Come back! They will shoot us all!"

I didn't budge. Neither did my shadowy companions. I could see two soldiers holding on to the train. They were looking ahead, not down. They must have been concerned about the unexpected stop. Did they suspect a partisan ambush? I was astonished when as suddenly as it stopped, the train began to move. One soldier passed so close to me that it seemed I could have reached out and touched him. I held my breath. In no time, the train picked up speed and disappeared down the tracks, its rear lights rapidly growing dim.

33

For a few moments, we stood speechless and motionless, still not believing that the train was gone, leaving us behind. It didn't take long before I was hugging Inka and repeating with elation, "We're free! We're free!"

There were four of us. In the dim light coming from distant railroad lamps, I saw two women still pressed against the wire fence. One of them stepped forward and, pointing to her companion, murmured, "My daughter, Teresa." I was confused at first by Teresa's grey hair and only when she came close, I realized she was not much older than me.

"We're very exposed here." Inka voiced the concern of us all. "The railroad must be heavily guarded. We have to find a shelter for the night."

Straining our eyes, we saw at a fair distance ahead the outline of a row of small houses. There was no light in any of them. Yet we hoped that if we could manage to brave the open area separating us from them without being noticed, we might count on help from our fellow countrymen.

Fortunately, as far as we could see, there wasn't a single soul anywhere around. Encouraged, we crossed the railway tracks and in total silence walked toward the houses.

I was leading the way. All of a sudden, I stopped abruptly, alarmed by a flicker of light reflected from a metal object. Could it be the helmet of a German soldier patrolling the railroad?

For a long while, all four of us stood as though chiseled in stone, fully aware of what easy targets we were. But nothing happened. Moving ahead with extreme caution, I realized that the object that had scared me was a metal waste paper basket attached to a pole. As we were getting closer to the row of houses, we saw light coming from a window of a small one-story house standing off alone. Unaware of the obligatory blackout, we turned toward it, hopeful that our rescue was at hand.

I left my companions concealed in darkness at the side of the house and cautiously made my way to the door. I raised my hand and was about to knock when the figure of a man appeared on the other side of the window. I froze. Through the filmy gauze curtains, I saw the profile of a relaxed German officer in full uniform. In his extended hand, he held a glass of red wine, gazing at it approvingly. Terrified, I backed away from the door and disappeared into the darkness of the night. I rejoined my companions and briefly explained what a narrow escape we'd had. The light in the house had attracted us like moths drawn to a flame. We crept away in a hurry, frequently looking nervously over our shoulders to see if any German guards were in pursuit.

Once we reached the road, we passed the first two small houses and stopped at the third. It stood in a little fenced garden. In the darkness, a gate loomed up before me.

Unfortunately, it was locked. Without thinking, I climbed over the high fence. Thank God that growing up with my brothers and cousins had prepared me for the challenge.

Inka and Teresa could probably have climbed over the fence too, but Teresa's mother, heavy as she was, even with our help, gave up. So I left them on the other side of the fence and went straight to the door. I strained my ear and listened. Quiet. Then I knocked.

No answer.

I knocked louder, but the only sound I heard was my pounding heart.

Still I didn't give up. I knocked once more, and in as loud a voice as I thought prudent, I cried, "For heaven's sake, open the door!" No answer.

My nerves were now strained to the limit. At last, at last, the door was opened just a crack, and I saw a short middle-aged man holding a candle.

"Who are you? What do you want?"

"Please! Only shelter for the night."

"Are you from Warsaw?"

"Yes. Please. Let me come in."

"I cannot! Don't you know what they will do if they find you here? They will shoot me and my whole family or put the house on fire with us inside."

"I beg you! Just for tonight. Tomorrow morning, I swear, we will be gone." There was a pause, and then the man opened the door intending to motion me inside.

"There are four of us, all women," I said. "The gate is locked so they are waiting on the other side of the fence."

He frowned, obviously trying to decide what might be the greater danger, having us in his house or leaving us outside, violating the curfew, and inevitably attracting attention of the guards. He hesitated for a moment, went back inside, and promptly returned with a key. In the darkness, he reached the gate, unlocked it, and quickly let the women in.

Once inside, I was astonished to find that there were other refugees in the house, a couple of them sleeping on the floor of the small entrance hall. I don't know where our host put my companions. He directed me to the kitchen where a woman handed me two sheets. Without undressing, I stretched out on a narrow couch and immediately sank into a deep sleep.

∽o∾

I was awakened to the sound of a crowing rooster and the cackle of the hens. I didn't open my eyes, sure that I must have been dreaming. But the crowing sounded again. I strained my ears in disbelief. The soothing tranquility that followed was even more astonishing. After days of shooting, shelling, and explosions, I felt I must be at the gates of heaven.

This blissful sensation was short-lived as I became aware of a multitude of itching bites from the fleas that had shared my bed overnight. I jumped off the couch and rushed straight to the window. A rustic country garden was bathed in sunlight. With a deep sigh of relief, I took in the beauty of that glorious summer morning. It was so calm and peaceful that everything I had recently gone through seemed unreal. My whole heart rose up in thanksgiving.

Just then, Inka came into the kitchen. "Good morning!" she said cheerfully.

"Good morning! I can't remember when I've slept so soundly!" I replied.

Our hostess must have been on her feet for some time since she was apparently the one who opened the kitchen shutters. In no time, two mugs of steaming hot coffee with milk were put on the table, and by each one, a thick chunk of country bread with cottage cheese. Before we gobbled up this feast, Inka and I managed to wash our faces and hands in a large wash bowl filled with cold, refreshing water. But the promise had to be kept. It was time to say good-bye to our benefactors.

"Whatever your destination, you have to first get to Prushkov," our hostess instructed us. "The station is just a short walking distance."

"Be very cautious," her husband warned us. "You were extremely lucky getting out from the train unnoticed. The Germans are shooting escapees on the spot. They are on full alert, trying ruthlessly to prevent the spreading of the Warsaw rebellion."

So we set out for the station, seeking the cover of the fences and houses. When we reached the station, we found that our train had just arrived, but having no money to purchase tickets, we crammed our way into a car as free riders. I was following Inka as she elbowed her way through the crowd when suddenly, all heads turned the same direction. To my horror, I saw an army truck loaded with a detachment of uniformed Germans stopping abruptly at the station.

We must have looked somehow different since a man standing beside us asked, "Are you ladies from Warsaw?"

"Yes," Inka confessed, frightened.

Words passed from mouth to mouth, until they reached the conductor, and instantly, the train pulled out. We were told it left three minutes ahead of its scheduled departure. I saw the SS policemen rushing to the platform and had a glimpse of a train just arriving from the opposite direction. Once again, we had been fortunate to slip out of the Nazi's clutches. Even so, I grieved that some of the passengers on the arriving train might not be so lucky.

We got off the train in Prushkov safely but not sure what to do next. Inka was positive that there was no direct train from Prushkov to Glovno. A gentleman just passing by noticed our confusion. He approached us and asked courteously, "May I be of any help?"

We recognized him at once as the man who had notified the train's conductor about the Varsovians on board.

"Oh, yes," Inka's worried face brightened. "We have been trying to figure out how to get to Glovno."

"Don't worry," he said reassuringly. "We'll find out what is the best way to get you there."

We followed him until he stopped in front of a couple of railway workers smoking cigarettes. He apparently knew them well. After a short conversation, they came up with a plan.

"Be here at three o'clock," one of the rail workers told us. "We will take you on the freight train as far as Skiernievitse. Don't worry. We've been through this before. From Skiernievitse, you will have to make a connection to Lovich, and from Lovich, take a train to Glovno."

We had a few hours to hang around the town, but my only memory of it is the busy marketplace with booths loaded with fresh vegetables, flowers, and above all, tempting-looking fruit. Passing and re-passing us were women offering single items for sale: here, a damask table cloth, or there, a beautiful nightgown. Neither Inka nor I had money to buy even an apple.

At three o'clock, we were at the appointed place behind the station, trying to be as inconspicuous as possible. The railway men led us to a flat car loaded with lumber. A small cave was arranged just large enough for Inka and me to lie down. Once we were snuggled inside, they covered the load with a tarp. It was not long before we felt a gentle bump as the train headed out of the yard.

All the way to Skiernievitse, we were squeezed like sardines in a can but didn't complain, knowing that we were in trusted hands. And the ride was free! The train stopped briefly before entering Skiernievitse station just long enough for us to be helped out of our hiding place, exactly as planned. In no time, it was moving down the track and out of sight. Only then, dumbfounded, we could see in the distance that the station building was guarded by German soldiers. Obviously, our benefactors had not been aware of that. Anxiety reared its ugly head once again.

We pressed our bodies against the pillars supporting an overpass, hiding behind them. There was no one on the platform except the two of us, but for how long? Crossing the railroad tracks would surely catch the attention of the guards. We were trapped! My head was spinning as we stood there totally helpless. Minutes dragged on interminably. All of a sudden, we heard steps and saw two women and a man entering the platform.

Aware of our presence, one of the women moved straight toward us. With a sigh of relief, I saw an armband on her sleeve with the familiar letters RGO. They stood for the Polish Welfare Organization, approved by the German authorities.

"You need help," she said gently, seeing our frightened faces.

"Yes," I nodded, "we are from Warsaw. We had been smuggled here in the freight train."

She explained that the train with the children from Warsaw would be going soon through the station, and she and her companions were here to pass some refreshments to the passengers. "You need to get out of here as soon as possible." She reached in her pocket and brought out two RGO armbands, handing one to Inka and one to me.

"Put them on, try hard to look relaxed, and follow me." She let us out through the door in the fence by the station building. It was guarded by a German soldier, but seeing our armbands, he let us through.

The woman led us to her home, conveniently located not far from the train station. It was late afternoon, and the sun was shining on the poplars shading the house. As we found out, our hostess, Mrs. Marysia, was a respectable woman of great heart and admirable courage.

During the supper, we were joined by two other refugees from Warsaw—a distinguished professor and his nineteen-year-old son. During the day, they stayed in a camouflaged recess of the attic. At night, they slept out under the stars, hiding in a nearby cornfield. The Nazi police were in constant pursuit of Varsovians, and pre-emptive raids of young men were common.

The two men disappeared after supper, and the rest of us stayed, debating how to get Inka and me to Glovno as soon as possible.

"I can purchase the tickets with no problem. I know the ticket agent well," Mrs. Marysia offered. "But how do you get through the strict control of the identification papers?"

The station had been guarded around the clock because Skiernievitse was, at that time, the headquarters of General von Vormann, commander of the *Wehrmacht's* Ninth Army fighting the Soviets on the other side of the Vistula River.

"One thing is sure," I said. "We cannot stay here. Mr. Guderian, my guardian, is the only person we can turn to." After a moment of reflection, I came up with a plan.

"Everything depends on our wits. Inka, who is a native Varsovian, will travel with my *kennkarte* while I will try to get by with an official paper stating I am legally moving from Lubartov to Glovno. Fortunately, Mr. Guderian handed it to me when we were parting in Warsaw."

"It's a noble offer," Inka broke in, "but think first of your safety. We are all aware of the strict order that everyone over fifteen years old has to carry the identification card all the time. Nobody would dare to travel without one, official or false." Nevertheless, I stood my ground. There was no better option.

After a good scrub in a tub filled with hot soapy water, my first bath in many days, I was led to "my room" by Mrs. Marysia. Seeing the soft bed with lots of pillows and beautiful embroidered linens, I was as excited as a child.

"Ahh! How marvelous! Thank you for your gracious hospitality. I haven't slept in a bed like this for years!"

The first thing I noticed next morning was that my blouse and underwear were neatly folded on a chair by the bed. They had been washed, dried, and ironed overnight. I was deeply touched. Inka, who was several years older than me, braided her hair and put on my outfit. I laughed seeing her pretending to look like a teenager.

Though I could fit in her elegant woolen suit, the skirt was too loose, and we had to take it up with safety pins. One glance in the mirror and I hardly recognized myself. I looked so grown up! After breakfast, Mrs. Marysia accompanied us to the station, bought the tickets, and bade us a warm farewell. We thanked her wholeheartedly for her courageous help and hospitality.

As agreed, I was to go first, and Inka was to follow a few minutes later. I noticed that the soldier checking documents at the station entrance was young. Handing him a single sheet, written in German, I tried to distract him with my nicest smile. He glanced at the official stamps and signature and promptly returned the paper, smiling. He must have had a good breakfast.

As soon as I passed him, my smile faded. I took a quick nervous look behind me toward the entrance door and tried not to think of what might happen if Inka couldn't make it. But it wasn't long before I saw her braided hair, and I immediately relaxed. We boarded the train, taking the same car. I found a seat in a compartment as far from Inka's as possible. Soon, the train was hissing and clanking, and we were on our way.

Listening to the chattering of the passengers, I remembered that it was not uncommon for German police to burst into a train, totally unexpected, looking for anyone without proper identification papers. We were just approaching a small station, and I felt the pangs of alarm. Outwardly, I sat calmly on my seat, but inside I was on tenterhooks. To my relief, the train passed the station without stopping. Still tense, I moved to the corridor and stood by a window, watching the fleeting scenery, so soothingly peaceful.

A couple of minutes later, a passenger from our compartment joined me. A presentable man, probably in his early thirties, he had been sitting across from me and may have noticed my nervousness. We started a conversation. I told him that I was going to Glovno to join my guardian, appointed after the death of my father. He was eager to hear about the unrelenting fighting in Warsaw and had been deeply shocked by the Nazi atrocities committed there on the civilian population.

He introduced himself and said he was the administrator of an estate near Lovich and would be getting off there. "Why don't you join me and be our guest until the war is over? It cannot be long now. I live with my mother, and I am sure she would enjoy your company."

I was very lonely, and nothing could have pleased me more than his attention. I looked into his serious eyes, and like any teenage girl, I felt flattered. Nevertheless, I gently declined, convinced that I had to go my own way. Our train was entering Lovich station when he handed me a card with his name and address, saying encouragingly, "If you find Glovno is not to your liking, feel free to join us. Our home is always open to you."

The last leg of our journey must have been uneventful because the only thing I remember is some people in the station hall greeting the arriving passengers with hugs and kisses.

Nobody was there to welcome us.

I approached a droshky driver and asked for directions to the address given me by Mr. Guderian. Of course, we planned to walk there.

"I live next door," he said, amused. "I know Mr. and Mrs. Guderian. Where are you coming from?" he asked, aware that we had no luggage or even a handbag.

"From Warsaw," I replied.

"From Warsaw!" he exclaimed. "I will take you any place you want to go, and the ride is on me!"

Climbing the stairs to the Guderian's apartment, I felt unsure how I would be received, arriving empty handed and bringing with me an unexpected companion.

34

We need not have worried how we were going to be received by Mr. and Mrs. Guderian even though Inka was a complete stranger to them. I counted on their reputation in Lubartov, where they were both active in the welfare organization approved by German authorities.

They welcomed us kindly and very correctly. There was no display of emotion, but I knew better than to expect that. After hearing about our experiences in Warsaw, Mr. Guderian nodded his head in sympathy. Enterprising as he was, he procured without delay a field bed for Inka. I was going to share a room with her at night, but during the day, the room would continue to serve as dining and living room for all of us.

In this new situation, I felt more at ease since when still in Lubartov, Mr. Guderian had asked me to contribute (from Dad's remaining savings) to expenses of finishing the apartment he had rented in the newly built house in Glovno.

That night, as we made ourselves comfortable in our beds, Inka said reflectively, "How lucky we have been to get out of Warsaw with our lives and unharmed."

"We must be thankful to God," I muttered, drifting off to sleep.

Since our house was located on the outskirts of town and we rarely ventured downtown, we lived a rather secluded life. I seldom saw a uniformed German, which was a great relief. As Mr. Guderian had been a good provider and his wife an established cook, I was eating good, nourishing food for the first time in many months. While I helped Mrs. Sophie with cooking and household chores, Inka mended and sewed clothing for the Guderians and the Czarneckis family, our next-door neighbors.

The days passed at a snail's pace. Our whole existence was temporary as we anxiously waited for the end of the war and our return home to Ino. For me, settling down to this quasi-normal life was particularly hard. I was again separated from Yanush. What happened to my little brother after I last saw him? How was he faring? To think about it was utter madness.

Somehow, I managed to get the addresses of major concentration camps and was busy in the evenings writing cards inquiring about my brother, Emil. I wrote the notes in German with Mr. Guderian's help. But I didn't receive a single reply.

"You must adjust to the new circumstances. Everything will eventually settle down," Inka offered me advice. "As for myself, I have made a decision to start an independent life. There may be a limit to the Guderian's hospitality. I'm leaving Glovno tomorrow. When I get back, I'll let you know."

She dropped out of sight. After her departure, my loneliness became even harder to bear. Inka was older than I, but there was a special bond between us after the ordeal we had been through. Only after she was gone did I realize that I knew practically nothing about her. I had never asked her straight out, "Who are you?" Was she Milek's acquaintance or a girlfriend? I promised myself I would ask when she returned.

Summer was coming to an end when one unforgettable evening Mr. Czarnecki, who was employed as an administrator of an estate near Glovno, brought the news, "The Parisians have spontaneously risen. American forces are approaching Paris. Paris has been liberated!"

For a few fleeting moments, I relived the ecstasy of the first days of the Warsaw Uprising. Yet all we knew was that the lonely, unyielding fighting stubbornly continued.

The days went by uneventfully. It was a crisp October day when Mrs. Sophie, who was suffering from hot flashes, sent me downtown to run some errands. The autumnal chill was seeping through my light coat. I was just about to cross the street when I heard a woman's voice behind me, calling my name. I turned abruptly and stared at a friendly face I could not quite recognize.

Seeing my hesitation, she gave me a smile. "We met in Warsaw only days before the Uprising," she said casually. "You came with Emil and Yanush…"

"Of course!" I now recalled that Sunday afternoon. "Milek had some urgent message to deliver to you. You lived just off the Union Square…who could have guessed that the next time we would meet in Glovno of all towns!" We moved to an unobtrusive place and continued our conversation.

"I'm so glad you made it out safely," she said.

"And what fortunate winds brought you here?" I asked.

"One cannot describe it in a few words. During the Uprising, I served as a nurse in the Old Town. You may have heard the heart-warming song: All the boys want to be wounded, after all, the nurses are so pretty," she intoned softly.

"After capitulation, I managed to sneak out of the transit camp in Prushkov." Her voice suddenly turned serious. "Do you have any news about Emil?"

"He was imprisoned in Paviak."

"Oh, I know that from Yanush…"

"Yanush?" I felt the whole world reeling before my eyes. "When did you see him?"

"This is what I wanted to tell you in the first place. Do you know that he was wounded during the fighting in Town Hall?"

"It must have been after we lost contact with each other," I mumbled.

"They brought him to our makeshift hospital in the basement. He was scheduled to have his leg amputated the next morning."

My heart quickened. "His leg amputated?" I echoed, still not sure I had heard those dreaded words.

"You see, by that time we had run out of antiseptics, they tried to save him."

"And did they do it?"

"I honestly don't know. As head nurse, I was assigned somewhere else the next morning, but I tried to prepare him for the operation as best I could. We prayed together."

She took me in her warm embrace. "I had to tell you this. I know how painful it is. Pray for him. Miracles do happen. I saw that often enough."

With my head spinning, I went directly to the nearby church. It was early afternoon, and the empty interior was plunged in semidarkness with only two people praying. I approached the main altar and knelt in the first pew. Before me, the tabernacle with the Holy Eucharist glistened in a soft glow. Deeply grieved by anguish and sorrow, I began to pray for the Lord's compassion for my little brother.

"O Lord," I was repeating through my parched lips, "keep my brother under your protection!"

∽o∾

Inka reappeared in Glovno, elegant and warm in her monkey fur coat. She invited me to a small apartment in the basement of the neighboring house. While we drank the *ersatz* tea, Inka shared the news with me.

"You cannot imagine how fortunate was our escape from the train," she said, sitting down. "That train was on its way to the concentration camp in Pruskhov."

I looked at her in surprise.

"We were in Pruskhov for several hours and didn't hear a word about a concentration camp there."

"That's right, we didn't know. We were not aware of its existence when those friendly railway workers smuggled us under the shipment of lumber, practically under the noses of the camp's guards."

"I brought some news you may want to hear. It is a sad story," Inka's gaze tightened on me.

With trembling hands, I set the teacup on the saucer. For a while, I couldn't say a word. Her voice calm, Inka told me that thousands and thousands of Varsovians went through that horrid transit concentration camp—starved, exhausted, and sick. Some had been released, but most had been deported to the concentration camps or to Germany for compulsory work. Thinking of Yanush, I felt my heart jump. I asked her about the fate of the insurgents.

"I have heard that they were granted the status of Allied Forces combatants."

I told her what I had recently learned about Yanush and that I had no word about Milek's whereabouts. In silence, I was staring at my plate with its still untouched cookies. Inka's steady voice reached me in my desolation, "It will not be long now. The Germans are retreating on both fronts." She presented me with a beautiful crystal bowl.

I didn't question how she acquired it, deeply touched by her thoughtfulness. Back home, not knowing what to do with it, I put the precious gift in the little suitcase I kept under my bed, together with my few other worldly possessions.

Some days passed. I was at home alone. The wind was whirling outside, and the rain was pelting heavily against the window pane. Feeling very lonesome, I resolved to go see Inka. I was at her door in no time. I knocked and knocked, but no one answered.

"You are looking for Inka? She has gone," a neighbor told me.

I backed away and rushed home, leaving my umbrella behind. Drenched with rain, I sat down on the edge of my bed and burst into tears. I covered my face so nobody would see my eyes full of tears. I was deeply hurt. I felt I had been robbed of something precious, of my confidence in Inka. I never saw or heard from her again.

I desperately needed a haircut, so Mrs. Sophie graciously agreed to take me along when she went for her appointment at the beauty salon.

Her hairdresser, and owner of the place, was a pleasant, middle-aged woman. When she learned I had recently come from Warsaw, she was very intrigued. As soon as I was seated in the large rotating chair and covered with a black drape, she started a chitchat.

"Your story of escaping from the train is just fascinating. I would like to help you. We have connections in town. Do you need a temporary job?"

"What I would really like to do is continue my studies," I said. "I didn't have a chance in Lubartov to properly complete the program of the fourth grade of gymnasium."

"No problem," she said with assurance. "Here in Glovno, we also have an underground gymnasium. I know the professor. It shouldn't be a problem to get you enrolled. But of course, not a word of this to a soul. I'm sure you understand that."

"That's wonderful news! I would like to start as soon as possible."

As she was brushing the hair from the drape, I saw in the mirror the reflection of my suddenly saddened face. I just realized that I had no money to pay the tuition, and I had nothing of value to sell. Mrs. Guderianowa and I were about to leave the shop when the hairdresser's little daughter came running in. She was about five years old and very cute. One glance at her and it occurred to me that I did have something I could sell—my doll! The Guderians had sent it along with my bed and their furniture before we left Lubartov.

"You have a darling daughter," I said and then added slyly, "Would you consider buying my big, gorgeous doll for her? This could help me pay the tuition."

She nodded sympathetically.

"By all means, bring it in as soon as you can. Christmas is coming, and I am sure we can make a deal."

Parting with Eve turned out to be harder than I anticipated. She was my only remaining link with Lubartov and our Christmas celebrations there with Dad and my brothers.

I had no doubt that when the hairdresser saw the doll, she would be eager to buy it. Just then, it occurred to me that winter was fast approaching, and perhaps I should use the money for a warm coat. No, I made a quick decision. Nothing is more important than continuing my studies.

By November, I joined a small group of Glovno's teenagers taking courses in Polish literature and history. The high school education for Polish youth was forbidden here as in Lubartov, and our classes were held in private homes. I was happy to meet my new classmates. One of them became my best friend. Her name was Danka. During long wintry evenings while the old-fashioned stove glowed and the Guderians and Czarnieckis played bridge, I sat at the end of a long table and was engrossed in my studying: reading and writing.

I loved poetry. I copied the poems and verses in my homemade assignment note book (I still have it), learned them by heart, and lulled myself to sleep reciting them to myself in the solitude of long winter nights.

January 1945 was bitterly cold.

The class that day was held at Danka's home. She invited me to stay over and study together. We were taking turns reading Wyspianski's drama, "The Wedding Feast," when her older brother, Bolko, burst into the room in a cloud of blowing snow.

He was greatly animated. "The Russian units have crossed the Vistula, entered Warsaw!"

Momentarily, the expression on his face changed. "Our capital is nothing more than a sea of deserted ruins... mercifully blanketed by snow."

He stopped, gasping for air. "I've also heard that the Red Army is in a full offensive. They could be here anytime."

Danka and I sat stunned and, for some time, speechless.

Thoughts were racing through my head: Warsaw liberated...in days, we'll be free...something we had waited for through five years of tribulation. And yet, strangely enough, there was no enthusiasm, no outburst of joy. This "liberation" by the Red Army was scary. We couldn't trust Stalin. Didn't he cooperate with Hitler in the partition of our country in September 1939?

I broke the silence.

"At the end of July, when the Red Army units were approaching Warsaw, the Russian radio urged the Varsovians to rise against the occupiers, only to abandon us once the Uprising started."

"I agree with you wholeheartedly," Danka said pensively. "This mistrust has deep roots."

Bolko was very serious as he said, "I am still hopeful that our Allies will abide by their pledge and the Red Army is not going to stay."

There was no doubt that the Germans were hastily retreating. One evening, a *Wehrmacht* officer was billeted with the Czarnecki family. Since his hosts spoke fluent German, he confided how deeply depressed he was by the turn of events and seemed convinced that all was lost for Germany. He stayed only one night.

It was one of the following mornings that I was stunned to see a truck parked practically under my window. It apparently had been abandoned by the Germans since the neighbors were happily unloading its cargo of food. No one bothered to stop them. That day, just down the hill, where the residents went to empty their slop buckets, two German *Wehrmacht* soldiers, obviously the truck drivers, lay dead on the snow, their faces up. I couldn't bear to look at them, so dishonored.

It must have been the same day, when walking with Mrs. Guderianowa down the street, we were stopped by a Soviet patrol and directed toward a rounded up troop of soldiers. They were Soviet volunteers in German uniforms, all with obvious Asiatic facial features. With some other passersby, we were forced to witness the horrifying scene of their execution by the squad of their own countrymen. This was how I learned that the Red Army "liberated" Glovno.

The Red Army's pursuit of the retreating German troops was spectacular. After crossing the Polish pre-war western frontier, they took Frankfurt on the Oder River and were advancing toward Berlin. The Nazi Third Reich collapse seemed inevitable.

"What are we waiting for?" Mr. Guderian asked Mr. Czarnecki one February evening as we were assembled around the table sharing the day's events. The next morning, they rented a truck, and at last, all eight of us were on our way back to Inovrotslav.

35

The only thing I remember about my journey back to Ino was a feeling of tremendous excitement. It seemed like I was waking at last from a long nightmarish dream. When I was a child, Mom would enter my room with a smile on her face, and all would be well again. Just to think that in hours, I would be back home after more than five years of exile from Ino!

I could even imagine myself impatiently ringing the doorbell and Milek opening it, Yanush throwing his arms around me, just the way it was when we were reunited in Warsaw shortly before the Uprising. After all, miracles do happen.

My room, of course, was not going to look the same. The books, my diary, and albums would have been thrown out a long time ago. I knew that a German family who resettled from a Baltic country had occupied our apartment and Dad's store. But my piano, I hoped it was still there.

As our truck entered Ino, at first glance, the town seemed remarkably untouched by the war. When we reached Holy Ghost Street, my street, I tried to be more realistic. It could well be that the German family had fled to the Reich, I thought to myself, panic-stricken by the rapid advance of the Russian army. Perhaps they even had time to loot our home, taking everything with them.

Even if everything was gone, I could still picture myself standing on the balcony and looking out over Town Square. Perhaps I would even grow petunias in the flower boxes again.

We stopped at the house where Mr. and Mrs. Guderian had lived. A neighbor gave them the keys to their flat on the second floor. To their great relief, they found that their furniture was still there. It seemed as though they had just returned home from a long, tedious journey.

"I'm going to run on ahead," I told Mr. Guderian, impatient to get to our house, only a block away on the corner of Holy Ghost Street and Market Place. I was walking briskly down the street looking ahead for the familiar balconies, but there was no sight of them. Only moments later, I suddenly stopped, deeply shocked. Where our house once stood, there was only a skeleton of burned-out walls. I felt the ground sink under my feet. That house was the only link with my past, a safe nest filled with the happy memories of my childhood. And now, all my expectations were buried in its ruins.

I tried hard to keep back my tears. Fate was so unpredictable. How many times since the outbreak of war had it robbed me of home? And now, when the Nazis' evil empire was about to collapse, came this final blow. I stood motionless, my heart broken and in deepest despair, unable to bring myself to think about what I should do next.

Somehow in the midst of this, I saw again in my memory whole blocks of Warsaw's houses gutted by fire.

"O my god, how easily I am losing my confidence!" I said to myself. Am I the only one struck by the misfortunes of war? I have been spared by Providence, not to so easily give up but to face bravely the challenges looming ahead, however daunting they seem to me right now.

Looking at the ruins with a calmer eye, I realized that the foundation of the house remained intact. The stairs leading to the basement were accessible. I walked down several steps and stopped off. The basement was flooded with water. It must have happened when the firemen were extinguishing the conflagration that might have engulfed the whole block of houses. Nonetheless, our six stores on the ground level and six spacious apartments above were all "gone with the wind of war."

When the war is over, I promised myself, trying to brave the blow, our house will be rebuilt like so many others. Back in the Guderian's apartment, I found them busy unpacking and arranging their possessions. They already knew that our house was burned out.

"We have just heard that your Uncle Stefan is in town," Mr. Guderian said in his reserved yet polite voice.

I knew what he meant. Now that we were back in Ino, he felt that his responsibilities as my guardian had come to an end. I must admit that I didn't mind that at all, wanting to be on my own anyway. I thanked both of them for so kindly putting up with Inka and me in Glovno—two more mouths to feed.

On the way to Uncle Stefan's, I was passing our burned-out house. All at once, it occurred to me that Mom's last letter as well as her jewelry might still be buried in the basement.

The scene from the past suddenly came back: Dad holding the jar in his hand and echoes of his words, "Whoever of you will be back after the war is over…"

∽∾

Although surprised by my unexpected appearance, Uncle Stefan received me warmly. The next day, after I told him about the buried jewelry, he procured two pair of wading boots, a small flashlight, and a sturdy pickaxe, and we were on our way. The door to our cellar, which consisted of three compartments, was wide open. Wading through water halfway to our knees in total darkness, pierced only by a weak beam of light, I had trouble finding the exact place where Dad had buried the two jars.

After a few discouraging trials, we were about to give up when at last, Uncle hit the right location, and it didn't take long before we had our hands on the jars. One had been slightly cracked, but the other, holding the jewelry, was intact. On top of the jewelry, neatly folded in a leather case, was Mom's last letter, written on the day before her operation.

I removed it gently and, after handing the jar to Uncle, pressed the letter to my lips. Moving the beam of light along the lines of familiar handwriting, I started to read, my eyes dimmed with tears, "My beloved children…"

I was not aware of anything around me. My mom was again with me. I heard her warm voice, felt the gentle touch of her hand tying a fancy ribbon in my unruly blond hair, and looked in her beloved eyes gazing at me with profound affection.

"Oh, Mom, how I have missed you all these years!" I murmured, overwhelmed by a feeling of her presence. Uncle Stefan's calm voice brought me back to reality.

When we emerged from the basement and faced the grey winter sky, it occurred to me that it was the last day of February, the sixth anniversary of Mom's death.

I shared my thoughts with Uncle Stefan.

"What an amazing coincidence, indeed!" I still remember hearing him say.

I stayed only a few days in Uncle Stefan's small apartment. While there, I received a totally unexpected visitor. Obviously, the news of my return was quickly getting around. It was Mirka, a niece of Mr. and Mrs. Bukowski, who had been my parents' best friends. They had also recently come back, found their home in perfect condition, and were busy reopening their store. Aware of my misfortune, they invited me to stay with them. I was offered full board and a beautiful room with a piano in return for helping them in the store.

This was a fortunate beginning for my new life in Ino. They treated me like a member of the family, and having two young, energetic, and loyal girls, Mirka and me, waiting on customers didn't do the sales any harm. I got along with Mirka just fine, as she was a good-natured, pretty girl. However, I was particularly fond of her aunt, Mrs. Bukowska, a respected lady of great sensitivity and gentleness.

Life seemed to be gradually returning to some kind of normalcy, at least on the surface, and business was brisk. Since the store, at the corner of Market Place and Church Street, was located in the heart of town, I often had a chance to meet our family's former acquaintances. These were mostly happy occasions—except for one. I had been waiting on a customer when I noticed a man entering the store. His figure was somehow familiar, but perhaps because of his pale, emaciated face, I couldn't quite place him. Upon seeing me, he walked straight in my direction. When his turn came, he introduced himself courteously.

"I don't know if you remember me. I lived in the apartment in your parent's house on the third floor."

Of course, I recalled the sharp-looking lieutenant who moved in with his young wife a couple of years before the war. Milek's room was next door to their apartment, and in fact, they shared an entryway.

"I was in the *Gross-Rosen* concentration camp," he told me.

"How glad I am to see you home."

"While there," he continued, "I came in contact with Milek."

My initial enthusiasm quickly turned to apprehension. I had heard nothing about Milek since I received his short message about being deported from Gestapo *Paviak* prison to an unknown destination on the day the Warsaw Uprising broke out.

"Oh my God! Did you really see him…talk to him…was he working alongside you in the quarries there?"

"We did see each other during inmates' roll calls in Breg sub-camp—"

I interrupted, anxiously. "But recently. Have you seen him recently? Is he planning to come back home?"

A shadow fell across his face. I could tell he was making an effort to speak calmly.

"In January, a rumor went through our camp about an escape of a large group of prisoners. The SS-Command was in the midst of preparations for a massive evacuation of thousands of inmates from *Gross-Rosen*. One day, an official announcement was made that all the escapees had been caught."

His voice trembled slightly when he said, "They were summarily executed by the SS squad in full view of the prisoners assembled to discourage anyone who might contemplate escape." He lapsed into a long unbearable silence.

"I thought you would want to know," he resumed, "that Milek was one of them."

I felt a profound numbing shock that was immediately followed by disbelief.

"How could you be so sure about Milek? From a distance, all of the inmates might have looked alike…shaved heads… the same striped uniforms…shadows of men?"

"I saw it with my own eyes."

It was completely illogical to dismiss such a trusted eyewitness. Nonetheless, I could not shake the deep conviction that Milek was still alive. I had been put to the test so many times in recent months. I wasn't going to give up easily. I felt my face turning crimson as I insisted, "I don't believe it!"

"I hope you are right," he murmured. "It is all in the hands of God." He left hastily.

Struck by the crushing news, I ran to my room. Mrs. Bukowska had been obviously watching us and must have guessed what I was going through. She followed me there and, without a word, gently put her arms around me. The tormenting pain lessened in her warm embrace.

That night, I couldn't sleep. I thought I would go out of my mind. First, the news about Yanush, now about Milek. In the midst of this deep distress and anguish, the only thing to do was to put my trust in God.

A few days later, Mrs. Bukowska invited me to go with her to visit her sister and her family in Walbrzych. A week of vacation, my first vacation since the beginning of the war! Of course, I said, "Yes."

It was how I met Zenon, Mirka's brother. He was an intelligent young man, maybe a couple years my senior. I enjoyed talking to him during our long walks. On the last evening of an idyllic week, a formal family dinner had been served. Toward the end of the meal, Zenon proposed marriage to me. I was stunned. I looked at Mrs. Bukowska, who seemed unsurprised and pleased. How could I reject the nephew of the woman who had been so good to me, my mother's best friend? Zenon evidently interpreted my silence as acceptance and so presented me with a gem-encrusted ring.

I knew what I should say, "I am not ready for marriage," yet I knew that arranging that marriage had been an act of kindness on Mrs. Bukowska's part. I returned to Ino still dazed, hoping that with time, I would be able to clarify the misunderstanding. I was convinced that the most important for me was to get to the university.

A few months later, I received a telegram from Zenon, who wanted to know the wedding date! I sent a telegram saying I was planning to enroll in the university. In that way, I ended my unwanted engagement. Later, I returned the ring.

∽०∾

May was coming. How welcome was the spring, my first spring back in Ino. In Solanky Park, I followed a familiar gravel path under trees heavy with budding leaves. On the lake, swans were floating majestically like white clouds. How emerald green was the grass, how sweet the song of birds! The rebirth of nature brought hope for my own new beginning.

In the meantime, the town was pulsating with vibrant life. More and more people were returning home. And most important, the schools opened their doors again. Without hesitation, I enrolled in the Jan Kasprowicz gymnasium, the one Milek had attended before the war. It was co-educational for the first few months because of a shortage of professors. Some of the boys in my class, who during the Occupation hadn't had a chance to continue their education, were Milek's pre-war classmates. It was so wonderful to be back in school!

School and work occupied practically all of my waking hours. Mr. Bukowski was proud of my academic accomplishment, but when the Girls' High School opened its doors and classes started in the mornings, naturally, my absence from the store during the busiest hours did not go unnoticed. Sometimes, I felt I was being pulled in opposite directions, trying to satisfy the demands of both school and work.

36

May 3, Poland's most important national holiday, was approaching. The students had been notified by an official announcement that on Sunday, we were going to attend the traditional Mass and then march in the parade. It was going to be the first such celebration since the outbreak of the war in September 1939.

Sunday morning was not as warm and sunny as I hoped. Nonetheless, I had put on my new light blue summer dress. The solemn Mass was celebrated in St. Mary Church. Its vast interior was packed with youth. The concluding hymn still reverberated in my ears as I followed the fluttering school banners down the aisle. But once outside, I was dismayed seeing that the banners quickly disappeared, and there was no leader in sight to commence the parade. Instead, some men in civilian clothes appeared out of nowhere and began circulating between the groups of youth, ordering, "Disperse…go home!"

What was going on? Since we had no idea who these men were, we ignored them. The school announcement had been clear. After Mass, there was to be the traditional parade celebrating our Constitution of May 3, 1791. Generations of Poles had been proud of this written body of law proclaiming the rights of citizens and instituting sweeping political and social reforms some years ahead of the famous Napoleonic Code instituted in France.

Our reaction was spontaneous. The order to "go home" was a slap in our faces. We had survived the war and could not be easily intimidated. So we marched on, and passersby on the sidewalk cheered. Once we turned the corner of Solankova Street, the men, who turned out to be Internal Security agents (UB), started hauling away the parade leader in an attempt to dispirit and disband the marchers. Another leader stepped up, but soon, he was also arrested.

When I heard the murmur of a fearful girl suggesting we disperse, something stirred up within me. Acting on impulse, I began singing the patriotic "Varsovienne," and the marching youths quickly took it up:

> *At last the day of blood has dawned*
> *May it be the day of our deliverance!*
> *See the white Eagle in all its splendor...*

More young people were joining our march. When yet another leader was pulled out, I hurried to replace him. The song rose in volume, an outburst of deeply felt, determined protest:

> *Long live, Freedom,*
> *Long live, Poland!*

I led the marchers toward the school. Once we reached the school yard, we sang the national anthem.

As the students started to disperse, four uniformed security policemen approached me. I was told I was arrested for something I couldn't quite understand—like disturbing the peace. They escorted me to the street. The news of my arrest must have spread with lightning speed since a huge crowd of agitated youngsters was soon following us. The fury of defiance mounted as my escort turned the corner of Solankova, and it became obvious that I was being led to the security building.

When we approached the building, the students rescued me by kicking the knee of each escort. When the guards bent over to check their knees, the students swooped in, and I found myself being lifted by strong young hands and carried away. The rest of the throng closed in behind us, blocking any attempt at pursuit.

"Let me go!" I begged my rescuers. "I want to take responsibility for my action."

Somewhere behind us, we heard pistol shots. The boys let me down but held my hands tightly and rushed me on to safety. Only hours later, I learned that more men in suits had poured out of the building with pistols drawn, firing into the air. At that time, the UB did not have the guts to shoot at Ino's youngsters. Sometime later, I heard that the army, called to help disperse our parade, had declined to interfere.

With a number of gymnasium students in jail, the atmosphere in town became tense. At spontaneously arranged town meetings, the resolution was reached that the students'

action was motivated by frustration over cancellation of the traditional parade.

Some days later, the arrested students were freed. I was shadowed for some time by a UB agent but was never openly harassed. Perhaps the fact that for the following two weeks, I was escorted to and from school by the older well-fit classmates acted as a deterrent.

Certain memories retain their intensity forever. These were the days when we were awakening to reality that our expectations for an independent and sovereign Poland had been bitterly suppressed.

During that turbulent time, on May 8, the news of Nazi Germany's final collapse and unconditional surrender swept through the town. But the feeling of huge relief was overshadowed by a deep fear of the Communist regime forcefully imposed on our country while we, citizens, firmly resisted everything that Stalinist Communism stood for.

On a sunny late spring day, Ziho showed up unexpectedly. It had been almost a year since I had seen him on that memorable morning when he came to say his final good-bye just before I left Lubartov. After all I had recently been through, that seemed like another lifetime.

Yet there he was standing before me, tall and handsome. He had some youthful charm about him which held my eyes. I was genuinely pleased to see him again. Puzzled, I wondered how he had found me. He couldn't have known our address in Ino, and anyway, our house no longer existed, but find me he did.

I led him to my room. Seeing the shiny black piano, his eyes sparkled. I knew his passion for the violin and was not surprised when he said, "Play something for me."

Later, when we were going up Solankova Street, I listened eagerly to his news. For long months, I had heard virtually nothing about what was going on in Lubartov.

"The grade schools and gymnasium were reopened last September," he said. "You might like to know that Prof. Perczynska is teaching French. Having trusted teachers from the underground gymnasium, of course, we like our school a lot."

There were so many things I wanted to know about Lubartov. "While I was still in Warsaw, I heard that Lubartov was liberated shortly after I left."

"July 22!" Ziho's whole face lit up. "That was a day I will never forget."

"Tell me…tell me all about it!" He smiled at me, knowing how I may be pleased to hear the story.

"Since morning," he started, "the Germans were fleeing in panic. The armored units of the SS rumbled through Lubelska Street. Then by afternoon, the AK partisans marched into town, followed shortly by units of the 27th Volhynian Infantry Division of the Home Army (AK). You must have heard about that Division."

"It was a glorious summer day. In no time, the streets were overflowing with people, the girls hugging and kissing the worn-out soldiers, the women with tears running down their cheeks presenting them with flowers from quickly denuded German gardens. And do you know what they did? They proudly stuck them in the barrels of their rifles."

He paused for a while and then continued, "Heavy shooting could still be heard when a field kitchen was promptly installed in the courtyard of the school vacated by the Germans, and the volunteers were busy cooking a meal for our starved liberators."

"Oh, I should never have missed that day!" I exclaimed, overwhelmed with profound joy.

We walked for some time without speaking. Crossing Solanky Park, we reached the bridge over the lake. We stood there, close to each other, leaning over the parapet, watching the luminous surface of the water reflect the blue of an almost cloudless sky. I felt a long suppressed sense of deeply felt joy.

But the moment I gazed at Ziho, I noticed that his face had turned suddenly somber. Instantly, I had a premonition that something else besides seeing me had brought him here from Lubartov. He must have been aware of my inquiring look because he said, "I stopped here on the way after visiting my father in Vronki."

"What is your dad doing in Vronki?" I was greatly surprised.

"He is in prison there...with hundreds of other Home Army patriots."

I felt like someone had hit me without warning. My hand gripped the bridge railing tightly. He took it in both of his hands.

"I didn't want to spoil your joyful mood so I was in no hurry to continue my story. Nevertheless, I have to tell you that July 22 was the only day of freedom we knew in Lubartov."

A dead silence followed. I knew well that he usually kept upsetting news to himself and probably was reluctant to distress me. We found a bench shaded by a willow tree. With my eyes on the water, I sat close to Ziho, not to miss any of his words and to feel his reassuring presence.

The Soviet tanks arrived the following day, he told me as his face clouded, and took up strategic positions in the town. A small group of Communist partisans followed. One of the men formally introduced himself—first in Russian and then in Polish—as the new administrator of Lubartov! He ordered the Home Army forces stationed in the town to withdraw by the afternoon. It would have been pointless to fight. Behind that obscure Communist stood the all-powerful Soviet army.

"It was then," Ziho tried to control his voice, "that we realized we had simply exchanged one tyranny for another."

I shuddered. Instinctively, like a child seeking protection, I moved closer to him. He embraced me gently and kissed me on the lips with an intense emotion. I liked him. I liked him very much. I trusted him. He was part of my life for five years of the war. He was my link with Lubartov and the people there were dear to me. We had shared a hope for our country to be free again. But now, our expectations had been crushed.

However, we were young, and we had faith. It was our moral obligation to believe that Polish state would be reborn. After finishing high school, we had planned to continue our studies at the university—Ziho in Lublin and I in Poznon.

The sun was slowly sinking as I walked my trusted friend to the train station. On the way, it was my turn to answer his questions about how I had fared over the past year and what had happened to Yanush and Milek.

"I will be back," Ziho assured me just before boarding the train. "In the meantime, remember me!" He handed me his photo taken while playing the violin. I have that photo to this day.

∽o∾

The news about what was going on in Lubartov after the town had been taken by the Soviet Army kept coming, and it was devastating. The Home Army soldiers of the 27th Volhynian Infantry Division, who had bravely fought through the German lines, managed to reach their comrades-in-arms in Lublin district. After liberating a few towns from Germans, Lubartov included, the units concentrated in the well-known to me village of Skrobov. Their spirited marching song reflected their passionate dedication:

We are fighting through our way, and fate has to follow,
And if not, we will overcome the fate…

It still rang in Lubartovian's ears when the compound was surrounded by Russian tanks. The division was ordered by the Soviets to disarm. A few hundred officers and cadets were singled out and promptly arrested. The rank and file were ordered to join the Polish army under Soviet command. The captured officers were interned in the barracks in Skrobov, where I remember well, not so long before the Germans held Russian POWs. From there, they had been deported to detention camps in the Soviet Union.

By then, there was no doubt that the primary goal of the Soviet NKVD, following closely behind the advancing Red Army, was to annihilate the Polish Home Army and break the Polish spirit of freedom and independence. Yet no less painful was the news about the persecution of Lubartovians so well-known to me.

At the beginning of August 1944, Yatsek's father, Stefan Dumalo, pre-war captain of artillery, and during the Occupation, a member of the Command of AK in Lubartov, enlisted in the First Polish Army, which was under Soviet command, assuming it soon would be on the way to help the Warsaw insurgents. But a few days later, he was arrested in Lublin, along with scores of other Polish officers and civilian administrators. He was imprisoned there in Majdanek, the well-known Nazi concentration and later also extermination camp that was remembered with horror by the Lubartovians. Only a few weeks earlier, the SS guards there massacred the prisoners just before withdrawing. Captain Dumalo for some time had had some secret contact with his family in Lubartov. But at the end of the month, several hundred Polish officers and Home Army political leaders were loaded on a freight train and deported to a detention camp in the Soviet Union.

In the fall of 1944, new waves of arrests swept through Lubartov County. In December, Karol Skaruch, an active member of the Home Army during the Occupation, and Ziho, his older son, were detained and incarcerated. The same day, UB agents brought to an adjoining cell Prof. Maria Fryczowa, who taught the largest group of youngsters in our clandestine gymnasium and was one of the local leaders of the Resistance Movement against the Germans. Through the walls of his cell, Ziho heard the tortuous interrogation his professor was subjected to in the middle of the night.

Ziho was eventually released, but his father was found guilty, sentenced by a decree of the Regional Court in Lublin and sent to the prison in Vronki in western Poland. Prof. Fryczowa was held for a long time in the former Gestapo prison in Lublin Castle, and when finally released, had been deprived of the right to teach for life.

This news was greatly disturbing. It seemed evident to me that anyone who actively stood up for freedom and independence of Poland during Nazi Occupation had been regarded as a potential threat to the Communist regime imposed by Moscow.

37

The new year of 1946 arrived. The past fall, I set myself a goal to finish Lycee, the last two years of high school, in one year. But the more time I devoted myself to my studies, the less time I had for work. I began to feel that I might be wearing out my welcome by Mr. and Mrs. Bukowski. Oh, God, how I longed for my own home and my own family. Sometimes, I felt utterly alone. All the time in my mind was a thought of Yanush and Milek.

Months had passed since the war ended, and I still had no word from them. The uncertainty of what had happened to my brothers was nearly unbearable. Often, I awoke in the night tormented by dreams. When that happened, I comforted myself by repeating, "God is merciful! God is merciful!" There was nothing else I could do.

And then, how vividly I remember that wintry Saturday when I opened the door, and there stood Milek! Alive after all!

It was a moment of total surprise and indescribable joy. How comforting was my brother's warm embrace! He did not have the emaciated look of some of the survivors of the concentration camps, who often appeared to have had the life sucked out of them. I was facing a dashing, vital young man with a bright smile on his face.

"I am so happy to see you doing well," he said affectionately.

"And you, heaven sent, where have you been…where are you coming from?"

"I came to Poland as a member of an official American delegation," Milek said. He lowered his voice to a whisper. "But that is only a cover for my special mission here." His eyes had sparkled when he continued, "On the way to Warsaw, we stopped in Prague. There I had a chance to practice my English during the formal reception. When in Czechoslovakia," Milek smiled, "I visited Aunt Maria in Bogumin. She is as nice as ever."

He stared at me intently. "Do you have any news from Yanush?"

"So far, not a word. But what about yourself? Do you plan to settle here?" I asked, looking at Milek intently.

"I would if I could," he said enigmatically. "Tomorrow, I have to be back in Warsaw."

"I was sure…" I murmured, as the surge of hope that he had come home to stay suddenly vanished.

"That's all I can tell you right now." Milek said. "We'll talk more later. Now let us see Mr. and Mrs. Bukowski."

Mirka must have passed word of Milek's arrival to Mrs. Glowinska, Mrs. Bukowska's sister, since she invited us all for dinner. Glowinski's two daughters were our childhood friends. I couldn't help noticing that the older attractive Chrissie seemed especially delighted with Milek's presence.

At the end of the meal, when we were all still sitting around the dinner table, everyone was eager to hear the story of Milek's daring escape from the concentration camp.

He hesitated to revive his recent nightmarish experiences, but eventually he began.

"Well then, let us move back in time. As you know, in July 1944, the Soviet offensive was approaching Warsaw. Just before the outbreak of the Warsaw Uprising, the *Paviak* prison had been evacuated in a hurry. We were packed in standing position into cattle cars that had been previously pulled up on the sidetrack."

"During the trip, no food or water was provided. In the August heat, it didn't take long before prisoners started dying," he murmured. "It took five torturous days to reach the destination—the *Gross-Rosen* concentration camp in Silesia."

Milek explained that *Gross-Rosen*, by the summer of 1944, had become the hub of several sub-camps. With a large group of newly arrived *Paviak* inmates, he had been dispatched to Brieg, south of Breslau where the newcomers had been immediately put to work enlarging the airport.

"There had been so much misery and death around that I wondered how I was going to survive." He lapsed into a long silence.

Within a few days, he found out that there were more than a dozen former Polish officers in the camp and at least twice as many sub-officers. A secret resistance cell was planning the escape. Expecting that Soviet tank forces would soon be rolling into Silesia, they started secretly digging an underground tunnel leading out of the camp.

There wasn't a sound in the room, everyone listening spellbound.

"Unfortunately, the tunnel was discovered by the guards," Milek returned to his story. "Deeply discouraged, we firmly resolved not to give up."

The next chance came when trucks loaded with booty from the *General Gouvernment* started to arrive. The unloading proceeded outside the camp's perimeter. A selected group of the secret cell members promptly volunteered for the job. Milek was one of them.

"We planned to seize a truck and make our way down to the border of the GG. In the Polish occupied territory, we could count on help from the population. It was a desperate gamble."

Milek paused again.

The decision to act had been taken on January 4. While the assigned group had been busy unloading the truck, the leader, Captain *Zapora* (Mieczyslaw Dukalski), had watched every movement of the guards. At the right moment, he had given a signal to lure the guards to the truck one by one.

"We disarmed each one with our bare hands and seized their weapons," Milek said with an intense voice. "Sasha, the only Russian insider, jumped into the seat behind the wheel with Captain *Zapora*, wearing an army overcoat by his side. In no time, some twenty of us piled into the back, and the truck was racing down the road on the way to freedom."

My heart beat wildly. My eyes concentrated on Milek's lips.

When they had come to a checkpoint on the viaduct in Opole, they had ignored the German command to stop. But some miles down the road, they spotted a car loaded with gendarmes (German police) coming their direction. It had been a tense moment. However, unshaken, Captain *Zapora* coolly ordered Sasha to stop the truck and let the car pass. Yet some not initiated escapees panicked and started running away. The alarmed gendarmes had opened fire on them, thinking they were helping their comrades in the truck.

"A few blasts from our shotguns," Milek said very quickly, "settled the gendarmes down, but that accidental encounter meant the beginning of a terrible ordeal for us."

Fleeing now on foot, the escapees vanished into the woods. They knew the Germans would be pursuing them. Night had fallen, and they were already under fire. Those who survived headed toward the Polish border proceeding only under cover of the night. It was bitterly cold, and they were starved and sometimes disoriented. The fourth day of escape, an SS detachment, aided by local foresters, had rounded up the escapees. In the exchange of fire, several of them had been killed. The situation was desperate.

Milek and his companion had fallen into the hands of the *Volkssturm* (Home Guard), armed with shotguns. Night was falling so they had locked the escapees in a barn, obviously planning to turn them over to the authorities the next morning. But before dawn, a woman had unlocked the barn and left some bread and milk by the door. They were gone long before daylight.

For a while, Milek seemed to be lost in his thoughts. And then his voice rang out. "For once, luck was on our side."

What a relief it was to hear that he and his companion made it into occupied Polish territory and were rescued by partisans from the underground *Holy Cross Brigade*. It was then Milek learned the Red Army's winter offensive was in full swing. Soon it had become obvious that after "liberating" Polish territories, the Soviets kept them in their grip. The horror stories about disarming, arresting, and persecuting Polish Resistance fighters were passing from mouth to mouth.

"To safeguard ourselves from the Communists," Milek went on, "we proceeded toward the West as fast as we could, being joined on the way by scores of Polish partisans fearful of the approaching Russians."

On the way, they had liberated a women's concentration camp near Pilsen in Czechoslovakia. It had been the beginning of May when the units entered the American zone of Germany under General Patton.

"His antipathy toward the Russians and Communism is well-known," Milek concluded, smiling.

Oh! That was an unforgettable evening for all of us present. We felt privileged to hear Milek's story of the heroic escape of the large group of inmates from *Gross-Rosen* concentration camp. Most of them didn't make it, but my brother had survived to be witness of each enslaved person's craving to be free.

Heading back home, Milek and I walked for a while in silence.

"I didn't explain this before," he spoke with a calm, measured voice, "Although we came here on an official visit, we have been entrusted with a special assignment to spirit the wife and daughter of a Polish general to the West before the escape routes are closed by the *Bezpieka* (slang for "security forces"). But I also have a plan for you. Would you consider getting out of this Communist-run country? You speak French, and I have made certain arrangements in Belgium with the nuns who run a private high school with a tradition of its own. You could apply for a scholarship and continue your studies there. They have agreed to give you a place to stay. That is, if you wish to go."

After a short reflection, I made my decision.

"You know how much I would like to be close to you, but I will graduate from the Lycee soon and plan on enrolling in the University at Poznan this fall. Besides, I'm still hoping that Yanush may come back, and I want to be here when he comes."

Milek nodded with sympathetic understanding.

"If you change your mind or just want to keep in touch, here is my contact address in Cracow. The person there will help you."

"It was so marvelous to see you," I whispered.

He gave me a warm, encouraging embrace. Moments later, he disappeared into the darkness.

It would be eighteen years before I saw my brother again.

38

The autumn of 1946 was almost upon us. It was a nice crisp September day when one afternoon, Chrissie Glowinska and I returned to Ino from Poznan after being admitted to the university and signing up for our courses. It would be our last visit before the first semester of the academic year began. I still recall how proudly we were sporting our student fraternity caps.

We celebrated the occasion with Chrissie's mother and Mrs. Bukowska in the same little coffee house where some six years earlier I had been treated to my favorite dessert by Uncle Stefan. How merciful that we could not foresee then the near future, I thought to myself. Almost immediately, I pushed this thought away. Our group was a happy one, and Chrissie and I were brimming with joyful expectations about the challenge that lay ahead.

That was the atmosphere when Mrs. Bukowska adopted an enigmatic expression and began looking for something in her purse. I was wondering what she was up to when she pulled out a piece of paper and handed it to me. To my total surprise, it was a telegram from Yanush, sent to me on our pre-war address. I could hardly believe it was not a dream. I read and reread the message.

I have signed for repatriation to Poland. Am waiting now for my turn. It may be a while. Yanush.

So he was alive! I was overtaken with gratitude! My hopes and prayers had not been in vain!

Sometime after the New Year, when I was in the midst of my studies at the University, I received a letter from Yanush. It was posted in Alnwick, England. Enclosed was a photo with a short dedication to me on the reverse.

To dear Halinka. This is my little family here. We are just reading the letters from our friend. Yanush. Alnwick, December 17, 1946.

That was the best Christmas gift I could possibly have received. Never mind that it was delayed. From the happy faces and friendly embraces, I could see there was a genuine bond between Yanush and his buddies. That atmosphere of togetherness must have helped them overcome the long separation from families and homes. I felt truly comforted.

It was February of 1947 when Yanush arrived in Poznan, wearing an army uniform that had been stripped of all rank and distinction.

"I came here straight from Gdansk," he spoke with all the enthusiasm I remembered. "From the moment we landed on the shore, I couldn't wait to see you. Oh God, how I have missed my home and my family. We've been lost to each other for almost three years now."

"I'll never forget that morning of August 8," I said thoughtfully, "when you and Yurek came pounding on the door, warning me and those two young messengers from Jolibord that the Germans had started an assault on Senatorska."

"That's right. That was the last time, but I knew that you survived the Uprising. I wrote to Aunt Sophie from the Stalag in Germany. We were starving…she sent me a small parcel with bread, cake, and some cookies. It was a feast! She gave me your address in Glovno, and I wrote you a card."

"I never received it." Yanush's thoughts were obviously somewhere else. I sensed that he wanted to change the subject.

He said, "It's great to be back!" His face brightened.

My reunion with Yanush was different from Milek's brief appearance just one year earlier. We were like two happy, playful kids who had missed each other for so long and now enjoyed to be together again. Yanush came back with very few possessions; some *zlotys* that jingled in his pocket and a standard military farewell package with cigarettes (he didn't smoke), cocoa, and tea.

"You won't believe how generous the Repatriation Office in Gdansk has been," he smiled ironically. "I got a free ride here since I gave them your address as my home."

As penniless as he was, nevertheless, he presented me with a gift. Coming from Scotland, it was a raincoat, a very beautiful one.

"Azure blue to match your eyes," he said.

It actually turned out to be a very useful gift for years to come.

My dear brave little soldier! When I asked him what uniform he was wearing, he said briefly, "Honorably discharged from the Second Polish Corps under General Anders."

He had been serving with the famous Polish Corps that had fought with such incredible courage beside the British during the offensive in Italy. They were the ones who had captured the "invincible" German stronghold at Monte Cassino, the battle commemorated ever since in the heart-moving song, "The Red Poppies of Monte Cassino," that would forever be a deeper scarlet from the Polish blood shed there.

But Yanush stood before me with a big smile on his face. He did not want to talk about his war experiences, about bloody fights and gruesome months in the POW camps in Germany, but about the friendship and solidarity with his comrades in arms, emotions so essential to survival in combat and in captivity. He took particular delight in sharing with me the stories of flirting and dating pretty dark-haired Italian girls, so sweet and amusing.

I gazed at my brother in amazement. Yanush was radiant with youthful vitality. He seemed to be just returned home after some exciting escapade. His joyful mood was contagious. We all need to be loved just for ourselves, to go on with our own lives. The first thing he wanted was cold sour cherry soup (canned, of course) with a lot of fine homemade macaroni, exactly like a meal we had the day before he joined the ranks of the insurgents that memorable day of August, 1944. So we got busy shopping and cooking.

He planned to return to Ino and finish high school there. While stationed in Italy, he had graduated from a military school for non-commissioned officers and then managed to complete the fourth year of high school in San Natino near Galipoli. After graduation from Lycee in Ino, he hoped to enroll in the Institute of Technology in Gdansk. Luckily, I had acquired some money from our burned out house so I was able to help him with necessary shopping. All he had, literally, was the uniform on his back.

Only much later, during our occasional visits, Yanush would sometimes evoke his experiences of the last years of the war. Memories were flowing in.

Throughout August 1944, Yanush was fighting in the Old Town. First successful, euphoric days, the insurgents gaining in fierce combat control of some strategically important buildings and streets, the taste of freedom. But it didn't last long. Reinforced enemy units pushed the insurgents out of Vola. Old Town became cut off from Jolibord and City Center sectors. The surrounded, totally isolated defenders had found themselves under an unceasing heavy assault from artillery, mortars, and dive-bombers roaring just over their heads, bombs smashing block after block of houses. In the Bank Square, Yanush had been buried under the rubble of Polish Bank, an insurgent's redoubt.

"Bombs were falling all around us, and the artillery did not stop for a minute," I recall him saying. "Yet we survived being dug out by our dedicated comrades."

During the bitter fighting in the ruined Town Hall, Yanush had been wounded in his right knee. He'd been scheduled for amputation of the leg, but even with a wounded knee, he had escaped the underground makeshift hospital. "I was helped to the surface by my older caring comrade-in-arms, a native of Lvov," I recall him saying.

Yanush remembered his rescuer with gratitude ever after.

Pressed into an ever-smaller area, the decimated, exhausted insurgents were manning their barricades and posts to the last breath until they had been separated from the Germans only by the huge heaps of rubble from collapsed and smoldering buildings. It was then they had been ordered to abandon the Old Town.

"But it was never surrendered!" Yanush assured me. "We were leaving brokenhearted yet not feeling defeated, knowing what heavy losses we had inflicted on the Germans."

Some units fought their way to City Center sector, still in insurgent's hands, through the German positions, bleeding profusely. One unit, wearing captured German boots and camouflage jackets with red and white AK armbands on the sleeves, simply marched through the enemy stronghold in Saxon Gardens in darkness. It was an almost suicidal risk, but they had succeeded to reach the downtown barricade, dodging a hail of bullets once the Germans realized they had been duped.

Yanush was not sure if it was the first or second of September when he had been evacuated with hundreds of Old Town fighters through the sewers before the enemy realized the withdrawal had commenced. Although wounded, he was still able to walk.

"We entered the sewer[1] from a manhole on Krasinski Square, descending one by one. The going was extremely hazardous. You see, the sewers are narrow, low, pitch-dark, and filled with wastewater and stinking human waste. We held each other's hand so as not to get lost. My back rubbed against rough concrete. But the most paralyzing," Yanush shivered, "was our fear that the Germans, who knew we used sewers for communication, might at any moment drop a grenade into it."

That first wave of insurgents survived the passage and emerged from a manhole at the corner of Varecka and New World Streets in City Center. Yanush was first assigned to group *Kolo* and then to the Home Army 15th Infantry Regiment under command of Lt. Col. "Pawel" of Group City Center North. With unbroken spirit, he joined the fierce fighting on Chmielna, Vidok 9, and on Jerusalem Avenue.

On September 10, a day after a successful offensive on a German-held position, he was awarded the Cross of Valor and promoted to lance corporal. He was fifteen years old!

The fighting in City Center continued through September until the insurgents had run out of ammunition, grenades, food, and water.

The offensive of the Red Army, expected in July, never materialized. Marshal Rokossovsky had been standing passively on the other side of the Vistula River, preventing any access to the city from the east. The tragedy of the Uprising unfolded. On October 2, the surrender was signed. The surviving insurgents marched out proudly, leaving the Polish capital lying behind in ruins and smoke. Among them was a column of the youngest Warsaw combatants, including my brother.

"It was the saddest day of my entire life," Yanush freely admitted. "We had to lay down our arms, but we never took off our red and white AK armbands. After sixty-three days of fighting, we were all strained to the limit, exhausted, and hungry. Some of us were wounded or sick. But still, we were alive. Many of our comrades-in-arms were killed."

They were marched to the transit camp at Ozarov,[2] twelve miles away, escorted by *Wehrmacht* guards. Along the way at regular intervals, gendarmes and soldiers were posted with machine guns, ready to open fire on anyone trying to escape.

From the transit camp, the insurgents, by then recognized as combatants of fighting Allied forces, were transferred to *Stalag 344 Lamsdorf* in Silesia. The whole trip was macabre.

"We were packed in the cattle cars, standing during the whole trip, deprived of food and water. Upon arrival, they took all our identification papers. I just became number 103370."

While there, the boy-soldiers were particularly brutalized by their *Wehrmacht* guards.

"I saw the hate in their eyes," Yanush's voice was choked with emotion. "We have always heard that it was the SS who treated prisoners with inhuman ruthlessness, but we were prisoners of war in the hands of *Wehrmacht* soldiers, and they behaved like beasts, taking advantage of their prey. They had no regard or compassion for our young age."

Yanush did not know then that Milek was being held at the same time at a work sub-camp of *Gross Rosen* in Brieg, some twenty-five miles away.

It was the middle of November 1944 when most of the underage boy-soldiers were transported from Lamsdorf to *Stalag IV B* in Muhlberg. But they were not there long. At the beginning of January 1945, Yanush's group was dispatched to the work camp of *Stalag IV G Oschatz* in Brockwitz, Saxony. Known as *Lager zum Stein*, it was disguised as a glass factory. There they were forced into slave labor in the armament industries. The older boys were rousted out of bed at 4 a.m. each morning and transported to Niedersedlitz, a suburb of Dresden on the Elbe River, where they were put to work for long hours welding fuselages for Messerschmitt planes, a clear violation of their status as prisoners of war.

Yanush must have been there when Dresden was heavily firebombed in the middle of February 1945 since the image of people running like flaming human torches toward the river was locked in his memory.

"It still makes me shiver bringing back his emotional account. They were not aware that the phosphorus bomb fragments would continue burning, even under water."

The cruelty the boys had to endure in the camps defied imagination. They did their best to help each other, but still some were dying of starvation, cold, and disease, or were killed during desperate, but futile, attempts to escape.

"It would have been much easier and honorable to die defending Old Town," he once told me, "than to go through those months of hell in German captivity."

He desperately tried to push those nightmarish experiences out of his mind. He had to forget. That was necessary for the healing process that would let him regain the wholeness and determination to go on with his life.

The Red Army was advancing, and the young prisoners were forced to dig defensive trenches. Yanush's wounded leg, neglected for months, became infected, and he could not do the work. In April 1944, he was sent to a hospital for Anglo-American prisoners of war in Wurzen. Once there, maggots were applied to his wound to clean out infection. Then surgery was performed. To his great surprise, a bullet that had been embedded in his right knee for all those months was successfully removed.

Shortly after Yanish's operation, some American units liberated the hospital. As far as I remember, it was May 3, 1945, the same day I was arrested in Inovrotslav by the UB policemen for leading the May 3 parade.

From Wurzen, Yanush was transported to a military hospital in Soisson in northern France. He responded to the solicitous care by recovering quickly. His American physician took a fancy to this young patient and, when he learned he was an orphan, wanted to adopt him. Yet Yanush already had his own plans. As soon as he was released from the hospital, he headed to Paris and in *Casern Bassier* reported to the Polish military authorities. He was transferred to southern France and then to San Gorgio in Italy. "It was there that I enlisted in the II Polish Corps, faking my year of birth to be admitted," he said smiling, "and I was assigned to the 65th Pomeranian Infantry Battalion, 2nd Warsovian Armored Division."

In July 1946, a large group of Polish soldiers from General Ander's II Corps embarked the *Empress of Australia* on the way to England. After the years of ordeals, relaxing on the former luxury liner must have been, for Yanush, a wonderful experience. In England, he was assigned to a military camp in Barnsley near Manchester, and later transferred to Alnwick, near the Scottish border. There, given the choice,[3] he made a decision to join me and repatriate to Poland.

When Yanush arrived in Poznan in February 1947, we talked, of course, about Milek. I told him of Milek's brief visit in Ino and his successful escape from *Gross-Rosen* to the West.

"He gave me," I continued, "a contact address in Cracow. But my letter, sent from Ino in early spring, came back to me months later, with whole passages roughly underlined by some censor's pen."

Thinking back, I can imagine how relieved Yanush and I would have been knowing that only weeks ago, Milek immigrated to the United States after the Polish units serving as logistical support of the US Army in the American zone in Germany had been disarmed. I understood that, as much as he would want to, Milek couldn't have come back home.

German artillery destruction of Town Hall in
Theatre Square during the Warsaw Uprising.

Ruined Town Hall, one of the strongholds of the insurgents on
the north side of Theatre Square. Here Yanush was wounded.

Over a half million civilians from Warsaw were herded to a transit camp in Prushkov. From there some were sent to concentration camps, others, to slave labor in Germany.

Ziho with his violin, 1945.

My enrollment in the University of Poznan,
student's book. Fall, 1946.

Yanush (second from the right) with a group of
his buddies from the Polish Forces (fighting with
the British), Alnwick, England, 1946.

Milek, New York 1952

Zico and me in from of the cemetery gate in
Lubarto, 54 years after my departure for Warsaw
just before the Uprising. Photo taken by Ely.

Installation of the memorial plaque in the Gymnasiam
No. 1 in Lubartov on April 9, 2005. The plague is
honoring the professors and teachers who during the
Occupation secretly taught Lubartov's youth. Ely and
Yurek Kielczewski are presenting the flowers.

With a group of Catholic Intelligentsia from Warsaw, invited by Pope John-Paul ll to Castel Gandolfo. September 7, 1988.

Halina with children of Gdansk, 1989. The sign, which means "I Chose Solidarity" celebrates the first free election since the outbreak of WWII.

EPILOGUE

The end of World War II did not bring to our homeland the independence and sovereignty that was so courageously and selflessly fought for by the Poles during extremely oppressive Nazi occupation. The bitter truth of Poland's betrayal by the Western Powers in Teheran reached us late.

Stalin had a free hand to impose his domination over Eastern Europe. The Poles were now cut off from a traditional contact with Western European countries. The newly created Polish Peoples Republic, which lost Polish pre-war Eastern provinces to the Soviet Union, was ruled by the Communist regime subservient to Moscow. Stalinism was affecting every aspect of political, economic, and cultural life. Any suspected opposition had been ruthlessly persecuted. I still clearly remember that with Stalin's death, Moscow's direct dictatorship over Poland somehow lessened. Nevertheless, right from the beginning, the enormous task of rebuilding the country after the wartime devastation began with genuine dedication. The years went on.

It was August 1963 when I crossed the Atlantic on my way to the United States to take a position as a research associate at the University of Illinois, Urbana. I had been invited by my brother to stop in New York. Since I was coming from Montreal by train, Milek, whom I had not seen for eighteen years, was anxiously awaiting me at the station. It's impossible to express the emotion of our reunion.

Thinking of it now still brings memories of two happy weeks I spent with him and his wife, Mimi. By then, Milek was a successful interior decorator in New York. His lovely home in West Belmar, New Jersey, overlooked the Atlantic. He often gazed quietly out across the great ocean and spent most of his free time sailing in his boat.

One evening, our talk turned to war experiences. Yet Milek was not inclined to revive the painful memories. For a moment, he buried his face in his hands and then said very softly, "America has been good to me!" And yet I knew that in his heart, he yearned for Poland, and he never stopped hoping that the time would come when he would be able to settle in Gdynia on his beloved Baltic.

How unpredictable is fate! Only three years later, I married and was getting ready to move permanently to the United States. It was the year 1966, a grand year of nationwide celebration of the millennium of Polish Christianity. The faithful overflowed the churches, being reminded of our roots. The Communist regime, which was on a constant offensive against the Catholic Church—viewing it as an enemy of the state—snapped back with its own programs for the millennium of Polish statehood.

I settled in the United States. The years went on, but I kept in touch with Yanush, now holding a managerial position as a civil engineer, and his family. During my frequent visits to Poland, I always saw my friends. Particularly joyful and moving have been my reunions with the unique circle of friends of my youth. The winds of war had brought us by chance to Lubartov just for a few years, and yet the bonds of friendships established there have extended through our lifetimes. Proudly, we called ourselves "Lubartovians." I am glad that I didn't marry Ziho. His youthful, romantic love brightened the hours of our encounters for years to come.

When in Warsaw, I never miss a stroll through the Old Town. My pulse quickens when, walking from the Castle Square, I enter the familiar Senatorska Street. In the Theater Square, I aim straight for the magnificently rebuilt Grand Theater and stop in front of a memorial plaque mounted on the wall. It is always lit and adorned with fresh flowers. I stand there in total silence reading and rereading the words of the inscription I know by heart like a prayer:

THIS PLACE WAS SANCTIFIED

WITH THE BLOOD OF POLES WHO GAVE THEIR LIVES

FOR THE FREEDOM OF THE FATHERLAND.

ON THE DAY OF AUGUST 8, 1944,
IN THE RUINS OF THE GRAND THEATRE
THE NAZI EXECUTED 350 POLES.

I was one of those held captive here on the very day they died years ago.

And I am here...I am still here...why was I the one to survive? I ponder the burning question. But an answer never comes.

In the meantime, the Polish Peoples Republic was going through different political phases. With time, the opposition to the forcibly imposed system was gaining strength. O yes, I recall the outbursts in 1956 and 1970. The Warsaw Uprising, once declared by Stalin as "reckless adventurism," became a national legend, a "Polish Thermopylae"—synonym of man's unending quest for freedom.

With a declining economy, living conditions worsened. Frustration with the regime's injustice and the Polish Peoples Republic's malaise led to open confrontations, riots, and strikes. Bloody reprisals only mounted the resistance. A sharp increase in food prices was the final blow. The situation became extremely tense. Yet nothing, nothing changed the face of Poland more than the first pastoral visit of Karol Wojtyla, known to the world as Pope John Paul II. In June 1979, he challenged his compatriots with a daring message:

"You must be strong with the strength of hope. I beg you: never lose your trust...do not be defeated...do not be discouraged...always seek spiritual power from him from whom countless generations of our fathers and mothers found it. Never lose your spiritual freedom."

Millions came to see and hear the beloved Holy Father, the highest moral authority to all the Poles. For the first time in forty years, they became aware of their collective strength.

Lech Walesa, an unemployed worker in the Lenin shipyard in Gdansk, with John Paul II's message in his heart and mind, jumped over the shipyard fence, and commenced a strike that led to creation of the truly mass movement known to the world as Solidarity.

It was my good luck to be visiting in Poland when Lech Walesa was signing the act of recognition of the Solidarity Trade Union in the presence of government officials. I was there two years later, only months after Solidarity was banned on December 13, 1981, and brutally repressive martial law was imposed on my native country.

Life is a quest. After many challenges and suffering, endurance, and perseverance, on June 4, 1989, my Polish friends, with millions of my compatriots, hastened to their voting booths in the first free elections since the war broke out in 1939. We eagerly awaited the results. And oooh! What an unforgettable summer of celebration and thanksgiving it had been! The overwhelming victory of Solidarity crowned the years of nonviolent resistance. The election of Lech Walesa as president of the Polish Republic followed. My beloved native country was free.

GUIDE TO MODIFIED GEOGRAPHICAL NAMES USED IN THE TEXT AND THE ORIGINAL POLISH NAMES

Auschwitz	Oświęcim
Bank Square	Plac Bankowy
Bilgoray	Biłgoraj
Breslau	Wrocław
Brieg	Brzeg
Bydgosh	Bydgoszcz
Capuchin Church	Kościół Kapucynów
City Center	Śródmieście
Crooked Street	Ulica Kręta
Castle Square	Plac Zamkowy
Chechoslovakia	Czechoslowakia
Chenstohova	Częstochowa
Cemetery Street	Ulica Cmentarna
Citadel	Cytadela

Cracow	Kraków
Cracow Faubourg	Krakowskie Przedmieście
Frog Street	Ulica Zabia
Galizen	Galicia
Gdansk (Danzig)	Gdańsk
General Gouvernment (G.G.)	Generalna Gubernia
Gnievkovo	Gniewkowo
Goose Farm Jail	Gęsiówka
Great Poland	Wielkopolska
Glovno	Głowno
Holy Ghost Street	Ulica Swietego Ducha
Honey Street	Ulica Miodowa
Inovrotslav (Ino)	Inowrocław
Iron Gate Square	Plac Żelaznej Bramy
Jerusalem Avenue	Aleje Jerozolimskie
Jolibord	Żoliborz
Katyn	Katyń
Katovice	Katowice
Kovel	Kowel
Kozlovka	Kozłówka
Kuyavy	Kujawy
Lamsdorf	Łambinowice
Linden Street	Ulica Lipowa
Lisov	Lisów
Lodz	Łódź
Long Street	Ulica Długa
Lovich	Łowicz
Lubartov	Lubartów
Lvov	Lwów
Lublin Castle	Zamek Lubelski
Macieyovitse	Maciejowice
Motlava River	Motława, Rzeka

Naklo	Nakło
Ohota	Ochota
Old Town	Stare Miasto
Ozharov	Ożarów
Paviak Jail	Więzienie Pawiaka
Poland	Polska
Pomerania	Pomorze
Poznan	Poznań
Prushkov	Pruszków
Queen Yadviga Street	Ulica Królowej Jadwigi
Railway Street	Ulica Kolejowa
Saxon Garden	Ogród Saski
Schuch Avenue	Aleje Szucha
Silesia	Śląsk
Skiernievitse	Skierniewice
Skrobov	Skrobów
Solankova Street	Ulica Solankowa
Theatre Square	Plac Teatralny
Tehev	Tchew
Tomashov	Tomaszów
Torun	Toruń
Town Square	Rynek
Union Square	Plac Uni Lubelskiej
Vilno	Wilno
Vistula River	Rzeka Wisła
Vloclavek	Włocławek
Vola	Wola
Volhynia	Wołyń
Warsaw	Warszawa
Willow Street	Ulica Wierzbowa
Zamost	Zamość

GUIDE TO MODIFIED FIRST NAMES USED IN THE TEXT AND THE ORIGINAL POLISH NAMES

Alexander	Aleksander
Anthony	Antoni
Angela	Aniela
Bolka	Bolesław (Bolko)
Boleslaw	Bolesław
Chris, Chrissy	Krystyna (Krysia)
Casimir	Kazimierz
Danka	Danuta (Danka)
Dick	Ryszard (Rysio)
Edek	Edward (Edek)
Ely	Elżbieta (Elzunia)
Eve	Ewa
Francis	Franciszek

Genia	Genowefa (Genia)
Georgy	Jerzy (Jerzyk)
Helka	Helena (Helka)
Jane	Janina
John-Paul II	Jan-Paweł II
Josephine	Józefa
Leshek	Lech (Leszek)
Lutek	Lucjan (Lutek)
Marius	Mariusz (Marius)
Marylka	Maryla (Marylka)
Martha	Márta
Marysia	Mária (Marysia)
Milek	Émile (Miłek) Bratck,
	Polus Piasecki, Piasecki
Nicholas	Mikołaj
Renia	Irena (Renia)
Romek	Roman (Romek)
Sasha	Sasza
Sigipmund	Zygmunt
Sophie	Zofia
Stanislav	Stanisław
Stenio	Stanisław (Stenio)
Tad	Tadeusz (Tadek)
Timothy	Tymoteusz
Vaclav	Wacław
Vidok	Widok
Vitek	Witold (Witek)
Vladka	Wladka
Vladyslav	Władysław
Yada	Jadwiga (Jadzia)
Yadviga	Jadwiga
Yanush	Janusz

Yasio	Jan (Jasio)
Yatsek	Jacek
Yulek	Juliusz (Julek)
Yurek	Jerzy (Jurek)
Zbig	Zbigniew (Zbyszek)
Zenek	Zenon (Zenek)
Ziho	Zdzistaw (Zdzicho)
Ziutka	Józefa (Ziutka)

GUIDE TO FAMILY NAMES
USED IN THE TEXT

Bialy	Biały
Dumalo	Dumalo
Giedroyc	Giedroyć
Glowinska	Głowińska
Jablonowsky	Jabłonowski
Jastrzebska	Jastrzębska
Jeziorowna	Jeziorowna
Kecikowna	Kecikowna
Perczynska	Perczyńska
Pilsudska	Piłsudska
Pilsudski	Piłsudski
Skrzypinski	Skrzypiński
Wisniewska	Wisnieska
Wroblewski	Wróblewski
Wrobel	Wróbel
Wyspianski	Wyspiański
Zelazny	Żelazny

NOTES

CHAPTER 3

1. In the Polish language, the ending of surname of wife and daughter changes, e.g., the wife and daughter of Pilsudski is Pilsudska; the wife of Bratek is Bratkowa and the daughter is Bratkowna.

2. The crucial factor in Pilsudski's victory was the breaking of the Soviet's military code that made it possible for him to pinpoint the position of the Soviet Army. Later, in the 1930s, Polish mathematicians deciphered Germany's military code and made a precise replica of the *Enigma* machine. It became the foundation for the British code-breaking system *Ultra*, permitting the Allies to read German military messages throughout the war. Poland never received proper credit for this contribution to the war's success. (That information is drawn from the book by Lynn Olson and Stanley Cloud—see Bibliography.)

CHAPTER 4

1. The common endings of first names with "ek" indicates the lovely tendencies of Polish language to diminutives. Example: Emil to Milek, Julian to Yulek.

CHAPTER 5

1. Polish units courageously defended our beloved Hel, at great cost to the Germans. One of the officers, named Kazimierz Wierzynski, who participated in the defense of Hel Peninsula, wrote an account about it, which was published shortly after the war by Henry Steele Commager. (See Bibliography.) I have quoted from it:

Hel was defended as fiercely as one defends a most ardent love…Cut off from the mainland on the fourteenth of September, Hel had not much more than two thousand soldiers for its defense, and from the first day of the war, it had been subjected to the most trying ordeals. First came the air attacks, which set fire to the pine forests made dry by the continued hot weather. In this conflagration… fell bombs and artillery shells…At one time, thirty-five bombs were dropped on the submarine Sep (Vulture) and fifty-three on the Rys (Lynx)…

Hel didn't have any airfield and was forced to defend itself from the ground. Its anti-aircraft gunners performed wonders. Every plane shot down was rewarded by loud shouts from all the units…

The trawlers which had not yet been sunk went out each night on unbelievably difficult missions among the German ships to lay mines in the Bay of Danzig (Gdansk), which seemed to be completely occupied by the enemy.

By land, the foe was repulsed by counter attacks. Headquarters was forced to try its last chance—to blow up the narrowest portion of the peninsula and cut themselves off from attacking Germans…The torpedo heads were arranged in chessboard fashion—connected by a detonating fuse…As Germans began their attack, ten tons exploded underground…the water rushed in… the German attack was halted in that chasm. Hel became an island…

Hel lived through to the first of October until provisions and ammunition were exhausted. Five minutes before activity ceased, Polish artillery brought down one more plane. It was our fifty-third plane shot down in defense of the sea.

2. Decades later, reading Robert Payne's book on Hitler (see Bibliography), I could hardly believe my eyes. Horst Wessel was actually a pimp, living on the earnings of his mistress, Erna, whom he had stolen from another member of the National Socialist Party, Ali Hoehner. On January 14, 1930, Ali burst into their apartment and shot Horst in the mouth. Shortly thereafter, Ali and Erna mysteriously disappeared, and the false life story of Horst Wessel was published in the paper.

CHAPTER 6

1. Shortly after the war was over, I participated with a group of Ino's high school students in the ceremony of exhumation of the victims killed on the bloody Sunday night of October 22, 1939. One of the victims was Apolinary Jankowski, Inovrotslav's meritorious president, arrested some days earlier with the vice president, Vladislav Juengst, father of my classmate, Andrew.

CHAPTER 7

1. When in Sachsenhausen, Father Vladislav Demski was beaten to death by the SS toughs for refusing to tramp on his rosary.

2. During the Prussian Partition, many thousands of German families had been resettled in Polish western provinces. After Poland regained independence, only some of them left.

3. Under the command of Reinhard Heydrick, Chief of the German Police, the label took on a totally new meaning. Besides the SCHUPO (regular police) and GENDARMERIE, it included the SIPO (Sicherheitspolizei), the Security Police, headed personally by Heydrick. After the Polish campaign was over, its mobile EINZSATZ GRUPPEN became static GESTAPO (State Security Police) and KRIPO (Criminal Police), an instrument of tyranny unparalleled in German history. SIPO's measures could not be contested by law.

4. The following information and quotes are drawn from the book by Heinz Hohne, p. 301-306 (see Bibliography).

CHAPTER 8

1. Bogumin (in Czech Bohumin) in Zaolzie (Trnsolzia) was inhabited by Poles, Slovaks, and Czechs. In 1920, while Poland was in the midst of war with the Bolsheviks, the Czechoslovak army occupied Zaolzie, breaking earlier agreements. Poland seized it, ingloriously, in October 1938.

CHAPTER 11

1. Some time passed when one day, a starved Benjamin Cytrynblum stopped Adam Majewski in the busy market and implored him to advance some money as rent for the house from which he had been expelled. Without a word, Majewski whipped out his gun and shot him in plain view of horrified witnesses.

CHAPTER 12

1. The Jews who fled to Poland in the Middle Ages to escape persecution in Western Europe enjoyed autonomy and flourished as financiers, merchants, and skilled artisans. In the nineteenth century, during the partition of Poland, new waves of Jews (called Eastern Jews) kept arriving in Polish territories, now under the Russian rule, forbidden to live in the Russian Empire's central provinces. They had no understanding of Polish culture and eagerly

embraced rapidly spreading Hasidism, an ultra-orthodox form of Judaism that further hindered their assimilation into Polish life.

2. The choice of victims was not accidental: two criminals, two judges, two lawyers, two professors of Lublin Catholic University, two directors of the gymnasium, and two county mayors.

CHAPTER 13

1. English translation from Norman Davis' God's Playground, A History of Poland, Vol. 1, p. 151.

CHAPTER 14

1. Polish and German ethnic groups had inhabited industrial Upper Silesia for several centuries. After the First World War, following three successive Polish Risings there in 1919, 1920, and 1921, the League of Nations Council of Ambassadors assigned the greater part of the disputed territories, (rich in coal), to the reborn Poland. When the Nazis came to power in Germany, they furiously denounced that decision.

2. After the Soviet invasion of Poland and incorporation of its Eastern provinces, hundreds of thousands of Poles had been deported in railway convoys to the labor camps in Siberia or Kazakhstan. The outbreak of the German-Soviet war put an end to this cruelty, but by then almost half of the deportees were dead.

3. By the end of 1941, some one-and-a-half million Poles had been forcibly deported by Germans from Poland's western territories. In the fall of 1939, when we still lived in Inovrotslav, Artur Greiser, Nazi Gauleiter of the Warthegau (Warta River's province) threatened that "everything that is Polish is going to be cleared out of the region!" His prediction was now pretty much accomplished. The persecution of the Poles went steadily on both sides of the German-Soviet divide.

CHAPTER 15

1. The official paper published in Polish.

2. Yanush probably had no idea then how right he was. During one of my visits to Lubartov after the war, I learned that one of the clandestine listening stations throughout the Occupation was in Stanislav Pikula's house at Cemetery Street, just across the courtyard from us. Two persons headed the operating group: Father Aleksander Szulc, the former school catechist we knew from the library, and Father Andrew, whom we often saw in the Capuchin Church.

CHAPTER 16

1. All through the Occupation, the manhunts proceeded with German brute force and efficiency. Some one million Polish youths, who should have been in school, were toiling on the farms and in the factories of Hitler's bellicose Third Reich.

2. Most probably School Inspector Jan Mangold.

CHAPTER 19

1. In Poland, traditionally not birthday, but nameday was celebrated on the day of the feast of one's own patron saint.

2. Wajsmel Sajndle was one of some five thousand Jewish children and teenagers saved during the German Occupation by Polish nuns.

3. One of the favorite puns of Hebrew scholars refers to the name of Poland. In Hebrew, Poland is Polin, and po-lin means "here one rests." (Quote from the book by Abram Leon Sachar. See Bibliography.)

CHAPTER 22

1. The toll of the Nazi preliminary project to colonize the Zamost Region by the Germans was a staggering 110,000 Polish peasants, forcibly and most cruelly evicted from approximately 393 villages. That included 30,000 children, most of whom perished. Some 4,500, who were fair haired and blue eyed, were sent to the Reich for Germanization. Only a few of them were found and repatriated after the war. The project had not been accomplished since the Zamolt Region peasants, organized in Peasant Battalions, fought back and challenged the Nazi, who lacked enough manpower to continue the pacification project. (The information by Czeslaw Pilarczyk—See Bibliography.)

CHAPTER 24

1. Before the war, Capt. Jan Derecki had been a staff officer and Vice-Military Attaché of the Polish Republic in

Bucharest, Romania. From the beginning of the war, he was active in the underground ZWZ (Union for Armed Struggle). Under the pseudonym of Karol, he served as First Commander of the Espionage Department for Warsaw and the District of Warsaw. In February 1942, ZWZ was renamed Armia Krajowa (Home Army). It was Europe's biggest Resistance Movement with unquestionable legal ties with the Polish Government in Exile.

2. The verse written by me in Polish is on p. 20 of Ely's (Elzbieta Derecka-Chalat) memoir. (See Bibliography.)

CHAPTER 25

1. The story of his arrival in Lubartov became known only after the war. Stefan Dumalo, captain of artillery, fought the Germans in the September campaign. His army, "Lublin," after losing the battle in Tomashov, retreated to Zamost, in Lublin district. Here the soldiers were soon captured by the Soviet Army invading Poland from the East. Capt. Dumalo managed to escape the detention camp and reached Lubartov, where he joined his wife and son, who had earlier found refuge in town. He didn't know that by escaping, his life had been saved.

CHAPTER 27

1. In July 1944, the Polish Underground Home Army (AK) counted over 40,000 trained members in the Warsaw district alone. However, only some of them were armed.

CHAPTER 28

1. The little egg-shaped grenades were manufactured by the Home Army in secret places, usually in the basements of apartment buildings.

CHAPTER 29

1. Mayor Starzynski served as the Civilian Commissioner for the City's Defense during the September 1939 siege of Warsaw. In his last radio address, with his beloved capital in smoke and flames, he said, "Warsaw fighting in the defense of Poland's honor is at the pinnacle of her greatness and glory."

2. One of the brave AK fighters killed on that day was Krzysztof Kamil Baczynski, Poland's most talented young poet. From his post in a window of Blank Palace, he had managed to shoot two Germans before an enemy bullet smashed his head. He was buried in the palace courtyard.

CHAPTER 32

1. They were men from the Dirlewagner SS Brigade. J. K. Zawodny, in his book Nothing But Honour writes, "This unit was unusual in several respects: 50 per cent of its soldiers were common criminals, and 40 per cent of its officers were volunteers from the Soviet Union...non-Germans in German uniforms."

2. The earliest text, written in Greek in the year 250, was used in Coptic liturgy.

3. On the fifth day of Uprising, the Germans had waged a major offensive on Vola. In a few days, some 40,000 civilian population of Vola district were slaughtered, en masse condemned to death. They were indiscriminately rounded up and mowed down by machine guns. Those who sought protection in the cellars were ripped apart with grenades. The bodies were piled up and burned.

CHAPTER 38

1. During the Warsaw Uprising, the insurgents used the sewer system to communicate and move around between different sectors of Warsaw.

2. The information on Yanush's experiences in the POW camps in Germany is from his personal recollections shared with me and from the book Underage Soldiers of the Warsaw Uprising in Nazi Prisoners of War Camp in Lamsdorf (now Lambinowice), written in Polish by Damian Tomczyk. (See Bibliography.)

3. Shortly after the war ended, relations between the Western Allies and the Soviet Union became strained, and some four hundred thousand Polish soldiers in the West, who fought for others and our freedom, hoped that in case of an armed conflict, they would be able to rescue their homeland from Soviet domination. But by the summer of 1946, it became clear that such hopes were futile.

BIBLIOGRAPHY

Commager, Henry Steele, *The Story of the Second World War*, Brassey, Washington, D.C., 1991. Originally published by Little, Brown, Boston 1945.

Davis, Norman, *God's Playground. A History of Poland, Vol. II*, Columbia University Press, New York, 1982.

Davis, Norman, *Rising '44, The Battle of Warsaw*, Viking Penguin, 2004.

Derecka-Chalat, Elzbieta, *Czasy pokoju lata wojny, Memoir, 1927-1944* Manuscript, 24 pages, Number 8, Lublin, April 2004.

Dobosz, Bogdan, sob.01/05/2008 *Do Konca Niezlomny Kapitan 'Zapora'* published in Polish on the Internet at http://www.prawica.net/node/10355.

Domanska, Regina, *Pawiak Wiezienie Gestapo, Kronika 1939-1944* (p.488), Ksiazka i Wiedza, Warszawa 1978.

Dumalo Ryszard Jacek, *Wojna, Okupacja, Wyzwolenie, Lubartow 1939-1949*, Polihymia, Lublin 2003.

Hohne, Heinz, *The Order of the Death Head. The Story of Hitler's SS*, Penguin Books, 2001.

Ligeza, Zdzislaw, *Lubartowskie Drogi Armii Krajowej*, Norbertinum, Lublin, 1998.

Olson, Lynn and Cloud, Stanley, *A Question of Honor. The Kosciuszko Squadron, Forgotten Heroes of World War II*, Alfred A. Knopf, New York, 2003.

Pilichowski, Czeslaw, selected information quoted from *Zamojszcyzna-Sonderlaboratorium SS* (The Zamosc Region – Special SS Laboratory) Collection of Polish and German documents from the period of the Nazi Occupation. Czeslaw Madajczyk, People's Cooperative Publishers, Warsaw, 1977.

Sachar, Abram Leon, *History of the Jews*, Alfred A. Knoph, New York, 1964.

Tomczyk, Daniel, *Nieletni Zolnierze Powstania Warszawskiego w Hitlerowskim Obozle Jenieckim w Lambinowicach*, ed. Opole, 1994.

Zawodny, J.K., *Nothing but Honour. The Story of Warsaw Uprising* 1944, Hoover Institution, Hartford, California, 1978.

Lubatow i Ziemia Lubartowska, Collections of articles, editions of 1993, 1996, 2000, 2006, edited by Lubartowskie Towarzystwo Regionalne.